THE
HOME
COOKBOOK

THE HOME COOKBOOK

MONTY & SARAH DON

PHOTOGRAPHY BY MARSHA ARNOLD

BLOOMSBURY

LONDON · BERLIN · NEW YORK

SINCE THE EIGHTEENTH CENTURY the British have regarded foreign food as by definition superior to home fare. Go out for a meal in London and you will have the choice of every cuisine in the world – yet a restaurant that serves just British (let alone local or seasonal) food will be hard to find. Where other countries openly celebrate their own cuisines, the best of British food is usually to be had in people's homes.

Enjoying good food at home is easy, cheap and fun. But it means cooking daily, buying ingredients as near as possible to their harvested state. It means making the preparation of food an important and rich part of daily life rather than a chore. It means eating meals at a table rather than in front of a screen or in the car, and wherever possible sharing them with other people who are also eating the same meal. It means eating food that has as little packaging as possible with ingredients that need no faddish advertising to promote them. It means trusting and enjoying the long heritage of traditions and recipes that have resonance to you and the place where you live.

Almost all food is seasonal, and the best food is a marker of its season. Asparagus in early summer, peas, new potatoes and soft fruits in high summer, tomatoes and plums in late summer, apples and pears in autumn, and parsnips and broccoli in winter – these are part of the outpouring of a garden. But not so long ago lamb was a treat for summer, goose for Michaelmas and Christmas, and eggs rare or even non-existent in winter. To everything its season. Some foods, like grains, store easily so can be consumed the year round, but even their growth and harvest has a rhythm and pattern dictated by the seasons, climate and geography. To live as though these things are not important is an impoverishment. This is why

it is so rewarding to try to grow something edible, even if it is only some
herbs in a small pot on the windowsill. It connects you to the living reality
of food, with its dependence on sunlight, water, soil and, as often as not,
human care and skill. The flow from the cultivation of the ground and
the planting of a seed through to the harvest, cooking and consumption
is continuous.

Food has meaning in geographical context – where it comes from is as
important and interesting as how it is produced or prepared. To try to eat
only local food soon becomes a punishing exercise, but it is surprising how
good a diet can be had if the majority of your food comes from nearby.
I was once at a seminar where the discussion became very heated over
what defined 'local'. The answer, of course, is different for everyone
everywhere. 'As near as possible' will do well enough.

This means that all the foods that we cannot grow or produce in Britain
– like coffee, olive oil, lemons, oranges or spices – need to be brought from
far away. But it is important to find out where our food comes from and the
implications of sourcing it from there. Our current supermarket system of
central distribution, which takes food halfway across the country to sort and
package it, only to return it to a store a few miles down the road from
where it was produced, has so many lunacies that any stand against that,
by buying food as close to its place of origin as possible, with the minimum
middlemen or food miles, is always worthwhile.

Another factor that is inextricably bound up with good food is good
husbandry. Every time you put some food into your mouth, you are taking
an agricultural action and making an agricultural decision. The global food
corporations and supermarkets squeeze the land till it screams in pursuit
of the cheapest food possible, with maximum profits. This is at the expense

of animal welfare or ecological and human health, yet they always fall back on the claim that they 'are only providing what the public want', as though they were performing some kind of social service. Do we really want ill health, cruelty, pollution and bland uniformity? Probably not. The answer is to exercise your power of choice and take personal responsibility. This land is our land. We make of it what we eat. And good food begins at home.

Our own garden and farm are run organically and we believe that this is the best way to grow healthy, good food. But it is not a creed writ in stone. It is often better to buy from a local farmer who produces food in a sustainable manner but which is not certified organic than the same item that is technically organic but which is flown in from the other side of the world. This book has largely British ingredients and many of the recipes are based upon traditional British cooking, often from the countryside. It unashamedly celebrates our own immediate locality, not least our garden.

The recipes are the result of thirty years cooking for ourselves. Much of what we have learned comes from our own childhood tables; we were lucky enough to be brought up at a time when most food was prepared based upon knowledge that had been handed down the generations and shared communally. Although we both enjoy cooking, we tend to be very busy, and more often than not we prepare our meals in a hurry from what is to hand. We seldom entertain, and when we do it is usually an excuse to share the food that we particularly enjoy in that season. There is very little that is elaborate – everything is kept as simple as it can be.

Essentially this is private food to share with people you love. It is also food for those who are hungry and who will eat with relish. There are no jus, foams or tiny portions to tempt jaded palates. Unlike bad restaurant meals, home cooking cannot hide behind pretension. Of course home food has to look appetising, but the proof of any pudding is in the eating. Good food, prepared with love and eaten with those that we love in the warmth and privacy of our homes, is one of the greatest pleasures that life has to offer. It is the yardstick against which one measures all culinary experiences.

Monty and Sarah Don

Ivington, July 2010

Breakfast

I LIKE BREAKFAST. Taut-faced dieticians will tell you that it is the most important meal of the day, which it probably is, but they forget to tell you that it is also the best meal of the day. The thought of grabbing breakfast on the hoof whilst going to work is horrible, although I know many people seem to cope happily with this. But perhaps they have forgotten how good breakfast can be.

Here's my own recipe for the Complete Breakfast. Get up with the light. Don't dawdle. Washing and dressing should not take more than ten minutes. Straight downstairs and put the kettle on to make tea. Always tea with breakfast, lots of it, and always at least one cup before anything gets eaten. If it is a lovely day I might well wander outside for a bit, mug in hand. I can easily end up on my hands and knees deep in a border, the tea growing cloudy and cold, but the early sun warm on my back and appetite whetted. I might go to my desk for an hour or so, my mind at its clearest and relishing the absolute peace and silence of dawn.

I start with fruit and yoghurt, although last night's leftover fruity pudding makes a very good alternative. Best of all is stewed fruit from the garden with fat-free yoghurt from the local dairy and a trickle of honey from bees gathering pollen on the Black Mountains. There is nothing precious in this. These details are my own but you can substitute any that have meaning to you. In October and November a chopped-up apple or pear is delicious, and between July and October a handful of raspberries, picked with that first cup of tea, dropped into a white bowl of yoghurt, makes a perfect, clean taste. The toast has meanwhile been cut and put into the top oven of the Aga. This is the best way of making toast that I know, although I cannot see that it matters how you reach the desired end of bread that is crisp through, yet with some chew.

There should be a main course to any breakfast. In this household eggs feature strongly because we produce our own. If it is possible to keep hens – and even the smallest garden can sustainably accommodate a couple – then it transforms breakfast, because fresh eggs, eaten a day or two from laying, from hens fed only on scraps and grain and allowed to forage without restriction all day, really do taste better than any others.

Fried tomatoes, picked from the greenhouse and taken straight from garden to a frying pan, are an August treat. You can buy tomatoes and fry them for breakfast all the year round but the early home-grown ones have an intensity of taste that is stunning. They lose that intoxicating sweetness by mid-September but for the few weeks while the magic lasts it is worth setting the clock early for.

Ideally toast should be eaten with butter and homemade marmalade. Sometimes, when I'm feeling racy or clean out of marmalade, apricot jam gets an outing. It livens things up.

Breakfast is much better for being eaten alone. If there is company then it should be silent. This is not because mornings are thick with unsociable fug but because talk distracts from the absolute pleasure of the meal. At its best it has a solitary rhythm, although the *Today* programme and a newspaper are fine. I will often get up especially early simply to avoid sharing my breakfast with the hoi polloi. It should be noted that said hoi polloi – i.e. my family – regards this as fussy and obsessive to the point of ridicule. Sarah's ideal breakfast does not begin until tennish and my eldest son likes nothing better than last night's leftovers.

The important thing is to give enough time and attention to whatever works for you.

COLD BREAKFAST

The British eat an inordinate quantity of breakfast cereal. This is because it suits the kind of peripatetic, snatched meal that many people regard as normal as they hurry to work. I hate this. It wastes and abuses what can be the best meal of the day. Yet I accept that for many people – myself included – cooking anything beyond toast is not always practical.

But a cold breakfast need not mean a rushed affair eaten on the go. The secret is to make time specifically for the meal, whatever it consists of, to let breakfast breathe and receive the attention it deserves, not just fuel you for the morning ahead.

Some combination of fruit, yoghurt, granola and honey is one of my favourite dishes of all. I love yoghurt and it somehow always tastes better first thing in the morning. Although there are very good commercial yoghurts, it is easy and satisfying to make, and the only ingredient needed is good milk. Seasonal stewed fruit such as rhubarb, gooseberries, blackcurrants, raspberries or apples always accompany yoghurt perfectly. Muesli and granola can easily be made at home, and it is often possible to get really good local honey even in the middle of cities.

Add a pot of tea or coffee, and perhaps some freshly squeezed fruit juice, and the result is a meal that can be put together and eaten in under half an hour and remains subtly memorable for the rest of the day.

Stewed, baked or poached fruit

We try always to have a bowl of cooked fruit ready to spoon over breakfast yoghurt or muesli. Rhubarb, gooseberries, plums and apples are our favourites.

The first apple to crop is Arthur Turner which cooks into a glorious, frothy foam. By late autumn, apples still dominate and many varieties, such as Newton Wonder, can be stored, keeping well into winter. To stew them, simply peel, core and quarter several apples and simmer in a saucepan – with just enough water to stop them sticking – until soft. Use one variety at a time as they cook more evenly.

The stewing and poaching methods are interchangeable. Fruit can also be baked in the oven, often sweetened with sugar or honey. This method suits harder fruit such as quinces, although plums, gooseberries and late rhubarb cook well in this way too.

Baked fruit

Serves 6
1kg fruit, prepared
100–150g caster sugar, or 4–6 tablespoons runny honey

Preheat the oven to 200°C/Gas Mark 6.

Place the fruit in an ovenproof dish and pour over between 200ml and 500ml water. Watery fruit, such as rhubarb, requires little water, while stone fruits, such as plums, need more. Sprinkle over the sugar, or trickle over the honey. Cover with a lid or loosely tucked in baking parchment, leaving room for the steam. Cook for 20–25 minutes until tender. Harder fruits such as quinces will take longer, so keep checking every 5–10 minutes after the first 25 minutes.

Poached fruit in syrup

Adding fruit to a simmering sugar syrup and cooking until soft is ideal for more delicate fruit, such as pieces of early rhubarb.

500–750g fruit, prepared

For the poaching syrup:
100g caster sugar
1 stick cinnamon (optional)

Pour 200ml cold water into a saucepan large enough to take the fruit. Add the sugar and cinnamon stick, if using, and gently bring to the boil, stirring to dissolve the sugar. Simmer for a few minutes.

Add the fruit and gently poach until just soft. Delicate pink rhubarb is easy to overcook, so just as it starts to soften, remove it from the heat and allow it to cool in the syrup. Larger fruit cooked whole, such as pears, will need more poaching syrup, so adjust the quantities accordingly.

Yoghurt

I don't think there's a cleaner, more refreshing taste than yoghurt. Combined with fresh or stewed fruit (page 16), it's even better. There is nothing bracing about it. It's subtle without being the slightest bit bland. Homemade yoghurt's slight astringency and thinner consistency mean that it's best to start a meal with it rather than using it to accompany a pudding.

So whenever possible, I start my breakfast every day with a few generous tablespoons of yoghurt, accompanied either by honey or fruit. Rhubarb, gooseberries, raspberries and apples are all particularly good with yoghurt in their season. The key to this is that the fruit accompanies the yoghurt rather than the yoghurt being a health-conscious cream substitute to go on top of the fruit.

We have become used to buying very good yoghurts and I like many versions, from the thin tartness of the very low-fat types to the thick creaminess of Greek yoghurt. The secret is to find a local dairy or a commercial brand that makes it in a manner you like. It is, however, very easy to make yourself, although in my experience, no two batches ever come out exactly alike. All you need is a starter, which can be a pot of any active, live commercial yoghurt you particularly like, and organic whole milk. If you can get it, unpasteurised milk is best.

We were once given a yoghurt-making kit with a series of small jars and an electrical heater, but the best yoghurt I ever made was over a period of a year when I used a simple terracotta pot in an airing cupboard, never washing the pot and simply adding warm milk to the last of the previous batch. Worked a treat. In principle, anywhere that's suitable for rising bread dough is good for making yoghurt.

Makes about 500g
500ml whole milk
4 tablespoons live, active
    whole-milk yoghurt

In a pan over a medium heat, warm the milk to blood temperature. (Stick your finger in it. You should feel nothing other than wetness. If it feels at all cold, heat a little more. If you can feel warmth, put it to one side and leave it to cool.)

Put the starter yoghurt into your container. If you don't have a yoghurt-maker, use a glazed terracotta or earthen-ware pot, or a vacuum flask. Mix a third of the milk into this. Pour in the rest of the milk, stir gently and cover. Put in a warm place for at least 12 hours so the bacteria can set to work. I find that making it first thing in the morning means that it can be refrigerated last thing at night ready for the next day. Remember to keep some back to use as the starter for the next batch.

Smoothies

Muesli

Smoothies are a refreshing and easily digestible way to start the day. Use bananas as the basis of the drink and add a handful of other fruit, chosen according to the season, although it's a mistake to add too many different fruits at once. Mangoes are my favourite, and strawberries make a lovely, pretty drink in summer.

Raw muesli can be a bit daunting first thing in the morning but I love to eat it if the oats have been soaked first. The benefits of uncooked oats are still there, but they're more easily digested.

Muesli must be prepared from scratch, but it's really delicious and simple to make. I like the nuts to be lightly toasted. You can do this by warming them in a dry frying pan just until they become fragrant and slightly golden.

Serves 1
1 ripe banana
125ml (a small glass) apple juice
or freshly squeezed orange juice
125g plain whole-milk yoghurt,
or whole milk
A small handful of seasonal fruit
1 teaspoon runny honey

Serves 1
3 tablespoons medium or rolled oats
4 tablespoons apple juice or milk
1 apple
1 tablespoon chopped hazelnuts or
almonds, toasted if you like
1 teaspoon clear honey or brown sugar

Place all the ingredients in a blender or food processor and blend until smooth. Serve immediately.

To serve:
Yoghurt (see opposite)

Put the oats in a small bowl and soak in the apple juice or milk for a minimum of 20 minutes, or prepare and leave overnight. (You can use water if you like, but the flavour will be blander.)

Immediately before serving, grate the unpeeled apple and mix it into the oats. Add the nuts, spoon over the honey or brown sugar and serve with yoghurt.

Granola

This is absolutely delicious and very more-ish. The advantage of making it yourself is that you can add extra nuts (I love almonds), seeds and dried fruit such as raisins, sultanas and chopped, dried apricots. The commercial versions are often mean with these and tend to pad out the mixture with lots of oats. Eat it with milk or sprinkled on yoghurt.

The quantity here goes a long way as a portion of just a few tablespoons is enough for most people – although I find it hard to resist nibbling on it, so it quickly disappears. This makes the equivalent of several cellophane bags as sold in pricey delicatessens.

Makes about 600g
225g rolled oats
125g whole almonds
50g sunflower seeds
50g pumpkin seeds
25g sesame seeds
125g clear honey
3 tablespoons sunflower oil
50g sultanas, or other dried fruit,
  alone or in combination

Preheat the oven to 150°C/Gas Mark 2.

Mix all the dry ingredients together in a large bowl, except for the sultanas as they burn and become bitter little pellets if they are cooked with the granola.

Heat the honey and sunflower oil in a small saucepan over a medium-high heat. Bring it to the boil, whisking all the time until it amalgamates into a creamy liquid.

Pour the hot honey and oil over the dry ingredients and gently stir everything together until the liquid is evenly distributed and absorbed.

Cover a large baking tray with baking parchment and spread the granola mixture evenly over the surface. Place the tin in the oven and cook for 45 minutes to an hour, occasionally turning the mixture over to make sure it cooks evenly. It should be a lovely golden brown. Take it out of the oven, allow to cool, then add the sultanas. When the granola has cooled and dried out completely, store in an airtight container. It will keep for about a month in a cool, dry place.

HOT BREAKFAST

A cooked breakfast makes the day sing. Everything is invariably better for it. And, in practical terms, my own experience is that a breakfast with some protein in it keeps hunger at bay for longer.

For much of the year we have a supply of fresh eggs from our hens that live in the orchard. It is hard to beat a perfectly made poached egg, but these are always a bit of a punt and one that is even a fraction overcooked is spoiled. Boiled eggs also have an element of risk, but a fried egg is comfortingly reliable. Scrambled egg is delicious but rich and tends to be eaten for supper in our household. However, eggs have their season, which runs from early spring to late summer. Hens will not lay and moult at the same time; most birds begin their seasonal moult at the end of summer and do not start laying again properly before late January, rising to an eggy frenzy from March through to June, steadying a bit in summer, gradually declining into autumn. This means that a morning egg in midwinter is rare.

Everybody knows that the smell of bacon frying in the morning is irresistible, and the combination of salty bacon with a fried egg always transcends the sum of its parts. There is a huge difference, though, between mass-produced bacon and the really good stuff, not least in that factory pig farming is one of the more degrading human practices and should not be supported in any way. My own preference is for thick-cut, unsmoked back – I would rather pay two or three times as much for it and eat it half or a third as often. Ham for breakfast, with or without eggs, is our Christmas treat and eaten daily until it is all gone. I love a well-made sausage, and when I was a child we ate sausages for breakfast at least once a week – I do so now perhaps two or three times a year. If there is a kidney or a kipper to be had, then it is a red-letter day, but these treats are all the better for being eaten only every once in a while.

Porridge

Porridge oats are first rolled to flatten them, which means that they cook in a few minutes. Purists prefer pinhead oatmeal, which is considered more authentic, but it takes longer to cook and has a grainier texture. I love its nutty flavour but we tend to eat rolled oats more often as they are more readily available, and there's usually a packet of them in the cupboard.

If we're making porridge for breakfast, there's a ritual the night before of measuring out the oats into the saucepan, pouring over twice their volume of cold water and then leaving it until the morning. The oats swell up overnight and cook quickly the next morning, but they still need stirring for a few minutes for a smooth porridge. If we are less organised, it's made in the morning and cooked straight away, but the water is put in the saucepan first and the oats sprinkled on to the surface to prevent lumps.

I once worked with a designer who had been a student of American architect Frank Lloyd Wright. He told me how he had had to prepare the master's porridge at the summer school at Taliesin. The students were on a rota and had to get up at 4 a.m. to stir the great man's breakfast. It's unimaginable now to think of students with such discipline and deference to their teacher.

Serves 2–4
100g rolled oats, or a use a mug
to measure as we do
600ml cold water
A pinch of salt

To serve:
Cream and brown sugar,
or milk and honey

If the porridge has been soaked overnight, add a pinch of salt, bring to the boil and simmer for a few minutes, stirring constantly with a wooden spoon to prevent it catching on the bottom of the pan.

If you're making the porridge from scratch, it will need longer, slower cooking. Pour about 600ml water into the pan, sprinkle the oats on top, add the salt and bring to a simmer, stirring constantly. Precise cooking times aren't possible as it depends on the type of oats and how they are processed, but you want a nice, creamy mixture. I find it normally takes about 5 minutes.

Serve with a splash of cream and some brown sugar, or milk and honey.

Eggy bread

We have a surfeit of eggs in late spring as the hens at last begin to lay enough to justify the care and attention lavished on them over the unproductive winter months. We then eat a lot of eggs, which makes it all worthwhile.

I love hearing the hens clucking away with their throaty mutterings, happily scratching around the garden all day. Unfortunately, they are occasionally taken by brazen local foxes when they have young to feed and are very hungry. It is always devastating and we have to start all over again with new batch of hens and wait impatiently until they begin laying. In the meantime, I have to buy eggs, which feels really odd as we are so used to our own. But I do try to get hold of the freshest organic eggs sold locally. Having our own hens has spoilt me though, as nothing compares to our lovely fresh eggs with their dark yellow yolks. Anything cooked with them turns the most wonderful golden colour.

I often make eggy bread for myself for a late breakfast as it is so easy. The children enjoy cooking their own slices too. The best bread to use is a baker's white loaf with a soft, doughy interior. I usually fry eggy bread gently in butter, though it is also very tasty cooked in bacon fat. Eggy bread can be sweet or savoury, served with maple syrup or honey, or with salty, crisp bacon.

Serves 4
4 large eggs
1.2 litres whole milk
4 thick slices of white bread
100g unsalted butter or bacon fat

To serve:
Maple syrup, honey or crisp bacon

Whisk the eggs and milk together in a bowl. Pour the mixture into a shallow, flattish dish, big enough to fit a couple of slices side by side. Soak the bread slices in the mixture for a few seconds, turning them over to coat both sides. As you carefully lift each slice out of the eggy mixture, allow any excess to drip back into the bowl.

Heat the butter in a frying pan until it is foaming, then put one or two slices of the prepared bread in the pan and gently fry on both sides until golden brown and cooked through. Repeat with the rest of the slices.

Serve hot, with maple syrup, honey or crisp slices of bacon.

Pancakes

Pancakes are very quick to make, but you do need to let the batter rest for at least half an hour before cooking them. Be warned: the first pancake is usually a disaster but the rest should be fine. This recipe makes lots, but it can easily be halved if you prefer.

I like my pancakes with maple syrup and butter, or a squeeze of lemon and caster sugar, but the possibilities are endless, whether savoury or sweet.

Makes about 16 pancakes
250g plain flour
A pinch of salt
2 eggs
600ml milk
Unsalted butter, softened, for frying

To serve:
Maple syrup, butter, lemons, caster sugar

Sift the flour and salt into a medium-sized bowl.

Make a well in the centre of the flour and add the eggs. Start mixing with a wooden spoon. Add the milk a little at a time, stirring constantly, until you have a smooth(ish) batter. If it's particularly lumpy, use a whisk and beat until smooth.

Tip the mixture into a jug to make it easier to pour into the pan later. Allow to rest in a cool place or the fridge for at least 30 minutes and up to an hour.

Heat a 25cm frying pan over a high heat until a drop of water trickled onto the surface bounces and sizzles. Take a generous pad of kitchen paper and smear on some softened butter. Rub it onto the hot pan to give a fine coating. Repeat as necessary between pancakes.

Pour in a generous tablespoon of the batter, tilting and turning the pan to spread the mixture thinly. You are aiming at a thin pancake with slightly crisp edges, about the size of a tea plate. The moment bubbles appear on the surface, flip the pancake over and lightly cook the other side – you can do this with a spatula if you prefer. Once the pan is really hot, the first side will take no longer than 1–2 minutes, and the other side about another 30 seconds.

Pile the finished pancakes onto a plate and keep in a warm oven until you've used up all the batter, or serve immediately as you cook them.

Sprinkle them with sugar and a squeeze of lemon, or any other favourite combination.

Fried tomatoes

Tomatoes change in taste as the season progresses. The first ripe tomatoes of the year, especially if they are not 'beefsteak' varieties and not too big, seem to have more intense sweetness than those that follow a month or so later. In our own garden, the first tomatoes tend to be ready at the end of July, and the month of August is dominated by fried tomatoes for breakfast. Some varieties are especially good for this. Shirley is acknowledged by gardeners as a good, all-round tomato for growing organically and it fries very well. Black Russian is, I think, even better, with a delicious depth of flavour.

Tomatoes are ideal for breakfast because the taste lingers satisfyingly in the mouth without being overpowering. The British tend to treat them as a kind of breakfast vegetable, alongside the meat of bacon or sausage, and therefore don't value them enough. In high summer they deserve centre stage, and the only accompaniment they need is a little garlic and toast or fried bread.

I love to wander outside on a beautiful August morning – when the garden is dewy but already warming with a low sun – and go to the greenhouse to choose a handful of ripe tomatoes. It's rare to buy properly ripe tomatoes because when they are truly ready, they are fairly delicate and will not last or travel well.

A ripe tomato has a warm, musky aroma with skin that is taut and full, and perhaps even slightly split. It comes away from the vine easily with a little twist. I simply halve and fry them over a low heat in olive oil for about 10–15 minutes, depending on their size and ripeness – a small, ripe tomato will fry twice as quickly as a larger, slightly less ripe one – adding some chopped garlic for the final few minutes. The juices will run and mingle with the oil and garlic to create delicious, caramelised juices, which should be scraped out of the pan down to the last scrap and all placed on slices of good toast. The sweetness of tomatoes can take lots of salt and I sometimes, by way of variation, spread a little Marmite or Patum Peperium anchovy paste on the toast first.

Once you have eaten them like this, grown yourself and in their true season, you will seldom want to compromise with an inferior breakfast fried tomato again. I am very happy to have an intense, rather over-indulgent three or four weeks of them and then wait happily another 11 months for the season to come round again.

Kippers

Kippers are herrings that have been split, lightly salted then smoked over oak. They make a pleasingly savoury dish for breakfast.

Try never to buy artificially dyed kippers, only naturally smoked ones. It's best to buy them from a fishmonger who will not only verify this for you, but will probably know which smokery they're from too.

Serves 2
2 kippers

To serve:
Brown bread and butter

Kippers are simple to prepare. Just place them in a deep, wide-necked jug and pour over enough boiling water to submerge them. Leave them for 5–10 minutes, by which time the flesh will have plumped up.

If you don't have a suitable jug, place the kippers in a shallow pan and pour boiling water over them. Keep them on a low simmer until they are plump, about 5 minutes.

Drain them well and eat warm with brown bread and butter and a cup of strong tea.

Kedgeree

Kedgeree can be eaten at any time, not just at breakfast. For convenience, it can be made a few hours in advance and reheated. Kedgeree is also very good made with leftover salmon.

Serves 8
1kg smoked haddock
500ml milk
500g basmati rice, brown or white, rinsed
50g butter
2 medium onions, thinly sliced
2 teaspoons medium curry powder
4 eggs
A small bunch of parsley (tough stalks
*   discarded), finely chopped*
Salt and freshly ground black pepper

Place the fish in a large, shallow pan with the milk and 500ml boiling water, bring back to the boil and simmer for 5 minutes to poach. Allow to cool for 5 minutes off the heat, until the fish flakes away from the skin easily. Remove the fish from the poaching liquid and flake the flesh, discarding the skin and bones.

Strain the cooking liquid and reserve. Tip the rice into a measuring jug, note the amount, then measure out one and a half times as much cooking liquid. If there is not enough liquid left from cooking the fish, top it up with boiling water. Pour the rice into a saucepan with the liquid. Bring to the boil and simmer, partially covered,

until the rice is cooked. White basmati cooks quickly, so check often as it should cook within 10–15 minutes. Brown rice can take over 30 minutes, but I like it best. When cooked, fluff it up with a fork.

Warm the butter in a frying pan over a medium-low heat and cook the onions for about 5 minutes, until softened, then stir in the curry powder. Cook together for a couple more minutes.

If you are serving the kedgeree straight away, boil the eggs as you cook the onions so they're warm when you add them to the dish. Simply put them into a pan of cold water, bring to the boil and cook for 6 minutes before plunging them into cold water. This cooks the whites while letting the yolks remain slightly soft.

Now assemble everything in a heatproof serving dish: start by mixing the onions into the rice, forking them together gently. Add the flaked fish and season with salt and pepper. Peel the eggs, cut them in half and place around the dish, then sprinkle on the parsley. We like to eat the kedgeree with mango chutney and a squeeze of lemon.

If you want to prepare the kedgeree ahead, make as described in the recipe, leaving out the eggs and parsley. When you are ready, cover with foil and reheat at 180°C/Gas Mark 4 for 40 minutes. Hard-boil the eggs at the last minute, then sprinkle the dish with parsley before serving.

Fried kidneys

It seems that kidneys for breakfast are no longer fashionable. I suspect that this is down to a general squeamishness about offal. People associate it with blood and guts, and the nearness of the word 'awful' to offal casts further doubt. More fool most people I say, because I think kidneys on fried bread or toast make one of the best savoury breakfast dishes of all.

Always buy your kidneys very fresh from a good butcher. They're sold on a Tuesday in our local town, as the lambs go to the abattoir on a Monday, so if they're on our breakfast menu, it's always on a Wednesday.

Calves' kidneys are also very good and can be roasted whole in their fat, rather like a hedgehog in clay, but lambs' kidneys are probably the best for frying for breakfast as they are small and cook very quickly.

Serves 1
2–3 lambs' kidneys
About 3 tablespoons plain flour
Butter and/or olive oil for frying
1 large slice of good white or
  sourdough bread
Salt and freshly ground black pepper

Remove the membranes from the kidneys, then slice them in half and remove the pale core with a sharp knife or scissors. Season the flour with salt and pepper and toss the kidneys in the mixture, shaking off any excess.

Warm a large knob of butter and/or olive oil in a frying pan over a medium-high heat and fry the bread until golden and crisp. Place in a warm oven while you prepare the kidneys. (Frying the bread with the kidneys doesn't work. It tastes very good but the bread resists crisping.)

Add more butter and/or olive oil to the pan, raise the heat and when it's very hot put the kidneys in the pan. Sear them on both sides and fry for just a couple of minutes. They should be pink on the inside and the juices should still be fairly bloody. Serve immediately on the fried bread and pour the juices from the pan over them. Eat very hot.

TOAST, ETC

Twenty years ago we bought one of those big Dualit toasters. Very retro, sleek and, at the time at least, fashionable. Very expensive too. But not very good at making toast. It was forever jamming and burning, giving an unsatisfactory state of toastiness.

We have never used another toaster because the truth is that toasters do not make good toast – they are invariably designed for sliced bread, which is too thin for good toast, and something we seldom buy. (That said, the Central Bakery in Leominster will slice any loaf for you at one of three thicknesses, which is handy if you are making a lot of sandwiches.) The ideal thickness for a crispy exterior and chewy but unsoggy interior is about the thickness of my forefinger or a paperback novel.

So much for the serious science, but it begs two questions: what is good toast and, if not a toaster, what do you use to make it?

Whilst my good toast may not be your good toast (and certainly not Sarah's – she likes hers ridiculously undercooked), there are basic standards to be met. Toast should never be soggy. Toast should never be brittle-dry. Toast should not be too burnt, although a little charring is fine by me. Toast should rarely be warm. This I know is contentious, and there are occasions when you want the butter to soak into it so it becomes a warm, gooey mass. But at breakfast toast should be fresh but cool, so the exterior has real crispness and the interior is chewy.

As for making it, you need two things. The first is high heat. We always use the top oven of the Aga, which makes perfect toast as long as you remember to check it before it overcooks. Over the years dozens of slices of bread reduced to sleek black charcoal have been hurled out of the window. (But then dozens of dishes have been charcoaled through neglect in the same oven too.) If you have a grill (we don't), that works well too, as does an open fire and a toasting fork. As children we always made toast for winter tea with a toasting fork, loading them with dripping or butter and Marmite and stacking the pieces on a plate on a trivet by the flames to keep warm and infuse with the juices. The hotplate of an Aga or electric stove (or even a barbecue) will make perfectly good toast too, although perhaps it cooks a bit too quickly to be ideal.

The other essential for good toast is good bread, or at least the right kind of bread. Modern, industrially produced white loaves make terrible toast, as I am reminded every time I stay in a hotel. The crumb is cotton-woolly and collapses as you bite into it, making a sticky pulp. The best toast comes from dough that has risen slowly – which precludes all packaged and most supermarket bread – and, on the whole, sourdough bread is ideal, although it can take an age to toast if at all fresh. I suspect that the habit of eating toast for breakfast came from the fact that slightly stale bread is much improved if toasted – in fact, very fresh bread is never as good toasted as a loaf that is a couple of days old, but even very stale bread will make perfectly acceptable toast if dampened with cold water before toasting in the oven.

Finally, toast should never be laid flat until it is ready to be spread, otherwise the moisture remains trapped beneath it. Even the best bread, toasted with infinite care, will go unacceptably floppy as a result.

Oatcakes

We eat a lot of oatcakes. They are lovely for breakfast, as an alternative to toast, with cheese and almost anything savoury. Although bought versions can be very good, these, like most freshly baked food, have a taste and crisp texture that cannot be bought. It is worth noting that medium oatmeal is finer than pinhead oatmeal and is not like the easily obtainable rolled oats, which are unsuitable for this recipe. It's not very difficult to track down medium oatmeal, though. You can find it in health-food shops and in some supermarkets.

Makes 15–20 oatcakes
200g medium oatmeal, plus more
*   for dusting*
50g plain flour
¼ teaspoon bicarbonate of soda
A pinch of salt
50g unsalted butter, cut into cubes

Preheat the oven to 190°C/Gas Mark 5.

Put the dry ingredients into a bowl and add the butter. Rub it in until the mixture is the consistency of breadcrumbs, then pour over just enough boiling water to form a stiff dough, about 2 or 3 tablespoons should do, mixing with a metal spatula or knife. Dust the worktop with more oatmeal and knead the mixture to form a ball.

Roll the dough out thinly to a thickness of 6mm, adding more oatmeal to the work surface if necessary. Cut into rounds or squares and carefully transfer them to a baking sheet using a spatula. Bake for 20 minutes until crisp.

Cool on a wire rack and store in an airtight tin, where they keep quite well for a couple of weeks.

Marmalade

Marmalade belongs to breakfast as much as porridge and eggs. Which is to say that it can be eaten at any time and for any reason, but breakfast is where it is clearly most at home, especially if it's preceded by anything fried, as its bittersweetness cuts through the fattiness and leaves a satisfying balance in the mouth. This, incidentally, is why marmalade is the best accompaniment to sausages. Try it. It's no odder than eating redcurrant jelly with lamb and just as nice.

Montagu's paternal grandmother was Leila Keiller, whose family, from Dundee, marketed marmalade and Dundee cake in the nineteenth century. Unfortunately, the family fortune was all blown by Granny's cousin in the process of excavating the prehistoric stone circle at Avebury, and none of it filtered down to her. But this recipe for marmalade did, and it supposedly came to her as the original Keiller marmalade.

Makes about 6 x 450g jars
900g Seville oranges
1 lemon
1.8kg granulated sugar

Scrub the oranges and lemon, then squeeze the juice from the fruit and remove the flesh and pips, keeping all to one side. Slice the peel into strips, as thin or coarse as you like.

Tie the pips and flesh into a muslin bag and put into a large saucepan or preserving pan together with the peel. Add 2.25 litres of water and bring to the boil. Simmer until the peel is soft and the water is reduced by half (if there is too much water the marmalade will not set), checking to see that it does not burn. This can take anything between 3 and 6 hours, and fills the house with a wonderfully rich, slightly burnt orangey smell.

When the peel is soft, warm the sugar in a low oven for a few minutes and add to the liquid, stirring constantly. Do not allow to boil until all the sugar is dissolved (check by dipping in a wooden spoon – you shouldn't be able to see any sugar crystals on it when you take it out). When it is ready, boil hard without stirring for 15–20 minutes. While it is cooking, chill a couple of saucers in the fridge.

Test to see if the marmalade is ready by taking a teaspoonful and dropping it onto one of the cold saucers. When it has cooled down, it should wrinkle when pushed with your finger. If it is at all sloppy, it needs more boiling.

When it's ready, take off the heat and leave to stand for 10 minutes before putting the marmalade into warm, sterilised jars. You can sterilise them by putting them through the hottest wash in the dishwasher, and warm them in a low oven. Cover with wax circles and cellophane, or seal with lids. Label and store in a cool, dark place for up to 2 years.

Elevenses

ELEVENSES IS ONE OF THE NICEST words in the English language. It embodies the sense of a break from your labours – and the just reward for a period of good and valuable work – as well as a stepping-stone between breakfast and lunch. Yet there is a gentility in it that also hints at domestic or sedentary work that is not too testosterone-fuelled or back-breaking. Elevenses is accurate too. Eleven o'clock is just right. Unless you have been hard at work since seven, ten is too early and by midday lunch is looming.

Even as recently as fifty years ago, I remember elevenses serving almost as a little meal in its own right, with a large pot of tea on the kitchen table (never coffee) and everyone present sitting around it politely, drinking tea and dipping into the biscuit tin. That tin was reserved solely for elevenses (although I used to steal from it regularly), so the biscuits were a daily treat, even if they were usually Rich Tea or plain digestive. Chocolate biscuits were for very high days or teatime – and then only if there were guests. In fact, I realise that they were treated as proper food, unlike the modern class of snacks that get eaten almost in lieu of food. Even up until the mid-1960s, everyone was always just a bit hungry, so a couple of digestive biscuits had meaning.

There is no reason why elevenses food cannot be both delicious *and* belong to that little meal, fitting into the mid-morning culinary niche in the same way that bread and jam serves teatime, or porridge fits breakfast. It is the only time of day that I drink coffee, and strong, bitter coffee allies itself well to sweetness and chocolate. A chocolate brownie with a cup of coffee at elevenses feels like winning a prize.

Biscuits, plain cake, flapjacks and buns all work well and are easy to make at home. By 'plain cake' I mean the rather old-fashioned seed cakes and plain sponges that were traditionally eaten with a glass of Madeira or sweet sherry. I like the idea of the combination, although it can seem a bit like imbibing a deconstructed trifle. Personally, I would rather stick to a good cup of coffee with a spoonful of honey and a flapjack, a brownie or – if really going out on a limb – a cheese scone.

Flapjacks

Flapjacks are easy to make and really useful for lunch-boxes, picnics and long car journeys. This simple recipe is good, but you can adapt it to your taste, adding sunflower seeds, sesame seeds, pumpkin seeds and dried fruit at the same time as the oats. Add just a sprinkling, though – if you add too much the flapjacks might break up.

Makes 12
50g butter
75g soft brown sugar
3 tablespoons golden syrup
180g rolled oats

Preheat oven to 180°C/Gas Mark 4. Butter a shallow baking tin, approximately 18cm square, or a brownie tin.

In a saucepan, gently melt the butter, sugar and golden syrup over a low heat until the sugar dissolves, stirring frequently with a wooden spoon. Remove from the heat and mix in the oats until they are completely coated.

Spoon the mixture into the baking tin, flattening it down gently with the back of the spoon. Bake for around 20 minutes until it's a light, golden brown.

Leave to cool in the tin but cut into squares while still warm as the mixture becomes too hard to cut when cold. The flapjacks keep well in an airtight container for up to a week.

Honey cake

This cake has a mild but pleasantly old-fashioned taste, as it is a little spicy and not too sweet. Cut into slices and lightly toasted, it can be served as a quick, delicious pudding with poached fruit (page 16) in autumn and winter, or berries and ice cream in summer. Honey is a preservative, so the cake keeps quite well in a tin for a few days.

Serves 6–8
100g butter
50g soft brown sugar
2 tablespoons honey
2 eggs
150g self-raising flour
1 teaspoon mixed spice
50ml milk

Preheat the oven 180°C/Gas Mark 4. Lightly butter an 18cm cake tin and line the bottom with buttered baking parchment.

Cream the butter, sugar and honey together in a mixer or food processor, or in a mixing bowl with a wooden spoon, until they are light and fluffy. Add the eggs one at a time, beating well after each addition.

Sift together the flour and mixed spice and fold into the batter. Add the milk little by little and stir until you have a smooth mixture.

Pour the batter into the prepared cake tin, smooth the top gently with a spatula and bake for 35–40 minutes, until a toothpick or skewer inserted into the middle comes out clean. Remove from the oven and let the cake cool for a few minutes in the tin before turning out onto a wire rack to finish cooling completely.

Seed cake

There are many old recipes for seed cake, and examples vary from the rich to the very plain. We make a plain cake flavoured with caraway seeds, which have a subtle, aniseed flavour. The plant used to be common in the wild in England, but now it is very rare, although it will grow easily enough in the garden. This cake is quite dense, moist and buttery, and as a special treat, we like to enjoy it served in the traditional way, with a glass of fortified wine such as Madeira or Marsala.

Serves 6
150g unsalted butter, plus a little
  more for greasing
150g caster sugar
3 eggs
2 teaspoons caraway seeds
200g self-raising flour, sifted
1–2 tablespoons water or milk,
  if the mixture needs loosening

Preheat the oven to 180°C/Gas Mark 4.

Lightly grease a 15 x 10 x 7cm non-stick loaf tin with butter and line the bottom with buttered baking parchment.

Cream the butter and sugar together in a mixing bowl with a wooden spoon until they are light and fluffy. Add the eggs one at a time, beating well after each addition and adding a little flour if it looks like it's going to curdle. Sprinkle in the caraway seeds, then gently fold in the flour. Add a little water or milk if the mixture seems too stiff – it should drop easily from the spoon.

Spoon the mixture into the prepared baking tin and bake for 45 minutes, or until a toothpick or skewer inserted into the middle comes out clean.

After the cake comes out of the oven, let it cool in the tin for a few minutes before turning it out onto a wire rack to cool completely. Each slice should have a golden crust with a pale yellow crumb, speckled with caraway seeds. It keeps well in a tin for several days.

Madeira cake

Madeira cake is due for a revival. Its simplicity is its virtue, making it the perfect antidote to legions of sickly, over-adorned cupcakes. This plain cake, embellished with strips of lemon, is lovely served in the middle of the morning with a glass of Madeira or sweet wine. In fact, the only time I have eaten it in Madeira itself, it was served with the local vinho verde, a slightly fizzy, very young, light white wine. The crumb is slightly dry and the texture more dense than a sponge cake. It keeps well in a tin for several days.

Serves 8
175g unsalted butter, plus a little more
 for greasing
1 lemon
175g sugar
4 eggs
275g self-raising flour, sifted
A splash of milk, if the mixture is too dry

Preheat the oven to 180°C/Gas Mark 4.

Lightly butter a 20cm cake tin and line the bottom and sides with buttered baking parchment.

Remove two strips of lemon peel, approximately 1 x 4cm, with a vegetable peeler or a very sharp knife, and grate the rest of the zest, being careful not to remove any of the bitter white pith.

Cream the butter and sugar together in a mixing bowl with a wooden spoon until pale and fluffy. Add the eggs one at a time, beating well after each addition, and adding a spoonful of the flour with the third and fourth egg to prevent the mixture curdling. Gently fold in the rest of the flour and the lemon zest. If the mixture seems a little dry and doesn't drop easily from the spoon, stir in a tablespoon or two of milk.

Pour the mixture into the lined baking tin and smooth the top with a spatula. Bake for 30 minutes before placing the strips of lemon peel on the surface. Put the cake back into the oven for a further 30 minutes, or until a skewer stuck into the middle comes out cleanly. Remove from the oven and leave for a few minutes until the baking tin can be handled before turning out and leaving to cool completely on a wire rack.

Store-cupboard brownies

These are easy to make from ingredients most of us usually have to hand, and are satisfyingly chewy. This is a great basic brownie recipe, with the combination of chocolate and nuts that I love. For a more luxurious version, try rich brownies (page 49).

Makes 16
100g butter, plus a little more for greasing
50g cocoa powder
2 eggs
225g caster sugar
1 teaspoon vanilla extract
50g flour
60–75g walnuts, roughly chopped

Preheat the oven to 180°C/Gas Mark 4.

Butter a 20 x 20 x 5cm tin and line the bottom and sides with buttered baking parchment.

Melt the butter in a saucepan over a low heat, then stir in the cocoa powder. Leave to cool.

While the butter is cooling, beat the eggs and sugar together in a bowl until light and creamy, then stir in the vanilla extract and the butter mixture. Sift the flour over the mixture and fold it in gently with a spatula. Sprinkle the walnuts over the bottom of the tin and spoon the brownie mixture over them.

Bake for about 25–30 minutes, being careful not to overcook as the brownies are meant to be chewy with a soft centre. A toothpick or skewer inserted into the middle should come out with a few crumbs still clinging to it. Cool in the tin on a wire rack before cutting into squares.

Rich brownies

Here is a richer version of the store-cupboard brownies (page 47). Use the best-quality chocolate you can find and savour each brownie as a luxurious treat. I like to use hazelnuts in this recipe but you can use walnuts if you prefer.

Makes 16
150g hazelnuts or walnuts
250g dark chocolate, at least
    70 per cent cocoa solids
250g unsalted butter, plus a little
    more for greasing
6 eggs
375g caster sugar
1 teaspoon vanilla extract
150g plain flour, sifted

If you are using hazelnuts, you will need to toast them first. Place them on a tray in an oven preheated to 180°C/Gas Mark 4 and toast blanched nuts for about 7 minutes, unblanched ones for 10 minutes. Keep an eye on them, as they burn easily, and give them a shake halfway through so they toast evenly. Wrap unblanched nuts in a clean tea towel when you take them out of the oven, leave for a minute, then rub them quite vigorously to remove the papery skins.

Chop up the toasted hazelnuts or the walnuts.

Preheat the oven to 180°C/Gas Mark 4. Butter a 20 x 20 x 4cm baking tin, and line the bottom and sides with lightly buttered baking parchment.

Break the chocolate into small pieces and put into a heatproof bowl with the butter. Place the bowl over a pan of barely simmering water (the bottom of the bowl should not touch the water) and melt, stirring until smooth. Cool for a few minutes.

In a mixing bowl, beat the eggs and sugar with the vanilla extract until light and fluffy. Stir in the cooled chocolate and butter, then gently fold in the flour.

Cover the base of the tin with the nuts and pour over the brownie mixture. Bake for 20–25 minutes, until a toothpick or skewer inserted into the middle of the brownie comes out with a few crumbs clinging to it. Cool on a wire rack in the tin before cutting into squares.

Cheese scones

Sweet scones (page 225) are perfect for teatime, but a cheese scone is very good with a mid-morning cup of coffee or served with soup for lunch. This recipe is very quick to make – within half an hour you have a plate of golden, crusty scones to fill the gap between breakfast and lunch.

Makes 6–8
225g self-raising flour, plus extra
   for dusting
1 teaspoon English mustard powder
A pinch of cayenne pepper
A pinch of salt
60g unsalted butter, chilled and cut into
   small cubes, plus a little more for
   greasing
100g strong Cheddar cheese
150ml milk

Preheat the oven to 220°C/Gas Mark 7. Lightly butter a large baking sheet or tray.

Sift the flour, mustard powder, cayenne pepper and salt into a mixing bowl and add the cold butter. With a light touch and cool fingers, rub in the butter until the mixture is the consistency of coarse breadcrumbs.

Grate half the cheese into this mixture and stir. Make a well in the middle and pour in the milk. Quickly mix it together with a metal spatula or knife into a sticky dough. Turn it out onto a lightly floured surface and pat the dough into a disc about 2.5cm thick. Dip an 8cm cutter in flour and cut the dough into rounds, flouring the cutter each time. Try to keep the sides straight, or the scones will be lopsided as they rise. Any scraps can be briefly kneaded together and cut into more scones.

Carefully place the scones on the baking sheet or tray. Cut the rest of the cheese into thin slices or grate it coarsely and place it on top of the scones. Bake until they are golden brown, about 15 minutes.

Using a spatula, carefully transfer the scones to a wire rack and allow to cool before splitting them open and eating with butter.

Lunch

SOME OF MY HAPPIEST MEMORIES as a child are of playing outside and being hungry, and then hearing the muffled resonance of the gong for lunch. This was as effective a way as any other of getting five children to come to the house from dens, tree-houses and across the fields. Lunch was always good, not least because I was always hungry for it. I still am, every day.

No other meal adapts so well to a huge range of menus and circumstances. Lunch remains lunch whether it is a pork pie and an apple or a nine-course banquet. For children it is the main meal of the day, which is why, I suppose, we still call it school dinner – although in its reduced, packed form it is lunch.

One of the best things about working from home is the way that lunch, the most malleable of meals, can be shaped into as personal a form as time, invention and the fridge or store cupboard will allow. Lunch at home clearly falls into two distinct styles. There is the much rarer formal meal, especially prepared for guests or festivity, and then there is the everyday lunch, quickly put together from what you have to hand.

Lunch is one of the great incompatibles that our marriage has had to learn to negotiate. Sarah loves lunches with good food and company, a relaxed atmosphere and a sense of occasion. But on a day-to-day level she would happily ignore lunch, and considers my insistence on it an intemperate interruption of her day. Her timetable is Tudor whereas mine is Victorian; I would no more deliberately miss lunch than stay up all night. Both have been known to happen, but there is always a price to pay.

There are fixed rules to my lunch. Its default position is at one o'clock. Earlier is fine if it fits the rhythm of that day, but much later than one stretches things to the point at which the situation is barely retrievable, and anything past two o'clock is always a case of salvaging the wreckage of the missed meal. But such intolerance is balanced by an absolute acceptance of whatever is available and edible. I have been known to lunch perfectly happily on half a cold baked potato spread with homemade chutney for first course, and the other half spread with jam for pudding.

It is a short step up from this to relishing reassembled leftovers. In fact, the creative use of leftovers is part and parcel of the enjoyment of lunch, when dishes like the last of the stew fried and served on toast, or cabbage and potatoes hashed together with chilli and Worcestershire sauce, which would never be placed before a guest, can be genuinely delicious. It is a very unmodern idea to prepare and cook, as opposed to unwrap, a snack. But this is essentially what many lunches amount to, and it can be traced back to the earliest roots of the meal.

Lunch evolved – and is perhaps still evolving – as a result of the steady drift of dinner from the Tudor 11 a.m. to the Victorian 8 p.m. or even later. Until dinner moved past late afternoon, there was no need to break up the day with another meal. In fact, throughout the sixteenth and early seventeenth centuries dinner matched the hour that we would expect to take lunch, and was followed about six hours later by supper, so the pattern of the meals, if not the content, was modern. As people increasingly worked away from home, breakfast was taken earlier, and it became common to take an informal snack between breakfast and dinner. But it did not seem to acquire its name – luncheon – until the beginning of the nineteenth century; by the time Jane Austen referred to it in *Pride and Prejudice* in 1813, the word seemed to have entered common use, with the first known shortening of 'luncheon' to 'lunch' occurring in 1829. But once the Victorians took hold of the idea of lunch, it became a daily fixture.

SOUP

Soup is a good thing. Every time I have it I wonder why I don't do so for every meal every day.

But the truth is that making soup is like making bread. Deeply satisfying and easy once you get into the swing of it, but too much to take on if you are in a hurry or feeling slightly inadequate. It is worth clearing that hurdle, though, because homemade soup is always a really satisfying way of making a warming, filling, tasty meal out of very little.

The chef Raymond Blanc once told me how his mother would make soup for lunch every single day simply by going round the garden and seeing what was there. I imagine a neat French housewife gathering a few select leaves and adding them to a delicate broth in which all the elements remain clearly identifiable, yet harmonise to reach something more than the sum of their parts. But the real point he was making is that you need only a small amount of any vegetable to make enough soup for a family. My own mother demonstrated the Britannic flip side of this Gallic ingenuity, often putting the remaining vegetables and gravy from Sunday lunch into the liquidiser until they had whirred into a slush, which she diluted with water or milk and served for supper as soup. It was sometimes passable, but more by luck than culinary judgement.

The basis of any soup is a good stock. We often have some chicken stock in the fridge because we eat roast chicken regularly and make stock from the carcass. It can be rather strong for some soups, but is an ideal base for anything that fits into the 'hearty' category, which inevitably includes any soup with a touch of body to it. Some stock, some leaves (kale, chard, spinach or cabbage all serve well), perhaps a few rashers of bacon chopped up and fried, some onions, garlic or leeks (leeks always work well in soup), a boiled potato loosely chopped and boiled enough in the stock to heat through – all make a very humble but good lunch that will take no more than ten minutes to put together.

My grandfather always ordered consommé when he took us, his five grandchildren, out to lunch – which he did often. Consommé struck me then, and still does a little, as soup that has had the joy strained out of it. I can appreciate clear soups and soups that are subtle and delicate, but the ones I like best are those that Sarah makes up from whatever is to hand in the kitchen or garden. They have a kind of festivity and common sense about them that exemplifies all that is best about home cooking.

Vegetable stock

Chicken stock

I prefer the clean taste of a vegetable-based stock in most soups and risottos. This is not an exact recipe, but more a base for other flavours. Depending on the season, I like to add richness with different vegetables, such as tomatoes in summer or mushrooms in autumn.

> Makes approximately 1.5 litres
> *3 tablespoons olive oil or*
>   *40g unsalted butter*
> *450g onions, roughly chopped*
> *450g carrots, roughly chopped*
> *4 stalks of celery, roughly chopped*
> *450g leeks (tough green parts discarded),*
>   *roughly chopped*
> *6 peppercorns*
> *2 bay leaves*
> *A sprig of thyme*
> *Salt*

Warm the olive oil or butter in a large saucepan over a medium-low heat. Add all the vegetables and sweat them, stirring frequently, until softened, about 15 minutes.

Pour over about 1.5 litres of water, add the peppercorns and herbs, bring to the boil and simmer gently, partially covered, for 45 minutes. Strain the stock and season to taste with salt.

I rarely make chicken stock from scratch using a whole bird as I like the frugality of making stock from the remains of one. Most weeks we eat a whole chicken, leaving the precious carcass to be transformed into a steaming broth.

This is done by putting the carcass in a large pan and pouring over just enough water to cover, adding 2 bay leaves, ½ teaspoon peppercorns and a quartered onion. You could also slice a leek and a large carrot and include them if you have them to hand. Bring to the boil and simmer for about 1 hour, skimming off any scum that rises to the surface.

Strain and refrigerate the stock as soon as it is cool. It will set as a jelly with a seal of fat. Use it within 3 days, or freeze for up to 3 months.

Sorrel soup

It is said that a French housewife always has a sorrel patch outside her back door. Not knowing any French housewives, I cannot say whether this is true or not, but I do know that we have a patch of sorrel in our own vegetable garden. For much of the year, when the surrounding beds are over-flowing with produce, it is overlooked and overshadowed, but in early spring sorrel comes into its own as a useful green before there is much else to pick.

The leaves have a sharp, lemony flavour and, when young and small, can be eaten fresh in salads. They are also good sliced finely and added to the beaten eggs of an omelette, or to a creamy sauce to accompany fish. We make a spring sorrel soup to cheer us up after the long winter.

Serves 4–6
30g butter
4 small red onions, finely chopped
6 garlic cloves, sliced
6 small potatoes, peeled and thinly sliced
1.5 litres homemade chicken stock (see opposite), or stock made from Marigold organic vegetable bouillon powder
A strip of lemon zest, approximately 1 x 5cm, pared with a sharp knife or vegetable peeler
1 large colander full of sorrel leaves (coarse stems discarded), roughly chopped
Salt and freshly ground black pepper

To serve:
Crème fraîche and croûtons (page 67)

Melt the butter over a medium-low heat in a saucepan large enough to hold all the ingredients.

Add the onions and cook gently for 5 minutes, then add the garlic and cook for a minute. Add the potatoes and stir gently for a couple of minutes. Pour in the stock, add the lemon zest and season with plenty of salt and pepper. Cook for about 15 minutes, until the potatoes are soft.

Add the chopped sorrel and simmer for a minute or two. Liquidise the soup, either with a stick blender in the pan or in batches in a food processor. Reheat, being careful not to let it boil.

Ladle into warmed bowls and serve with dollops of crème fraîche and croûtons fried in butter.

Nettle soup

Not all vegetables come from a seed packet or are carefully tended and raised in a border, and not all weeds are unwelcome to the cook. Certainly, nettles can be both a vicious weed and a refined ingredient. We have deliberately left several large patches of nettles in the garden. Not only are they an important habitat for wildlife – butterflies love them – but in spring the young shoots make a nutritious soup.

The stalks are tough even after cooking, so restrict your harvest to just the newest leaves. I always take the top two. You can treat them as a cut-and-come-again crop, taking them right back to the ground as soon as they flower to encourage a fresh batch of young leaves. I wear my rubber gloves to avoid being stung, although nettle sting is apparently a long-standing treatment for arthritis.

Once cooked, the leaves lose all their power to sting. They reduce rapidly, rather like spinach, and can be treated in much the same way. They were greatly valued by country people as a source of goodness – especially after a long winter, when fresh greens were scarce – and they are very rich in iron, vitamin C and minerals.

Serves 4
80g unsalted butter
4 medium onions, finely diced
1 large potato, peeled and cubed
4 garlic cloves, minced
2 litres chicken stock (page 58)
1 carrier bag full of nettle tips,
    well washed
Salt and freshly ground black pepper

To serve:
Crème fraîche (optional)

Melt the butter in a large saucepan over a medium-low heat and sweat the onions for about 5 minutes. Add the potato, stir and soften for another 5 minutes, then add the garlic and cook, stirring for a minute or two, taking care not to burn it.

Pour in the stock, bring to the boil and simmer for 10 minutes, until the potatoes are tender and squash easily with a fork. Add the nettles and simmer for 5 minutes. Cool slightly, then liquidise the soup in batches until smooth.

Return the soup to the pan, reheat gently (do not let it boil) and add seasoning to taste. If using crème fraîche, add a good dollop to each bowl before serving.

Minestrone

We always try to have a lump of Parmesan cheese to hand as it's so useful. Although I have tried to find a substitute, nothing compares to the flavour of an aged Parmigiano-Reggiano. Grated onto pasta and soup or shaved over salads, it has no equal. It tastes so good when it's fresh that it's tempting to break off little pieces to eat immediately, and it is certainly something to be savoured on its own with a glass of wine. If wrapped in greaseproof paper and a dampened tea towel, it will keep for a few days in a cool place, or for four weeks wrapped in greaseproof paper then foil in the fridge, but it is better to buy small amounts to use as you need it.

As Parmesan is an expensive cheese, I never want to waste a scrap. Once it has been grated down to the rind, I don't throw it away but keep it to add to minestrone soup to enrich the broth. The rinds keep well in a Kilner jar in the fridge, or even sealed in a bag in the freezer.

There are many ways to make minestrone and I have never cooked it the same way twice. But it should always be seasonal and fresh-tasting. The ingredients and quantities are influenced by whatever is available. In summer we use any combination of green beans, courgettes, peas, sorrel, little potatoes, asparagus tips and masses of fresh herbs. In winter we use cabbage or beet tops along with tinned tomatoes and cannellini or borlotti beans. The soup can be enriched with a little cream at the end of cooking, or a spoonful of pesto can be stirred into each bowl if you like.

Serves 4
2 tablespoons olive oil
1 red onion, roughly chopped
2 carrots, roughly chopped
4 sticks of celery, roughly chopped
4 garlic cloves
1.5 litres hot chicken stock (page 58),
*   or hot water*
A large pinch of salt
2 bay leaves
A sprig of thyme
1–2 pieces of Parmesan rind
A handful of pasta or Arborio rice
*   (optional)*
A small bunch of flat-leaf parsley
*   (tough stalks discarded), finely*
*   chopped*
Freshly ground black pepper

To serve:
Freshly grated Parmesan
Extra virgin olive oil

For summer minestrone:
Broad beans, peas, green beans, shredded
*   chard, shredded sorrel, asparagus tips,*
*   small new potatoes, fresh borlotti beans,*
*   diced courgettes*

For winter minestrone:
*Kale, 1 x 400g tin chopped tomatoes,
tinned borlotti beans or cannellini
beans, finely chopped leeks, shredded
beet tops, shredded cabbage*

To make summer minestrone, heat the oil
in a large saucepan over a medium-low
heat and sweat the onion, carrot and celery
until softened, about 10 minutes. Now add
the garlic and cook for a minute.

Add the stock and salt, bring to the
boil, then add the bay leaves, thyme
and Parmesan rind, which will soften
and swell.

Add the pasta, rice or new potatoes,
if using, and simmer until they are almost
cooked. Add the rest of the vegetables and
continue cooking for a few more minutes
until they are tender.

Discard the Parmesan rind, adjust the
seasoning, stir in the parsley. Serve in big,
warmed soup bowls, with extra virgin olive
oil trickled over the top and some grated
Parmesan.

For winter minestrone, heat the oil in a
large saucepan over a medium-low heat
and sweat the onion, carrot and celery
until they soften, about 10 minutes. Now
add the garlic and cook for a minute.

Strip the leaves from the kale and
finely slice the stalks before adding half of
them to the pan. Keep stirring to prevent
them from sticking, then add the tomatoes
and continue cooking for a few minutes to
reduce the liquid.

Add the stock and salt, bring to the
boil, then add the bay leaves, thyme
and Parmesan rind, which will soften
and swell.

Drain and rinse the beans and add to
the soup along with the pasta or rice, if
using, and simmer until the pasta or rice
is almost cooked. Add the rest of the
vegetables and continue cooking until
they are tender.

Discard the Parmesan rind, adjust the
seasoning and stir in the parsley. Serve in
big, warmed soup bowls, with extra virgin
olive oil trickled over the top and some
grated Parmesan.

Parsley soup

We grow rows of flat-leaf parsley, so I can pick it from spring to winter until the frosts have reduced it to sodden clumps of rotten leaves. It is possible, however, to buy big bunches in the market very reasonably. This bright green soup is one of my favourite ways of cooking parsley.

Serves 4
1 large leek
50g butter
1 medium potato, peeled and diced
*1.5 litres chicken or vegetable stock
  (page 58)*
*A large bunch of flat-leaf parsley,
  coarsely chopped*
Salt and freshly ground black pepper
2 tablespoons double cream

Wash the leek well, trim off the root and the tough green part, then chop into chunks and rinse again to remove any traces of grit. Warm the butter in a large saucepan over a medium-low heat and gently cook the leek and potato, stirring, for about 5 minutes. Add the stock, bring to the boil and simmer for 15 minutes, until the potato is soft.

Add the parsley. Simmer for 5 more minutes. Cool slightly, then liquidise in batches until smooth. Return to the pan, season and warm through gently. Stir in the cream and serve immediately in warmed bowls.

Cauliflower soup

This white and velvety soup has a subtle yet distinctive flavour. Cook cauliflower soon after buying because the delicate flavour becomes cruder with age.

Serves 4
25g unsalted butter
1 large onion, finely chopped
*1 small cauliflower, trimmed and broken
  into small florets*
600ml chicken stock (page 58)
300ml milk
Salt and freshly ground white pepper

To serve:
*Parmesan cheese or a white, salty cheese
  such as Lancashire*

Melt the butter in a saucepan over a medium-low heat and cook the onion slowly, stirring, for about 10 minutes. Do not brown as this will alter the flavour and appearance of the pale soup; add a tablespoon of water if it starts to colour. Add the cauliflower and cook with the onion for a couple of minutes.

Add the stock, raise the heat and simmer until the cauliflower is soft. Cool slightly, then liquidise until smooth. Return to a clean pan and add the milk. Heat gently until piping hot but not boiling, season with salt and pepper, and serve with the cheese grated or crumbled over the top.

Cock-a-leekie

This classic, Scottish winter soup was traditionally a one-pot way of serving a boiling fowl with vegetables.

I like to serve this in large, shallow soup plates so that all the ingredients can be shared out more easily. Any leftover poached chicken can be eaten separately in salads, coronation chicken (page 85), sandwiches or pies.

Serves 8–10
1 chicken, about 1.8kg
2 onions, halved
4 medium carrots, kept whole, or 2 large
  ones, chopped into chunks
4 sticks of celery, halved
12 peppercorns
2 bay leaves
A small bunch of thyme
12 small leeks, about 3cm in diameter
12 prunes, stoned
Salt and freshly ground black pepper

Place the chicken in a deep pan and cover with water. Add the onions, carrots, celery, peppercorns, bay leaves and thyme. Bring to the boil, then simmer gently for 1 hour, skimming off any scum that rises to the surface. Let the chicken cool in the stock.

Remove the chicken from the pan. Strain the stock (you should have about 2 litres), and discard the vegetables and herbs. Pour the stock back into a clean pan and set aside.

Clean the leeks, carefully removing any grit or soil, and trim off the ends (reserve some of the green tops for garnishing). Cut the rest of the leeks into 2cm lengths, put them into the stock and bring to the boil. Simmer until soft, at least 20 minutes. Add the prunes for sweetness in the last 5 minutes of the cooking time. Season and ensure the soup is piping hot.

Place a slice of the poached chicken in the bottom of each warmed soup plate, then pour over some of the stock, leeks and prunes. Finely slice the reserved green tops of the leeks and use to garnish the soup.

Potato soup with croûtons

Potato soup might not sound very glamorous, but it's utterly delicious, comforting and simple. I'd rather eat a bowlful of this than many more elaborate concoctions. It doubles or triples up well, so adjust the quantities depending on how many people you have to feed.

Serves 4–6

6 medium potatoes or 4 large ones,
  peeled and cut into 4cm cubes
1.2 litres whole milk
Salt and freshly ground black pepper

For the croûtons:
4 thick slices of bread, cut into 2cm cubes
70g unsalted butter

Put the potatoes into a saucepan with the milk and 300ml water, bring to the boil and simmer for 30–40 minutes, until the potatoes are very tender.

Mash the softened potatoes into the liquid with a potato masher. If you want a smoother soup, press through a sieve at this stage. However tempting it may be, it's not a good idea to purée potato soup in a blender as the texture becomes gluey and unpleasant. Return the soup to the pan and reheat.

Meanwhile, make the croûtons. Place the cubes of bread on a baking sheet and toast them lightly under the grill or in a hot oven, being careful not to burn them.

Warm 50g of the butter in a frying pan over a medium heat and fry the bread until golden. I find that making the croûtons this way, rather than just frying them from scratch, means they crisp up faster and soak up less butter.

Season the hot soup well with salt and pepper and stir in the remaining the butter. Serve in warmed bowls with the croûtons sprinkled over the top.

Leek and
potato soup

I like to think of our garden as a quicker and more convenient source of ingredients than any shop, but today the lure of the warm, dry supermarket is very tempting. As I write this, it's nearly lunchtime and it has been raining hard all morning. The ground is sodden and the cloud unbroken. However, I need to go out and dig up some leeks, so putting on as much waterproofing as I can, I head outside. My boots are clogged and the rain drips down my neck.

Sometimes little trays of prepared vegetables seem so much easier, but it's all worth it as the leeks are for this delicious soup. Nothing is simpler than this recipe. All you need are equal weights of trimmed leeks and peeled potatoes cooked in salted water and served with a little butter. That's it.

Serves 4
450g leeks, trimmed weight
450g potatoes, peeled
550ml water, or very light chicken or
  vegetable stock (page 58)
40g unsalted butter
Salt and freshly ground black pepper
Chopped chives, for garnishing

Wash the leeks well, peel off the outer layer and trim back to the white part. (I actually like a bit of the green part too, as long as it's tender.) Slice into 1.5cm rings and wash again to remove any traces of grit.

Cut the peeled potatoes into quarters and slice them again into small pieces.

Pour the water or stock into a pan, adding a little salt if you're just using water. (While this soup is delicious made with just water, you can make it richer by using stock, but if it is not *very* light, it will spoil the delicacy of the flavours.) Bring your chosen liquid to the boil and add the vegetables. Cook until the leeks are soft and the potatoes are on the point of breaking up, about 20 minutes. The soup should be rough-textured, not smooth.

Stir in the butter, test for seasoning, then ladle the soup into warmed bowls. Sprinkle with chopped chives before serving.

Pea and ham soup

Pea and ham soup is traditionally made with dried split peas. I have been served a bowl of it, which was no doubt authentic, consisting of a thick, beige-coloured gruel with gristly, dirty pink scraps of ham. If I were a starving peasant, I would eat it, but if I served it to my family today, they would probably spit out.

This version is, thankfully, an appetising green colour with a sweet taste. It's a good way of using up peas towards the end of their season as they begin to become mealy, and it works equally well with frozen peas. If you have stock from a ham bone or a few scraps of ham or boiled bacon, this soup is a great way to use them up. A thickly sliced rasher of bacon, ideally home cured by your butcher, works well if you're starting from scratch.

Serves 4
20g unsalted butter
1 onion, finely chopped
1kg fresh or frozen peas, shelled weight
1 litre light ham or chicken stock (page 58)
150g cooked ham or fried bacon
Salt and freshly ground black pepper

To serve:
Single or double cream

Melt the butter over a medium-low heat in a large pan and fry the onion until it is soft and translucent, about 15 minutes.

Add the peas and stock and simmer until the peas are soft – 15 minutes for fresh ones, 5 minutes for frozen. Cool slightly, then purée the soup until smooth using a stick blender or food processor.

Cut the ham or bacon into small pieces and add to the soup. Taste for seasoning, warm through and serve piping hot in warmed bowls with a splash of cream.

Beetroot soup

Earthy, economical and a fabulous colour, this is one of my favourite soups. It's easier to use small beetroots as they cook more quickly, and I prefer to roast rather than boil them as it intensifies their flavour.

You can save the discarded beetroot tops (see below) to make the recipe on page 96.

Serves 4
1.5kg beetroot (about 8 smallish ones)
A few sprigs of thyme
2 tablespoons olive oil
1 medium onion, finely diced
1 litre light chicken or vegetable stock
  (page 58), or water
2 bay leaves
Salt and freshly ground black pepper

To serve:
Yoghurt (page 18) or crème fraîche
1 tablespoon finely chopped chives

Preheat the oven to 200°C/Gas Mark 6. Scrub the beetroot well, cut the tops off and trim the roots. Leave their skins on and cut into halves or quarters, depending on their size. Place in a roasting tin with the thyme, season well with salt and pepper and pour over 1 tablespoon of the oil. Toss to coat. Cover tightly with foil and roast for about 40 minutes, until soft. When the beetroot is cool enough to handle, peel off the skin.

Alternatively, you can cook the beetroot whole by placing them, with their skins on, in a pan of cold water and bringing them to the boil. They are ready when a knife slides into the centre easily. This can take 30–60 minutes, or even longer, depending on the size and age of the beetroot. When cool, skin them by rubbing them under a running tap. Cut into halves or quarters.

Once you have prepared the beetroot, warm the remaining oil in a pan over a medium-low heat and sauté the onion until soft, about 15 minutes.

Place the cooked beetroot in a food processor with the onion and blitz until smooth. Scrape the purée into a pan, then add the stock or water and the bay leaves. Bring to the boil and simmer for 10 minutes. Discard the bay leaves and season.

Serve with dollops of yoghurt or crème fraîche and a sprinkling of chives.

Pumpkin soup

Pumpkins make a very good, nourishing soup and they retain their glorious orange colour on cooking. This is a comforting soup in the autumn, and we make it all through the winter with stored pumpkins. You don't have to roast the pumpkin, but I find it adds more flavour, which goes beautifully with the fried sage leaves. This recipe also works well with squash.

If I'm in a hurry, I used Marigold organic vegetable bouillon powder in this soup. If using a bought stock, check before adding any extra salt as they can be more salty than homemade stocks.

Serves 6
1kg pumpkin, prepared weight
4 tablespoons olive oil
1 small red onion, finely diced
2 big garlic cloves, minced
2 ripe tomatoes, peeled, cored, deseeded
  and chopped, or 2 tablespoons
  homemade tomato sauce (page 102), or
  2 tablespoons shop-bought tomato purée
1 litre vegetable stock or light chicken stock
  (page 58)
A good handful of fresh sage leaves,
  stalks removed
Salt and freshly ground black pepper

Preheat the oven to 180°C/Gas Mark 4. Wash the pumpkin and cut it into 8 slices, removing any fibres and seeds with a spoon, but leaving the skin on. Place the prepared slices in a roasting tin, drizzle over 2 tablespoons olive oil and season well. Roast for about 40–60 minutes (the time will vary depending on the size of the slices and the freshness of the pumpkin), until the flesh is soft.

Warm 1 tablespoon olive oil in a large saucepan over a medium-low heat. Add the onion and fry until soft, about 10 minutes, adding the garlic for the last minute. Stir in the tomatoes, sauce or purée and remove from the heat.

When the pumpkin is cooked, scoop the flesh from the skin and place it in the pan with the onions and tomatoes. Add the stock and simmer for 10 minutes to allow the flavours to blend. Next, either purée with a stick blender in the pan or cool slightly and purée in batches in a food processor.

Season and reheat the soup, but take care – it has a tendency to erupt, lava-like, into alarming bubbles when heating because it is very thick, almost a purée. Check that it's thoroughly hot before serving as it appears to be boiling long before it has properly warmed through.

Heat the remaining tablespoon of olive oil in a frying pan and fry the sage leaves until just crisp. Ladle the soup into warmed bowls and scatter some of the sage leaves on each portion before serving.

Savoury bread

We have been making bread at home for the past 25 years, but have never been very good at keeping it up. There are flurries of enthusiasm that last for a few weeks, then gradually fade away. That's because we tend to make such a performance of it and it takes over the kitchen. The resulting bread – slow-rising, chewy, long-lasting and delicious – is wonderful, but the price in terms of disruption is very high.

If you're daunted by the idea of making a traditional loaf, this might be the one to try as it can be made quickly and simply. The recipe is based upon Italian focaccia, which is made with salt, lots of oil and often flavoured with herbs. To give it a spongier texture, replace half the flour with semolina. It is the perfect thing with a bowl of hot soup.

Makes 1 loaf
500g plain flour, plus extra for dusting
1 teaspoon fast-action dried yeast
1 teaspoon salt
1 teaspoon caster sugar
1 tablespoon olive oil, plus a little more
  for oiling the tray

For the topping:
2 small potatoes
1 onion
3 tablespoons olive oil
Salt and freshly ground black pepper

Mix the flour, yeast, salt and sugar in a large bowl. Make a well in the middle and pour in 300ml warm water and the oil. Mix with your hands until it forms a ball of dough. The texture should not be too dry. Add extra warm water if necessary.

Sprinkle some flour onto a clean surface and knead the dough with the heel of your hand, folding over the corners, turning it 90 degrees and kneading it again. Continue this process for about 10 minutes. Oil a baking tray approximately 35 x 25cm and stretch the dough by holding it up and allowing gravity to pull it into shape – do not try to press it to fit. Place on the tray, cover with a cloth and leave to rise in a draught-free, warm place for 40–60 minutes, until doubled in size.

While the bread is proving, slice the potatoes finely and cook in a little water until just soft. Slice the onion and sauté in a tablespoon of the oil over a low heat until softened.

When the dough has risen, preheat the oven as high as it will go, at least 230°C/ Gas Mark 8. Press the tips of your outstretched fingers all over the dough to make indentations. These act as reservoirs for the oil. Cover the surface with slices of potato and onion and season well. Sprinkle with a little of the oil. Bake in the very hot oven for 15 minutes. Remove and pour over the remainder of the oil. Serve torn into chunks.

COLD LUNCH

It is entirely possible to have an elaborate and delicious meal that has no hot food in it at all, but it tends to be the exception. There is something about serving hot food that adds an expression of effort that cold dishes can never quite attain. But the nature of lunch is such that, in our household at any rate, hot food is less common than the limited but perfectly satisfying range of cold dishes that make up a quick and simple meal.

Bread and cheese is our standard fallback and I love it. A supply of bread and oatcakes is essential, and while it would be lovely always to have very good cheese, ordinary Cheddar can be made delicious with homemade chutney or pickles. Nipping outside and collecting salad leaves elaborates the formula. Sometimes we will have a single beefsteak tomato each, slightly warm from the greenhouse, eaten with salt, pepper and a little dressing, or radishes swished under a cold tap and eaten with unsalted butter and sea salt. Add in some fruit or the leftovers of last night's pudding and satisfaction is guaranteed.

A cold lunch might be the most informal of all meals but it still deserves to be fully enjoyed – there's no point apologising for what it does not aspire to. And it is a short step to elevate this a little – so when we have guests or the whole family is at home, the cheese might be augmented by pâtés or pies and a slightly more involved cold vegetable dish that needs some preparation. But half the fun of an informal lunch is the ad hoc nature of pulling things from the fridge or larder and assembling a meal in minutes.

Radishes with bread and butter

I prefer food that needs little preparation; however, I would rather eat an apple and a piece of cheese than a ready meal. Despite the pictures on the packets, they are always disappointing, and on the rare times I have had to eat one it has made me feel quite ill.

A bunch of fresh radishes, easy to grow in early summer, or bought from a greengrocer, make a summery meal with bread and butter. Choose a bunch with bright, pinky red, firm skin, no wrinkles, and fresh leaves. Of course, the bread matters too. Avoid buying industrially processed bread that comes with a long list of ingredients. It should be made from mainly flour, yeast, salt and water.

Serves 2
1 bunch of very fresh, crisp radishes
Sea salt
Good bread
Unsalted butter, chilled

Wash the earth off the radishes and eat them dipped in a little salt. Accompany with a slice of the best available bread and cool butter. Their peppery crispness contrasts with softness of the bread. Heaven.

Marinated aubergines

Although we do grow aubergines, they can be a bit hit and miss, so when we have a successful crop we prepare them with care to make the most of them. If I see them in the market or greengrocer's, they're irresistible to me. When you're buying them yourself, always look out for ones with bright, shiny skins free of blemishes and wrinkles.

In this recipe, I have cooked them as simply as possible, using a classic Italian recipe. Their light yet curiously substantial texture is more like a good field mushroom than any other vegetable. They can be eaten as a separate course or with cold meats. Sometimes I like to serve them with roast red peppers (page 80) and scattered with basil leaves – the sight of them spread out on a plate is a lovely.

Serves 4 as a side dish
2 large aubergines
2 tablespoons olive oil
2 large garlic cloves
1 small bunch of basil, stalks removed
1 small bunch of parsley, stalks removed
100ml red wine vinegar
Salt

Cut the stalks and bases off the aubergines and cut lengthwise into 1cm slices. Place the slices in a colander, sprinkle with salt and leave for at least 30 minutes to drain (droplets of liquid will form on the surface). Rinse with cold water and pat dry with kitchen paper, then put the slices in a bowl with just enough olive oil to coat them.

Heat a ridged griddle pan until hot and cook the slices a few at a time, turning them when they are lightly browned on one side, and taking care not to burn them. This will take about 3 minutes per side.

Chop the garlic, basil and parsley and mix together well. Place a layer of cooked aubergines in a shallow bowl and sprinkle some of the chopped herbs over each slice. Continue to layer the aubergines and herbs until you have used them all up. Pour over the vinegar, cover the dish with cling film and leave for several hours (or even several days) for the flavours to develop. If you keep the dish in the fridge, it will come to no harm. Remove and bring back to room temperature before serving.

Roast red peppers

We like to make this salad whenever we can get hold of really thick-fleshed Mediterranean red peppers. Unfortunately, the more readily available Dutch peppers don't work as well because they are watery and thin, and disintegrate after you roast them. Like lemons, there are some fruit and vegetables that we can't grow or buy from local producers, so we have to rely on imported supplies. The dark red peppers, with their almost meaty flesh, need more heat than we can provide.

Given the right ingredients, this is a very easy dish to prepare and hardly requires dressing as the roasted peppers have an oily, sweet essence that flavours them. One large red pepper per person makes a generous portion, but it's worth making plenty as the salad will keep for a day or two if covered and kept in a cool place or the refrigerator.

I always use a hot oven for this dish, but the grill can be used for cooking small quantities if you prefer.

Serves 4–6
6–8 large (or 12 small) red peppers
1 lemon
3–4 tablespoons finely chopped parsley

Preheat the oven to 220°C/Gas Mark 7.

Leave small peppers whole; cut large ones in half. Cram the peppers into a roasting tin in a single layer, with the skins facing upwards if using halved large peppers, and place them in the oven until the skin starts to blacken, at least 20–25 minutes.

Remove the peppers from the oven, transfer them to a shallow bowl while still hot, and cover with cling film. Alternatively, put them in a plastic bag and seal tightly. Set aside for 15 minutes as this will loosen the skin. Peel off the skin with your fingers – it should come away easily – then scrape out the seeds.

Tear or cut the peppers into long strips and lay them on a flat dish. Strain the juices over them to get rid of any remaining seeds, then squeeze over a little lemon juice and sprinkle with the parsley. Serve warm or cold.

Borlotti beans

Borlotti are the most ornamental of all beans. Their pods are a creamy white flecked with red, and the beans have a purply-pink speckled surface. They can be eaten fresh, or allowed to ripen fully, then dried and stored for months in a sealed jar. I love sitting outside in the late summer sunshine, listening to the radio while podding them.

The pods are flattish and flexible when unripe, but become stiff and split open easily when the beans have reached maturity. Although they're an Italian vegetable, in our experience they do very well in the British climate.

Serves 3–4 as a starter
2 tablespoons olive oil
200g borlotti beans, podded weight
2 garlic cloves, sliced
2 bay leaves
A sprig of rosemary
Extra virgin olive oil
A small handful of freshly chopped parsley
Salt and freshly ground black pepper

Warm the olive oil in a deep frying pan or large saucepan over a medium-low heat. Add the beans, garlic, bay leaves and rosemary and cook gently for a few minutes until the garlic is softened but not browned. The beans will absorb the flavour of the garlic and herbs as they cook.

Add about 250ml water, just enough to cover the beans, and simmer until the beans are soft but not breaking up. Keep an eye on them, adding more boiling water to ensure they're covered if they look like they're drying out. This should take 20–30 minutes. It's very important not to add any salt during the cooking process as this will toughen the beans (this is true of all pulses).

When the beans are cooked, remove the herbs and drain the beans. Season well, pour over some very good olive oil and sprinkle with fresh parsley. Treat these lovely beans like a delicacy and serve on their own as a starter or as an accompaniment to roast meats.

Variation:
Fresh borlotti beans can be blitzed to make an unexpectedly delicate and creamy purée – delicious spread on toasted sourdough bread. Cook until tender as in the master recipe, then drain and reserve the cooking liquid. Blitz the beans in a food processor with just enough of the reserved liquid to make a smooth, creamy purée, adding some chopped parsley, salt and pepper to taste. This method also works well with freshly podded broad beans, substituting mint for the parsley.

Grilled courgettes with lemon thyme

I am surprised when people complain about having too many courgettes growing at one time in their gardens, as they are so versatile. As long you pick them every day or so, when they are small, they are a manageable crop and you can always give away any surplus. They are a useful summer vegetable as they can be eaten raw, grated or shaved into long ribbons with a potato peeler, then dressed in olive oil and lemon and scattered with chopped parsley. The flowers are edible too (page 262), and even the odd marrow is good to eat in autumn.

Serves 4 as a starter or side dish
8 courgettes, about 15cm long
Olive oil, for brushing
Extra virgin olive oil, for dressing
Juice and a little zest of 1 lemon
Flaky sea salt and freshly ground
    black pepper
A small bunch of lemon thyme

Heat a ridged griddle pan until it is smoking hot. Slice the courgettes diagonally about 2cm thick, and brush both sides with a little olive oil. This will prevent them from sticking and make them crisp on the outside. Spread the slices across the pan and cook until there are attractive brown stripes on each slice. Turn them over and repeat the process with the other side. You will have to cook the slices in batches, but as this is a cold salad, there is no need to keep the cooked pieces warm.

Lay out the grilled courgettes on a big plate, dress with a trickle of extra virgin olive oil, lemon juice, salt and black pepper.

Discard any woody stalks from the lemon thyme and scatter it over the salad. Grate over some lemon zest just before serving.

Quick sardine pâté

Although this recipe is based on the humble tinned sardine, it's surprisingly good and has a light, almost delicate texture. It's the sort of recipe you find next to the tinned consommé in those post-war cookery books for busy housewives, which I love to collect because they're so full of delicious and frugal ideas.

Serves 4–6
2 x 120g tins sardine fillets, drained
Cream cheese
Juice of 1 lemon
Cayenne pepper

Drain the fillets and weigh them. Tip them into a food processor with an equal weight of cream cheese and add the lemon juice. Whizz together until you have a light paste. Place in one big bowl or individual ones, then sprinkle the surface with cayenne pepper, which gives bit of a kick to the pâté without overwhelming it. Serve with hot brown toast.

Coronation chicken

This recipe was passed to me by my mother-in-law – it's handwritten in pencil and called 'Cream of Curry Sauce for Chicken'. She often prepared it for family gatherings, served with a rice salad made with peas, chopped cucumber and plenty of parsley and chives. It makes a summery centrepiece and everyone likes it.

I poach the chickens following the method outlined in cock-a-leekie soup (page 65), which produces lots of tender, juicy chicken. Coronation chicken can be made the day before and kept in the fridge, though you should allow it to lose some of its chill before you serve it.

Serves 10
1 tablespoon sunflower oil
1 small onion, finely chopped
2 teaspoons medium curry powder
1 rounded teaspoon tomato purée
125ml red wine
2 bay leaves
1 lemon
A pinch or two of sugar
450g mayonnaise
2 tablespoons apricot purée, made with
*   poached, dried apricots, or strained*
*   apricot jam*
3 tablespoons lightly whipped cream
2 poached chickens
A couple of handfuls of watercress
Pinch of cayenne pepper
Salt and freshly ground black pepper

Heat the oil in a small saucepan over a medium heat, add the onion and cook gently for 4 minutes. Add the curry powder and cook for another 2 minutes. Add the tomato purée, wine, bay leaves and 100ml water. Bring to the boil and add a slice of lemon, 1 teaspoon of lemon juice, and salt, pepper and sugar to taste. Simmer for 10 minutes, then strain and cool. Stir in the mayonnaise and apricot purée, then fold in the whipped cream.

Strip the meat off the chickens (discard the skin) and cut into pieces of roughly the same size – you want them to be fairly generous, not bite-sized ones. (Save the discarded chicken carcasses to make stock, page 58.) Pour the curry sauce over the chicken, stirring gently to coat. Taste and adjust the seasoning, adding more lemon juice if it's not sharp enough.

Just before serving, arrange the watercress around the edges of a large plate, spoon the coronation chicken into the centre and sprinkle with cayenne pepper.

Chicken liver pâté

This is a lovely smooth pâté, and all you need to serve with it is toast and some cornichons. Oh, and a glass of wine. Because of its simplicity, it's important to source the freshest organic chicken livers you can.

Serves 6
500g organic chicken livers
190g unsalted butter
1 onion, finely chopped
1 garlic clove, chopped
2 tablespoons brandy
60g butter, clarified (see below)
Salt and freshly ground black pepper

Pick over the livers and remove any discoloured bits. Melt the butter over a medium-low heat in a large frying pan, add the onion and gently fry until it softens and begins to turn golden, about 10–15 minutes. Add the garlic and cook for a minute, being very careful not to burn it. Next add the livers, season with salt and pepper, and cook for 2–3 more minutes. They should be cooked on the outside but still pink inside. Pour in the brandy, stir and remove from the heat.

Tip everything into a food processor and blend until completely smooth. Leave the pâté to cool.

To make clarified butter, warm the butter over a low heat until just melted. Skim the scum off the surface, then strain the rest of the melted butter through a sieve lined with muslin or kitchen paper into a clean bowl.

When the pâté is cool, scoop it into a dish, pour over a layer of clarified butter to seal, and refrigerate for a few hours before serving with plenty of thin, crisp toast.

Chutney

Bread and cheese is a staple lunch for us, eaten winter and summer at the kitchen table, always with some type of chutney. If there's a bumper harvest of rhubarb, plums, beetroot, pumpkin or tomatoes, they are made into chutney and a morning spent making enough for a year's supply is certainly worth the effort. Chopped windfall apples are a good addition as they give a slightly thicker texture to the preserve. Chutney's also an excellent way to use up ripe tomatoes, but they need to be chopped first and simmered until reduced by about half to get rid of excess liquid. (This isn't necessary with green tomatoes.)

The quantity in this recipe should be made in a preserving pan, but for smaller quantities, use the largest, heaviest stainless-steel pan possible and reduce the amounts in proportion to one another.

There is no need to follow the recipe slavishly. Adapt and combine different ingredients according to what is available, as long as the basic proportions are kept. Part of the fun is the surprise of successful combinations made by accident or circumstance.

Chutney will keep for months in a cool, dry place and – served with cold meats, savoury tarts or pies, as well as cheeses – livens up most meals. It improves with keeping too, as this allows the flavour to develop. A jar of homemade chutney also makes a welcome present.

Makes about 15 x 370ml jars

10 cloves

2 teaspoons black peppercorns

2–3kg prepared rhubarb or plums, cooked beetroot, green tomatoes or reduced ripe tomatoes, pumpkin or apple

1kg dried fruit – raisins, currants or sultanas

1kg light muscovado sugar

600g red or white onions, finely chopped

1.5 litres cider vinegar

2 teaspoons salt

4 red chillies, finely chopped

Thumb-sized piece of fresh ginger, peeled and grated

1 cinnamon stick

Grind the cloves and peppercorns until quite fine. Cut the fruit and vegetables into small, even-sized pieces. Put all the ingredients into a large, stainless-steel pan and heat them up gently, stirring until the sugar dissolves into the vinegar and juices. Bring to the boil and simmer for about 40 minutes, stirring occasionally so it doesn't catch on the bottom of the pan. The mixture should thicken to the point where a wooden spoon drawn across the bottom of the pan leaves a clear line for a few seconds.

Pot up the chutney in warm, sterilised jars (page 37). Cover with waxed discs and cellophane, or vinegar-proof lids. Leave to mature for about 6 weeks before using. It will keep for up to 2 years.

HOT LUNCH

Lunch, for all its apparent simplicity, has subtle gradations. Sunday lunch is clearly a thing unto itself, loaded with expectations and traditions that bread and cheese or a bowl of soup do not fulfil. But a proper cooked lunch can span the gap between reheated leftovers – always a joy – to a carefully prepared meal, a bottle of wine, good friends and the afternoon to enjoy it.

The food we serve as a hot meal in the middle of the day is completely interchangeable with that of our evening meal. This is mainly familiar, comforting food that does not inhibit an afternoon's work nor prohibit a good night's sleep. These dishes are at the core of all home cooking because they exemplify the modest confidence that does not need public applause to validate them. They range from a glorified snack like tomatoes on toast, which can be put together in the time it takes a kettle to boil, to fish or cottage pie, which can be made well beforehand and reheated for subsequent meals.

If I seem reverential towards leftovers, then I have no apologies for that. Last night's supper reheated is surprisingly often an improvement on the first outing. Every kind of hot pie, sweet or savoury, can make at least two appearances, and stews famously improve with age. But to stolidly outline recipes for dealing with leftovers is mostly to miss the point. Leftovers should be free of culinary care. You make it all up as you go along, and if sometimes it ends up a mess, just feed it to the dog.

I love the sense of abandon that a really good lunch carries with it, based upon the knowledge that the rest of the day is, if not lost, then trailing in its wake. But the best lunches of all are a surprise. Every now and then I will wander into the kitchen at lunchtime contemplating bread and cheese to discover that Sarah has quickly and quietly 'just made a little something'. The day lights up.

Steamed purple sprouting broccoli

Purple sprouting broccoli is one of my favourite vegetables. At the end of winter, when it's in season, we prepare it in several ways. Lightly cooked and served with melted butter, it is as much of a treat as fresh asparagus and it's also good added to pasta as a sauce. It can be bought in bunches held together by elastic bands like purple posies in greengrocers or farmers' markets.

This makes an excellent starter, eaten like asparagus with your fingers, or an accompaniment to any meat or fish. To pick the florets, pull them towards you from the plant. They will snap cleanly with some stalk and young leaves, all of which can be eaten. The smaller they are, the tenderer they taste, although heads the size of a penny are probably best.

Serves 4–6
1kg purple sprouting broccoli florets
Salt and freshly ground black pepper

To serve:
Freshly squeezed lemon juice
Extra virgin olive oil

If you don't have a steamer, an ordinary pan with a colander placed over it and a lid on top works just as well – just make sure the water doesn't come above the bottom of the colander. Pour 5cm or so of water into the bottom of your steamer or pan and bring to the boil. Place the broccoli in the steamer or colander, put the lid on top and cook until the stalks are just tender, about 5–7 minutes. Season and serve immediately with a little lemon juice squeezed over and a trickle of olive oil.

Variation:
Gently sauté 2 finely chopped garlic cloves in 2 tablespoons of olive oil over a low heat for a minute. Add 1–2 chopped red chillies or ½ teaspoon chilli flakes and sauté for a further minute. Toss the steamed purple sprouting broccoli in the spicy, garlicky dressing just before serving.

Purple sprouting broccoli and anchovies on toast

Although this recipe is uncomplicated, I take care when making it as it's easy to overcook the broccoli heads.

The chilli you use needs to be reasonably hot to compete with the strong flavours of the anchovy and lemon.

The best bread to use here is one with a coarse, dense crumb. Sourdough is ideal, although any rustic-style bread will do. When toasted, it's like bruschetta, an Italian version of toast, which is rubbed with a clove of garlic, then dribbled with extra virgin olive oil before being covered with the vegetables.

Serves 4

750g purple sprouting broccoli, trimmed
4 garlic cloves, finely sliced
2 tablespoons olive oil
2–4 dried chillies, finely chopped
1 x 100g tin anchovies in oil, drained
4 thick slices of bread
1 garlic clove, halved
4 tablespoons extra virgin olive oil
1 lemon, halved
Freshly ground black pepper

Blanch the broccoli in boiling water for about 4–5 minutes, being careful not to overcook it. The stems should be just soft enough to bite into. Drain thoroughly and keep hot.

While the broccoli is cooking, add the sliced garlic to the cold olive oil in a frying pan – if you add them to hot oil, they can burn and turn bitter. Warm and fry gently for no more than a minute, taking care not to let the garlic brown. Sprinkle with the chillies and stir together. Add the anchovies and keep stirring gently over a low heat until they have melted into the sauce, then squeeze over the juice of half a lemon. I used to add the cooked broccoli to the sauce at this stage but found this made it too mushy. To retain the bite of the stems, it is better to pour the sauce over them at the end.

Toast the bread under the grill and lay it out on a board, ready for assembly. Lightly rub each slice of toast with the cut side of the halved garlic clove. Dribble some extra virgin olive oil over each piece. Divide the broccoli evenly between the slices of toast and serve on individual hot plates with the anchovy sauce poured over the top. Add a generous squeeze of lemon, some pepper and another slosh of extra virgin olive oil and eat immediately.

Hot cucumbers

Much as I love cucumber – especially finely sliced, lightly salted and sandwiched between thin slices of bread and butter – one or two at any one time would be enough. So in summer, I am always faced with the task of using up our cucumber glut in as many different ways as possible.

Cucumber salad is easy to make – simply sprinkle skinned and sliced cucumbers with a little sugar and vinegar. It is very refreshing and crunchy and the secret is to leave it for an hour to crisp up in the fridge before eating. It is especially good with any kind of fish.

Cucumbers are also a surprisingly delicate vegetable if cooked in a little butter, seasoned well and sprinkled with herbs. Hot, they are the perfect accompaniment to roast chicken or delicate fish.

Serves 4
1 large cucumber
A large knob of butter
1 tablespoon double cream (optional)
2 tablespoons finely chopped parsley
2 tablespoons finely chopped chives
Salt and freshly ground black pepper

Peel the cucumber – a potato peeler is ideal for this job – and cut lengthways into quarters. If the cucumber is young and female, there is no need to remove the seeds, although in older fruits they can become somewhat coarse, so it's best to remove them with a teaspoon. Divide the quarters into three equal lengths so you have 12 equal-sized pieces of cucumber.

Melt the butter in a frying pan over a medium-low heat and cook the slices until they are lightly browned but not soggy – this should take about 5–10 minutes. Season well, add the cream if desired and sprinkle with the chopped herbs. Serve hot.

Tomatoes on toast

Once the tomatoes start to ripen in late summer, we probably eat them in some form or another every day, making all the weeks of having to water the plants in the greenhouse worthwhile. Although they are fantastic just sliced in simple salads, tomatoes are also wonderful prepared like this – scattered with herbs and served on thick slices of toasted bread.

Later on in the autumn, if there is a glut of little tomatoes, I pull them off the vines and cook them in a little oil for a few minutes, which caramelises the juices, before spreading them over the toast. Towards the end of the season, we make them into sauces for the winter (page 102).

This is a very simple recipe as it doesn't have many ingredients, but each one is important – it relies on really good bread and oil and the freshest of herbs. Be generous with the tomatoes, piling them up high on the toast. Serve on individual plates or on one large, flat dish.

If you want to roast the tomatoes, preheat the oven to 220°C/Gas Mark 7. Scatter the tomatoes in a roasting tin, season and trickle over 2 tablespoons olive oil. Roast for about 30 minutes until the tomatoes are soft and starting to char slightly around the edges.

Toast the bread and while it's hot, rub the cut side of the garlic clove over each piece. Trickle over 2 tablespoons olive oil to moisten the surface.

Either divide the cooked tomatoes between the slices of toast or scatter over the raw tomatoes, then sprinkle over lots of basil leaves. Season with salt and pepper and add a little more oil. Slivers of Parmesan cheese shaved over the tomatoes with a potato peeler are a good addition, but not essential.

Serves 4
Very ripe tomatoes – about 4 large
  beefsteak ones, chopped, or
    24–30 cherry tomatoes, kept whole
2–4 tablespoons extra virgin olive oil
4 slices of good bread, such as sourdough
1 garlic clove, halved
A large handful of basil leaves
Sea salt and freshly ground black pepper
Parmesan cheese (optional)

Beetroot tops

I hate waste, especially wasted food. When we're all at home, any leftovers are usually eaten by the following day. In fact, we often cook more than we need so there is plenty for other quickly assembled meals or for dipping into when peckish. Any remaining scraps go to the animals. Vegetable peelings go on the compost, so eventually they are put back into the soil in a satisfying cycle.

We grow lots of beetroot, which are either roasted (page 129) or grated raw into salads. We also make them into soups (page 71) or boil them whole. The leaves are edible – we add the tiny, dark red ones to salads, and blanch the bigger leaves to serve as a leafy vegetable. In summer the leaves are prolific and tender, providing a useful source of greens. You don't have to grow your own, as bundles of small, fresh beetroot with their leaves still attached are easily available in markets and greengrocers.

This recipe is a by-product of our roasted beetroot, and we often serve the leaves cooked like this the next day. They are delicious with any meat, or can be seasoned with garlic and chilli and piled up on toasted bread.

Serves 4–6
750g–1kg beetroot leaves (from about
12 beetroots), including their soft,
tender stalks
4 garlic cloves, finely chopped
2–4 red chillies, halved, deseeded
and finely chopped
2 tablespoons olive oil, for frying
1 lemon
4 slices of good bread, toasted
2 tablespoons extra virgin olive oil,
for dressing
Flaky salt and freshly ground black pepper

Pick over the leaves and discard any old or tough ones. Trim the stalks if necessary, although they soften and cook down with the leaves. Bring a big pan of water to the boil and blanch the leaves for about 5 minutes. Drain well. At this stage, they can be seasoned and dressed with a little extra virgin olive oil before being served hot, just as they are.

Alternatively, add the garlic and chillies to a frying pan of cold oil and warm them gently until just soft – be careful not to burn them. Add the blanched leaves, and turn them in the oil mixture. Squeeze over some lemon juice, season and serve the leaves as they are, or on toasted bread, with extra virgin olive oil trickled over the top.

Swiss chard flan

Here's one of my favourite quick and savoury recipes. I often make it for lunch, and it looks so appetising as it comes out of the oven, puffed up and golden. I think chard is such an underrated vegetable here. In the south of France the thick white stems are considered a delicacy and cooked like asparagus. Luckily we grow it and I love the squeak as you pick the enormous fresh leaves. They can come in fabulous rainbow colours, with varieties such as Bright Lights, or Ruby, which has crimson stems and veins to the leaves, though they don't keep their colour after cooking.

The standard Swiss chard, with white stems and green leaves, is not that easy to buy in the shops, probably because the leaves wilt soon after picking, so they don't have much of a shelf life. The answer is to grow your own or seek out a local supplier. Spinach can be substituted for this recipe, which also makes good picnic food.

Serves about 8
2 heads of chard, about 750g
6 large eggs
250ml double cream
250ml crème fraîche
250g strong Cheddar cheese, grated
Salt and freshly ground black pepper
Butter, for greasing

Wash the chard and strip the green leaves from the stems. Cut the stems into 1cm lengths. Bring a large pan of water to the boil and blanch the stems for 2–3 minutes. Remove and drain. Now blanch the leaves for a couple of minutes. Drain and cool, then squeeze out any excess moisture. Roughly chop the leaves and stems together on a wooden board.

Preheat the oven to 180°C/Gas Mark 4. Meanwhile, beat the eggs in a large bowl and mix in the cream, crème fraîche and grated cheese. Season with salt and pepper, then stir in the chard.

Butter a large ovenproof dish, about 30 x 20cm. Pour in the chard mixture, spread it out evenly and bake in the oven for about 30–40 minutes, or until the top is golden brown and the inside is still a little soft and creamy.

We serve this warm or cold with chutney (page 87) and bread. It is also delicious with a slice of ham (page 294).

Bitter leaves with fried breadcrumbs

This way of preparing bitter leaves – either chicory or beautiful, red radicchio – makes a satisfying vegetable dish to eat in winter. The garlic in this recipe is a good addition. I prefer it used sparingly, but as Montagu likes to eat large amounts of garlic in most food, we use it often when cooking.

Fried breadcrumbs, using butter rather than olive oil and omitting the garlic, are also delicious scattered over the sweeter-tasting cooked chard, or even over steamed cauliflower florets, as a way of making them more savoury and interesting.

Serves 4
500g chicory or radicchio
4–6 tablespoons olive oil
Coarse breadcrumbs made from 1 or 2
   thick slices of good white bread
1 or more garlic cloves, finely chopped
   (optional)
Sea salt and freshly ground black pepper

Remove any damaged outer leaves from the chicory or radicchio and trim the base of each one. Cut the heads in half lengthways.

Blanch them in boiling water for 5–10 minutes, checking after 5 minutes as they should be tender but retain their shape. Drain them and keep them warm.

Alternatively, heat a tablespoon of the oil in a frying pan over a medium heat and wilt the chicory or radicchio by cooking for 2–3 minutes on each side. Remove from the pan and keep hot.

Warm the rest of the olive oil in a frying pan over a medium heat. Add the breadcrumbs and fry them gently until they are golden, stirring in the chopped garlic for the last minute. Finally, add the chicory or radicchio to the pan and heat, coating well with the crumbs. Season before serving immediately, piping hot.

Radicchio pizza

Radicchio is a beautiful, wine-red member of the chicory family, and very useful in winter when little else is available.

In New York a few years ago, we wandered into a restaurant that turned out to be deeply fashionable. What I remember most is their fantastic pizzas. This is my version of the one I ate there.

Makes 6 small, thin-crust pizzas
500g strong white flour, plus extra for
    kneading and rolling
1 x 7g sachet fast-action dried yeast
½ teaspoon caster sugar
1 teaspoon fine sea salt
2 tablespoons olive oil

For the topping:
2 heads of radicchio, roughly chopped
200g soft cows' milk cheese, thinly sliced
100g Parmesan cheese, shaved with a
    potato peeler
Olive oil
A generous handful of fresh thyme leaves
Flaky sea salt and freshly ground
    black pepper

If you have food mixer with a dough hook, combine the flour, yeast, sugar and salt in the bowl and stir for a few moments to combine. With the motor running at a moderate speed, slowly pour in the olive oil and 300ml warm water. Knead for 10 minutes, until it forms a smooth, silky dough.

If you are making the dough by hand, tip the flour, yeast, sugar and salt into a large bowl and whisk to ensure everything is thoroughly combined. Make a well in the centre and pour in the olive oil and 300ml warm water. Stir into a sticky dough, turn it out onto a floured surface and knead until smooth and silky, about 15 minutes.

Coat the ball of dough lightly with a little olive oil, then place in a bowl and cover with a damp cloth. Leave in a warm place for 1–2 hours, until doubled in size.

Preheat the oven as high as it will go, at least 240°C/Gas Mark 9, and put 3 large baking sheets into the oven to heat up. Knock back the dough and divide into 6 equal pieces (if you don't want to make so many pizzas in one go, the dough freezes well for up to 3 months).

Place the dough on a floured surface and, using a floured rolling pin, roll out as thinly as possible – about 4mm thick and 20cm in diameter. Scatter the hot baking sheets with flour and carefully put the pizza bases on them.

Sprinkle over the radicchio, then the cheeses, and splash a bit of olive oil on top. Season with salt and pepper and add a generous scattering of thyme leaves. Bake the pizzas in the oven for 8–12 minutes, until the crust is crisp and golden brown around the edges.

Roasted tomatoes

We have established a daily ritual over the years, which happens first thing every morning. I used to be reluctant to stick to any routine, but I now realise I get far more done, and anyway the garden and animals can't wait. I really enjoy it now as I walk through the garden, opening the two greenhouses, watering the pots and seedlings, and checking on anything that needs to be harvested. After letting out the chickens, I get a big basket and pick anything that is ready and put it in the larder to use later.

When there are far more tomatoes than we can eat raw, I roast them – either to enjoy immediately as they are, or to make into sauce. The sauce freezes well and is our winter staple, the equivalent of a tin of tomatoes in the store cupboard. We make the sauce with any of the half a dozen or so different tomato varieties we grow, but Gardener's Delight is especially good for roasting.

While this recipe is delicious as a simple pasta sauce, it's also great as a dip with bread. The most fantastic thing about this recipe, though, which seems so simple, is that it makes even watery English tomatoes taste sensational. Not surprisingly, then, it's one of the building blocks of all my cooking.

Serves 4, making about 800g
1.5kg ripe tomatoes
6 large garlic cloves, sliced lengthways
100ml olive oil
A good pinch of flaky sea salt
In summer: a handful of basil leaves
  and/or 2–3 sprigs of lemon thyme
In winter: a pinch of dried oregano
  and/or dried thyme
Freshly ground black pepper

Preheat the oven to 220°C/Gas Mark 7.

Pick over the tomatoes and cut any large ones in half so that they are all about the same size. Put the tomatoes and garlic into a roasting tin, pour over the oil and sprinkle on the salt. Roast for 30–40 minutes – it doesn't matter if the skins blacken a bit as this adds to the flavour.

Serve the tomatoes as they are, hot or cold, scattered with fresh thyme or basil and with some black pepper ground over the top. Alternatively, blend them into a smooth sauce to serve with pasta, or to spoon over pizza bases (page 101).

Variation:
Spread a thin layer of roast tomato sauce over pizza bases (page 101) and scatter over a selection of toppings and seasonings. Mozzarella, anchovies, Parma ham, olives and dried oregano all work well. When the pizza comes out of the oven, basil leaves or young rocket leaves are also good additions.

Pasta with chard
and mushrooms

Chard leaves can be used like spinach, and are delicious as a side dish, simply cooked in boiling water for a few minutes until tender, then dressed with extra virgin oil, lemon juice and seasoning. A pinch of dried chilli flakes fried in olive oil with one or two garlic cloves is also a good addition.

The rich, creamy sauce used here with the chard has a hint of garlic, and is a favourite stirred into pasta. Mushrooms are an unexpectedly successful combination with the silky green leaves, and help to make this a filling meal.

Serves 4
500g chard
2 tablespoons extra virgin oil
25g unsalted butter
500g chestnut mushrooms, sliced
250g double cream
6 garlic cloves, thickly sliced
50g Parmesan cheese, grated, plus a little
more for serving
250g dried pasta, such as pappardelle
or fettuccine
Salt and freshly ground black pepper

Prepare the chard by stripping the leaves off the stalks. Cut the stalks into 2.5cm lengths. Fill a large pan with 5cm water, bring to the boil, add some salt, and blanch the stalks for a minute. Add the rest of the leaves and cook until tender, about 4–5 minutes. Drain and reserve.

Heat the oil and butter in the same pan the chard was cooked in and fry the mushrooms over a medium heat until just soft.

Put the cream into a small saucepan, add the garlic and bring to the boil. Simmer for about 10 minutes, by which time the garlic will be soft. Stir the Parmesan cheese into the cream.

Bring a large pan of water to the boil, add salt and cook the pasta according to the packet instructions.

While the pasta is cooking, stir the chard into the mushrooms, warm through and season well with salt and pepper.

Drain the pasta and put into a warm serving bowl. Toss with the chard and mushrooms, then pour over the garlic cream sauce. Grate more Parmesan on top and serve immediately.

Pasta with cavolo nero

One of the most architectural plants in the vegetable garden is Tuscan black kale, or cavolo nero. The stalks grow to a metre tall and have plumes of dark, bluish-green leaves that resemble Prince of Wales feathers. We have a whole bed ready for harvesting from October, although it needs a frost to develop its best flavour. Pick the individual leaves from a number of plants and these will be replaced by fresh leaves all winter, so just a few plants provide a lot of meals.

Cavolo nero is unusual in that the leaves retain their colour, taste and texture even after long cooking, although the tiny young leaves can be used raw in salads.

Serves 4
450g cavolo nero
6 garlic cloves, peeled
300ml double cream
1 tablespoon extra virgin olive oil
50g Parmesan cheese, freshly grated,
* plus a little extra for serving*
400g dried pasta shapes, such as
* penne or farfalle*
Salt and freshly ground black pepper

Strip out the midribs from the cavolo nero and discard them before washing the fleshy leaves well.

Bring a large pan of water to the boil, add some salt, then blanch the leaves and the garlic for about 8–10 minutes, until tender. Drain well and place the leaves and garlic in a food processor with the cream and pulse quickly to blend. Put the mixture back into the pan with the oil and Parmesan, season well and warm through gently. The sauce will be pale green, flecked with the dark green cabbage.

While the sauce is simmering, cook the pasta according to the instructions on the packet. Drain, then toss in the sauce and serve immediately, with more Parmesan grated on top.

Simple pasta 'handkerchiefs'

As a family, we eat dried pasta in many forms with homemade sauces. A few months ago, while working in Rome, we were sitting alone outside Hadrian's Villa in an ordinary-looking restaurant, a bit late for lunch, so we both ordered pasta.

Soon two big bowls arrived with what looked like small squares of homemade egg pasta, a bit like little handkerchiefs, in a strange-looking, dryish sauce flecked with dark grains. The sauce turned out to be made from finely grated pecorino, the salty sheep's milk cheese, loosened with some cooking water from the pasta and olive oil. The dark flecks were simply ground black pepper, but more than I have ever seen in one dish. It was sensationally good.

It is said that the ancient Romans were obsessed with pepper, so I like to think we were eating a sauce that would have been familiar to them. The waitress said it had been cooked by her aunts in the hotel's kitchen. We ate versions of it again in Rome (the Italian name is *cacio e pepe*), but none were as delicious as the first.

I rarely make fresh pasta, and my pasta machine is gathering dust in a cupboard, so I was impressed by the simplicity of the aunts' pasta, made by hand with a rolling pin. Fresh pasta quantities are easy to remember: 100g flour per person, one egg and a teaspoon of oil. You can use this recipe to make any shape or type of fresh egg pasta, not just these squares. It doesn't keep, though, so cook it within a few hours of making it in plenty of boiling, salted water.

I haven't quite mastered the aunts' sauce yet, but this pasta is delicious served with good oil, Parmesan cheese and lots of pepper, or with tomato sauce (page 102) or pesto (page 172).

Serves 4
400g '00' pasta flour, plus a little more for dusting
4 eggs, lightly beaten
4 teaspoons olive oil
4 tablespoons salt

To serve:
Extra virgin olive oil
Freshly ground black pepper
Parmesan or pecorino cheese
Tomato sauce (page 102)
Pesto (page 172)

Sift the flour onto a cool work surface, make a well in the centre and put the eggs and oil in it. Using the fingers of one hand, gently draw the flour into the centre until everything has combined to form a dough. (It's also possible to do this by pulsing the ingredients in a food processor.)

Knead the dough for about 5 minutes, dusting the surface with a little more flour if necessary, until the dough is silky and soft. Wrap it in cling film and refrigerate for 30 minutes. Remove from the fridge and roll it out on a floured surface as thinly as possible – about 3mm. Cut it into 5cm squares with a sharp knife, or use a pastry cutter with a crinkly edge.

Bring 4 litres of water to the boil in a large pan. Once boiling, add the salt. (It might seem a lot, but Italians say the water should be as salty as the Mediterranean Sea.) Salt is essential because the pasta itself contains none and will be flavourless without it.

Add the pasta squares to the water and stir them once so that they don't stick together. They should be ready after boiling for 3–4 minutes. Drain them, reserving a few tablespoons of the cooking water to loosen the pasta sauce. Pour over a small amount of olive oil to prevent them from sticking together. Serve in warmed pasta bowls with good olive oil, lots of pepper and Parmesan cheese.

Alternatively, serve with one of the suggested sauces.

Wild sea trout
with samphire

Because we are so landlocked, I have to make a real effort to eat fish. Luckily, the fish stall at Hereford market is the best for miles around.

This recipe is a simple feast. Between June and September, when it's in season, ask your fishmonger for a bag of samphire, a type of seaweed, which complements the fish perfectly. It is also delicious served with a green sauce (page 170). Any leftovers are very good in fishcakes (page 114) or kedgeree (page 32).

Serves 4–6
1 wild sea trout, approximately 1.8kg,
   gutted (ask the fishmonger to do it
   for you)
2 lemons – 1 sliced, 1 cut in wedges
   for serving
A small bunch of parsley
25g unsalted butter
A small handful of fennel fronds (optional)
About 250g samphire
20g unsalted butter, if serving hot
Salt and freshly ground black pepper

Preheat the oven to 200°C/Gas Mark 6.

Season the fish inside and out, then place the lemon slices, a handful of parsley and the 25g butter in the fish's cavity. Sprinkle the fennel fronds, if using, over the top. Wrap the fish in baking parchment, then in foil, place in a roasting tin and cook for about 35 minutes. It is ready when the flesh is opaque and feels firm when you prod it.

While the fish is cooking, prepare the samphire. Bring a pan of water to the boil (no need to add salt, as the samphire is already quite salty). Blanch the samphire in it for a couple of minutes, then drain. If serving it hot, toss in a little melted butter.

Serve the trout hot or cold, with the samphire and wedges of lemon. If you like, you can present the fish on a long dish on a bed of samphire.

Smoked fish tart

Here is a rich, savoury tart that is relatively easy to make as the pastry doesn't need to be rolled out. Serve simply with a green salad and good bread to make it into a memorable lunch.

Serves 6–8
700g smoked haddock
500ml whole milk
2 eggs
2 egg yolks
300ml double cream
50g Cheddar cheese, grated
1 tablespoon finely chopped parsley
  and/or fennel fronds
A few gratings of nutmeg
Freshly ground black pepper
A few strips of smoked salmon (optional)

For the pastry:
100g butter, chilled and cut into cubes
175g plain flour
1 teaspoon icing sugar
A pinch of salt

Start by making the pastry. Put all the ingredients for it into a food processor and pulse until the mixture resembles coarse breadcrumbs. To make it by hand, place all the ingredients in a mixing bowl and rub the butter into the flour with your fingertips until the mixture resembles coarse breadcrumbs. There is no need to add any liquid: simply spread the pastry mixture over a 24cm loose-bottomed tart tin, patting it down evenly across the base and up the sides, and making sure it's not too thick at the edges. Place in the fridge for 30 minutes.

Line the pastry case with greaseproof paper and fill with ceramic baking beans or uncooked rice or pulses. Bake blind for 20 minutes, then remove the paper and baking beans and bake for a further 5 minutes or so, until the pastry is cooked through. Leave to cool.

Poach the haddock by placing it in a saucepan with the milk and 300ml water. Bring to the boil and simmer for 5 minutes. Let the fish cool in its liquid. When it's cool, drain and reserve 100ml of the poaching liquid. Break the haddock into flakes, discarding the skin and bones.

Preheat the oven to 180°C/Gas Mark 4.

Beat together the eggs, egg yolks and cream with the reserved cooking liquid. Stir in the cheese, parsley and fennel fronds, if using. Season with nutmeg and pepper. Mix in the flaked fish and the smoked salmon, if you're using it.

Place the tart tin on a baking sheet, pour the filling into the pastry case and bake for about 35 minutes, until the filling is just set – it should still wobble a bit in the middle. Serve warm.

Fish pie

This is a year-round favourite of ours and I think of it as a special treat. The ingredients are uncomplicated – fish cooked in a creamy sauce with hard-boiled eggs and topped with mashed potato – but it takes time and care to assemble.

In our house, which has few mod cons, there is no extractor fan to remove the obvious smell of fish. I don't mind at all, but the fussier ones do. To avoid the lingering evidence of poached fish, I tend to make the pie early in the day, ready to reheat before serving. Then I can relax with a glass of wine outside in summer, or by the blazing fire in the kitchen in winter. On most days I am usually standing by the cooker until the last minute preparing the meals, so to be this organised is a good feeling.

I prefer to choose the individual fish separately at the fishmonger's, as mixtures sold for fish pie are not always made up of the freshest fish, but they are better than nothing. We serve it with peas or a salad and the children always have to have ketchup.

Serves 6–8
750ml whole milk
1 small onion, halved and sliced
2 bay leaves
1–1.25kg fish, a 50:50 mixture of
*   smoked and unsmoked, e.g. smoked*
*   haddock, sustainable white fish, salmon*
*   and/or raw prawns*
6 hard-boiled eggs, quartered (optional)

For the topping:
1.5kg floury potatoes, peeled and cut into
*   even-sized pieces*
150ml whole milk
60g unsalted butter
Salt

For the sauce:
60g unsalted butter
60g plain flour
2 tablespoons finely chopped parsley
1 tablespoon anchovy essence
Freshly ground white pepper

Start by cooking the potatoes for the topping. Put them in a pan with enough cold water to cover them. Bring to the boil and cook them until they are soft but not falling apart, about 20 minutes. Drain well and keep them warm in a tea towel.

Pour the milk into the pan, add the butter and melt it over a gentle heat. Put the potatoes back into the pan and mash them with a potato masher. They should be quite stiff, not sloppy, or they won't cover the dish and will sink into the fish. Season with salt. Cover and set aside until needed.

Prepare the poaching liquid by pouring the milk and 350ml water into a shallow pan large enough to take all the fish except the prawns. Add the onion and bay leaves and bring it gently to the boil. Lower the heat. Put the fish in the liquid and poach until it is opaque and just cooked, no more than 10 minutes. Lift out the fish and remove the skin and any bones. Do this as carefully as possible because any bones left in the mixture can spoil the dish. Put the flaked fish into a large pie dish or gratin dish.

Sieve the poaching liquid into a large measuring jug and set aside.

To make the sauce melt the butter in a saucepan over a medium heat. Stir in the flour and let it bubble for a couple of minutes before pouring on a little of the reserved poaching liquid, stirring all the time. Slowly add the rest of the liquid, continuing to stir, until the sauce is thick and creamy. Mix in the parsley and the anchovy essence, and season with pepper. I like to use white pepper so that the sauce stays pale.

Preheat the oven to 200°C/Gas Mark 6 while you assemble the pie.

Scatter the hard-boiled eggs over the fish, then add the prawns if you are using them. Pour the sauce over the mixture and give it a gentle stir. Spoon the mashed potato over the top, smoothing the surface carefully.

Place the pie on a baking sheet and bake for 45–60 minutes, until the filling is hot and the top browned.

If you want to make the pie ahead of time, cover it with foil and refrigerate until an hour before the meal. Remove the foil and cook as above.

Fishcakes

I usually make fishcakes from scratch, but they are also a useful way of using up leftovers. They are a perfect example of simple ingredients transformed into a reliably good dish. Smoked haddock also makes an excellent alternative to salmon. Whichever fish you choose, don't be mean with the ratio of fish to potatoes – it should be at least half and half.

Serves 4
500g floury potatoes, peeled
500g salmon
Whole milk
2 tablespoons finely chopped parsley
2 tablespoons double cream
1 tablespoon anchovy essence
2 teaspoons English mustard
Salt and freshly ground black pepper
Plain flour, for coating
Sunflower oil, for frying

To serve:
Tartare sauce (page 180)

Boil the potatoes in salted water until soft, then drain and mash until smooth.

Put the fish in a deep frying pan and pour over a 50:50 mixture of milk and water, just enough to cover. Bring gently to the boil, then lower the heat and poach the fish for 5–10 minutes, until the flesh flakes easily away from the skin. Remove from the cooking liquid, allow to cool, then flake the fish and discard the skin and bones.

Gently mix the potatoes, flaked fish, parsley, cream, anchovy essence and mustard. Season the mixture and divide into four equal pieces. Using floured hands, form the pieces into cakes and rest them in the fridge for 30 minutes.

When you're ready to cook them, dust the cakes with flour, shaking off any excess. Heat up about 1cm of oil in a frying pan and fry the fishcakes over a medium heat for about 15–20 minutes, turning from time to time, until golden brown. Serve immediately with tartare sauce.

Leek pie

Leeks are one of the most useful vegetables in the garden, particularly in winter after frost has stripped the vegetable garden of its variety. The children have always loved them, especially cooked in the old-fashioned way, boiled and served with a white sauce. I think it is the slight sweetness of the leeks combined with the milkiness of the sauce that makes them truly comforting, as well as delicious.

This recipe makes a simple dish for lunch, or a starter before dinner.

Serves 4–6
2kg leeks, trimmed
75g unsalted butter
500g ready-made all-butter puff pastry
Flour, for dusting
3 egg yolks
280ml double cream
Salt and freshly ground black pepper

Thoroughly wash the leeks, removing any grit. Cut into 1.5cm sections, retaining only the white parts for this recipe. This might seem a waste, but you can use the green bits in soups or stocks, or put them around a roast to give flavour to the gravy.

Melt the butter in a large saucepan over a low heat and gently sweat the leeks until they are meltingly soft. Be careful not to burn them; you don't want them to take on any colour. Set aside to cool.

Preheat the oven to 180°C/Gas Mark 4. Butter a shallow metal pie dish, about 23cm in diameter.

Roll out the pastry on a floured surface, then place in the pie dish. Trim the edges.

Beat the egg yolks with the cream and season well with salt and pepper. Stir in the cooked leeks. Pour the mixture into the pastry case and cook for about 40 minutes, until the filling is just set and the pastry is golden brown. Cool for a few minutes so that the pie firms up a little, then serve while still warm.

Shepherd's pie

We tend to eat more shepherd's pie, made from lamb, than cottage pie, which is made with beef. The main reason for this is Montagu's longstanding dislike of anything made from beef mince since enduring years of watery mince at school.

I usually make shepherd's pie after we've slow-cooked a whole shoulder of lamb (page 159). As there's always plenty of meat on this particular cut, it's a good way of using up any leftovers.

Serve with simply cooked greens or a salad, and lashings of Worcestershire sauce.

Serves 6
1 tablespoon olive oil
3 carrots, diced
1 large onion, halved and finely sliced
1 stick of celery, finely diced
500g leftover roast lamb, torn into
  bite-sized pieces
250ml gravy or stock
1–2 tablespoons tomato purée or
  homemade tomato sauce (page 102)
Salt and freshly ground black pepper
30g unsalted butter

For the topping:
1.5kg floury potatoes, peeled and cut into
  small, even-sized pieces
150ml whole milk
60g unsalted butter
Salt

First make the topping. Put the potatoes in a pan with enough cold water to cover them. Bring to the boil and cook them until they are soft but not falling apart, about 20 minutes. Drain well and keep them warm in a tea towel. Pour the milk into the pan, add the butter and melt it over a gentle heat. Put the potatoes back into the pan and mash them with a potato masher. They should be quite stiff, not sloppy, or they won't cover the dish and will sink into the filling. Season with salt.

Preheat the oven to 180°C/Gas Mark 4.

Warm the oil in a large frying pan over a medium-low heat and gently soften the carrots, onion and celery together for 5 minutes. Add the meat to the vegetables and brown well before adding the gravy or stock and tomato purée or sauce. Season to taste. Let it simmer away for a few more minutes to allow the flavours to blend.

Spoon the mixture into a pie dish or gratin dish and cover with the mashed potato. Smooth over the top, then rough it up a bit with a fork. Dot it with butter, place on a baking tray and cook for about 30 minutes, until piping hot. If the top is not brown enough, turn up the oven or blast it under the grill for a few more minutes. Serve immediately.

If you want to make the shepherd's pie in advance, assemble it, cover with foil and refrigerate. Cook as above, increasing the cooking time to 40 minutes.

Flattened chicken

If I need to cook a whole chicken but haven't allowed enough time to roast it in the usual way, I cook it quickly by cutting it along the breastbone with a knife or poultry sheers and flattening it out.

Ever since a French friend made this for me, and served it with crisp little *frites* and a green salad, I have tried to replicate it. The mustard and cream and golden chicken are a winning, savoury and sharp combination. It doesn't look the most glamorous of dishes, so decorate it with lots of chopped parsley before serving.

Serves 4–6
1 chicken, approximately 1.6kg, preferably organic or free-range
3 tablespoons Dijon mustard
3 tablespoons double cream
Juice of 1 lemon
Salt and freshly ground black pepper
A small handful of parsley (tough stalks discarded), chopped

Preheat the oven to 180°C/Gas Mark 4.

Cut the chicken along the breastbone with poultry shears or a sharp knife and spread it out on a chopping board. Flatten it by pressing down firmly along the backbone. Trim off any loose skin and excess fat.

Mix the mustard, cream and lemon juice in a bowl and season with salt and pepper. Place the chicken in a roasting tin, skin-side up, and cover it all over with the mustard mixture, trying not to let too much overflow into the tray. Don't panic if a little ends up in the tray, though, as it will form part of the sauce to serve with the chicken.

Cook for 45–60 minutes, or until the juices from the thickest part of the chicken's thigh run clear when pierced with a knife, and the skin is golden and crisp at the edges. Place it on a warm serving dish while you make the sauce.

Deglaze the roasting tin by pouring in a little hot water and stir briskly with a wooden spoon to loosen all the delicious caramelised bits. Strain into a small saucepan and reduce to thicken if necessary.

Scatter the chopped parsley over the chicken before you bring it to the table. You don't need to carve the bird in the conventional way, just cut off pieces or pull the meat apart with a fork instead. Serve with the lemony sauce and a green salad. Homemade thin chips or sauté potatoes are good additions too.

SALAD

Sarah and I were both brought up in an age when British cuisine did its damnedest to make salads unappetising. I know now that we have grown a wide range of lettuces for the past four hundred years, but in the 1950s and 1960s a few rather damp, limp butterhead or crisp varieties dominated. Rocket and endive were practically unknown, and the Japanese salad greens, such as mizuna and mibuna, belonged to a future as remote as the Orient was to us then.

Salads were solid and stodgy, and lettuce was never to be trusted alone. In fact, a salad was measured in terms of the quantity of ingredients rather than the quality. So it might include boiled and sliced beetroot, hard-boiled eggs, quartered (never sliced) tomatoes, boiled potatoes, radishes, spring onions, celery, boiled peas or beans. This was all dressed with salad cream, with a 'French dressing' spoken of as though slightly saucy and definitely not for the likes of us. Maybe I'm being a little harsh. If the lettuce was a really crisp cos variety, like Little Gem, and the salad cream substituted by homemade mayonnaise, I would willingly tuck into a an encyclopedic salad of this kind.

Nowadays we eat a very simple green salad practically every day of the year, and often more than once a day, usually as a separate course. A bowl of fresh leaves always hits the spot. Add some good oil and a squeeze of lemon or, if preceded by a roast, the meat juices. It never fails.

To this end I try to have two or three different kinds of fresh green leaves growing throughout the year in such quantities that I can be carelessly generous with them. The reliable core is made up of green and red looseleaf (or salad bowl) lettuces, a few varieties of cos lettuce, such as Lobjoit's Green and Rouge d'Hiver, a couple of butterheads, like Merveille de Quatre Saisons and Tom Thumb, and rocket. Curly endive grows well for most of the year and adds a touch of tartness, and chicory comes into its own in autumn, when the brilliantly red radicchios are at their best. I also grow mizuna, mibuna, lamb's lettuce and land cress between August and June, and they are an important part of our salads in the very lean period from March to May.

The upshot of this variety in the garden is that we can whip outside with a knife and a basket and cut a big bunch of fresh leaves, rinse them, dry them in the whizzer thingy and have them in a bowl on the table ready for eating within no more than five minutes. I normally reckon that three different kinds of leaf is enough at any one time, but occasionally one will be so good – like young rocket in April, or a perfect cos lettuce – that it deserves your full undistracted attention.

Rocket salad

Parsley salad

Although we eat a green salad every day, the soft leaves of salad rocket are my favourite – simple but perfect. In spring the leaves of home-grown rocket are so tender and melting that you will need and want at least twice the quantity that you might expect to be served or want to eat in a restaurant. They're also very good dressed with the juices of a joint.

> Serves 2–4
> *A colanderful of rocket leaves*
> *1 tablespoon extra virgin olive oil*
> *½ a lemon*
> *Flaky sea salt and freshly ground*
>   *black pepper*

Toss the leaves in the olive oil, then squeeze over a splash of lemon juice and season with salt and pepper. Toss again and serve immediately.

Here's a good standby when there is no lettuce to pick, or a small green salad is all that's needed. Although we are lucky to have rows of flat-leaf parsley in the garden, I often see generous bunches in independent grocers selling for a reasonable price, so it's easy to get hold of in larger quantities than the paltry supermarket packets provide.

This salad is best when the leaves are still tender as the tougher leaves are too chewy and spoil the texture. It is delicious with cold roast beef.

> Serves 4 as a side dish
> *1 large bunch of flat-leaf parsley*
> *1 small red onion, halved and*
>   *very finely sliced*
> *1 tablespoon capers, rinsed*
> *2 large, sweet pickled cucumbers, finely sliced*
> *3 tablespoons extra virgin olive oil*
> *1 tablespoon cider vinegar*
> *½ teaspoon caster sugar*
> *Flaky sea salt and freshly ground*
>   *black pepper*

Pick all the tender leaves off the parsley, discarding any coarse stalks (save them for bouquets garnis and to flavour stock). Combine the leaves with the onion, capers and pickled cucumbers in a salad bowl.

Make the dressing by whisking together the oil, vinegar and sugar. Pour over the salad and season with salt and pepper. Serve immediately.

Hot spring salad with poached eggs

This mixed-leaf salad dressed with bacon and potatoes and topped with poached eggs makes a substantial meal. In late spring the bitter salad leaves provide a good contrast with the soft, creamy egg yolks. The secret of this lovely dish is to use the very best ingredients you can find and then assemble them as quickly as possible.

Serves 6
12 rashers of streaky bacon
Extra virgin olive oil
6 new potatoes, scrubbed and
*   cut into 1.5cm cubes*
1 teaspoon white wine vinegar
6 eggs
A handful of lamb's lettuce
A handful of radiccio leaves
A handful of endive leaves
A handful of mizuna or rocket
Balsamic vinegar
Salt and freshly ground black pepper

Cut the bacon into small strips and fry until crisp in a little olive oil. Remove and keep warm in a cool oven. Put the cubed potato into the same pan and cook in the oil and bacon fat for about 10 minutes, until cooked through and golden brown.

Bring a saucepan of water to the boil and add the vinegar. Poach the eggs a couple at a time by breaking each egg into a saucer and sliding it into the water.

Simmer for a couple of minutes until the whites are cooked and the yolks are still runny. Using a slotted spoon, gently lift the eggs onto a warmed plate covered with kitchen paper to absorb excess water.

Assemble the salad by placing a handful of mixed leaves on each plate. Dress with oil and vinegar. Add the warm potatoes and bacon and carefully place the hot poached eggs on top. Season and serve immediately.

Broad bean salad

Broad beans are my favourite early summer vegetable, which I love eating raw. The secret is to pick them when they are very young and tender. The first beans, sticking out from the main stem and no longer than a finger, can also be cooked whole in their pods. There are lots of delicious ways to prepare them, such as simmering them in a seasoned cream sauce dressed with little pieces of fried bacon, or even added to risottos and soups.

We grow broad beans in our garden, mainly the Aquadulce varieties, but they are readily available in greengrocers and farmers' markets in season. If you can't get hold of them fresh, frozen ones are a good substitute to use in any cooked recipe because they freeze well.

As the beans get older, they not only have to be podded, but popped put of their thick skins as well. When they have cooled sufficiently after a few minutes' cooking, simply use your thumbnail to make a nick in the skin, then squeeze them out. Skinned, they make a fantastic purée mixed with olive oil and masses of chopped mint – great on toasted bread. When they are young, however, skinning is unnecessary – it just takes time to pod them, so get everyone sitting around helping, preferably outside in the sunshine.

This recipe makes a lovely summer salad using the first pick of the very young, small beans and whole pods. Some slivers of ham or torn strips of Parma ham are a good addition too.

Serves 4
1kg very young broad beans in their pods
1 tablespoon olive oil
Juice of ½ a lemon
2 tablespoons finely chopped chervil
    or flat-leaf parsley
Flaky sea salt and freshly ground
    black pepper

Shell the larger beans, leaving the smallest in their pods. Bring a pan of water to the boil. Add the beans and the pods and cook for 5 minutes. Drain well and dress with the oil, lemon juice and salt and pepper. Add the chervil or parsley and gently mix everything together. Serve warm or cold.

Caesar salad

Caesar salad is a surprisingly rich dish, a useful way of transforming lettuce into a substantial main course. It's very simple to make well, but it relies on all the ingredients being really good: the freshest eggs, the crispest lettuce, the best Parmesan (please, never use ready-grated), the finest salted anchovies and carefully made croûtons.

Serves 4
2 heads of cos lettuce
4 thick slices of good white bread
6 tablespoons extra virgin olive oil
6 salted anchovy fillets
1 tablespoon white wine vinegar
2 large eggs
Juice of 1 lemon
1 teaspoon English mustard
1 garlic clove, minced
50g Parmesan cheese, grated
Salt and freshly ground black pepper

Pull off the outer lettuce leaves, keeping the hearts intact, then wash and dry them carefully. Slice the hearts in half lengthways and place in a salad bowl with the rest of the leaves.

Cut the crusts off the bread, then cut the soft part into cubes.

Warm 4 tablespoons of the olive oil in a frying pan over a medium-high heat and fry the croûtons until golden and crisp.

Soak the anchovies in water for a few minutes, then drain and pat dry.

Bring a small saucepan of water to a simmer, add the vinegar, then poach the eggs by gently breaking each one onto a saucer and sliding it into the water. Cook until the whites have just set and the yolks are still runny, no more than a couple of minutes.

Lift the eggs out with a slotted spoon and place in a food processor with the anchovies, lemon juice, mustard, garlic, salt and pepper. With the motor running, add enough olive oil, about 2 tablespoons, to make a runny sauce the consistency of single cream.

Assemble the salad by scattering the croûtons over the lettuce and pouring over the sauce. Sprinkle with freshly grated Parmesan cheese, then toss all the ingredients together and serve.

Florence fennel salad

Florence fennel has a delicate aniseed flavour. It is delicious cooked in a gratin with cheese and cream (page 311), braised whole, or roasted with pork. Used raw, it makes a crisp, refreshing salad which has a pure taste and doesn't need much attention, just an oil and lemon dressing. We serve it with cold meats – particularly pork – or on its own.

When buying fennel in late summer and early autumn, always go for the fennel bulbs that look the freshest, avoiding any wrinkly ones with brown patches.

Serves 4–6
3–4 fennel bulbs
2–3 tablespoons extra virgin olive oil
Juice of ½ a lemon
Flaky sea salt and freshly ground
  black pepper

Slice the fennel bulbs in half lengthways and cut out the coarse core at the base. Remove the outer layer of leaves if they are brown or damaged. Trim the stalks at the top, but keep the bright green, feathery leaves to strew over the salad.

Place the bulbs, cut-side down, on a chopping board and use a very sharp knife to slice each one widthways into the thinnest slivers possible. Place the fennel in a bowl, add the oil and lemon juice, then season with salt and pepper to taste, Scatter over the fennel fronds and serve.

Carrot and onion seed salad

This bright orange salad scattered with tiny black seeds is a useful recipe, especially in winter when there's not much around to make a fresh salad with. Black onion seeds are easy to find in the shops, and a small jar will be enough for three or four salads.

This salad is even better the next day as the juices run, making it more succulent. We often make it to go with cold meat and baked potatoes for an easy supper.

Serves 6
6 large, crisp carrots, peeled
1 tablespoon black onion seeds
Juice of ½ a lemon
A splash of sunflower oil
Freshly ground black pepper
3 tablespoons finely chopped coriander
  or parsley (optional)

Grate the carrots by hand or with the fine grater attachment of a food processor (the processor gives lovely fine strands). Put them into a serving bowl.

Put the seeds in a small, lidded saucepan and toast them over a medium heat for 1 minute, keeping the pan moving. Pour the seeds over the carrots, then squeeze over the lemon juice and add the oil and pepper. Scatter over the herbs, if using, mix together and serve.

Roast beetroot salad

More an assembly process than a cooked dish, this salad is nonetheless delicious. It looks lovely on the plate and is a very good and colourful winter salad. Be adventurous and try it with other kinds of beetroot, or a combination of pink, golden and deep purple roots.

It's easy to underestimate how long it takes to cook beetroot, so allow plenty of time. And cook a few extra too, as they keep so well in the fridge and you can use them in many other dishes.

Serves 6
6 medium beetroot
2 tablespoons olive oil
3 sprigs of thyme, plus extra leaves to finish the dish
2 medium red onions, halved and very finely sliced
18–20 pickled walnuts, sliced
A small handful of flat-leaf parsley, stalks discarded
180g Roquefort or a similar creamy, salty blue cheese, or feta
Salt and freshly ground black pepper

For the dressing:
3 tablespoons extra virgin olive oil
1 tablespoon white wine vinegar
2 teaspoons Dijon mustard
A pinch of sugar
Salt and freshly ground black pepper

Preheat the oven to 200°C/Gas Mark 6.

Scrub the beetroot well but leave the skin on. Place in a roasting tin, either whole or cut into equal-sized pieces. Toss in the olive oil and season. Tear up the thyme sprigs and strew over the beetroot. Add a splash of water, cover tightly with foil and cook for a minimum of 40 minutes and up to 1¼ hours, depending on their size. They are cooked when a knife slides easily into the centre. When the beetroot are cool enough to handle, peel off the skins.

While the beetroot is cooking, make the dressing by whisking the oil, vinegar and mustard together: the mixture will be thick. Season to taste with a pinch of sugar and salt and pepper.

To assemble the salad, quarter the peeled beetroot and place some on each of the plates – this salad is about proportion, so be generous. Sprinkle on some sliced red onion, pickled walnuts and parsley leaves. Trickle over some of the dressing, crumble over the cheese and sprinkle with the extra thyme leaves. Serve immediately.

Tomato salad

Tomato salad is self-explanatory; however, it is without doubt one of the best salads of all. There are so many variations, but most fundamental is the quality of the tomatoes. It is pointless making the effort to prepare the salad if the tomatoes are tasteless. I often see lovely Italian tomatoes for sale in street markets in the summer, their vermilion skins tinged with green and yellow, which I buy if ours aren't yet ready.

We don't have much success with outdoor tomatoes, so we dedicate an old greenhouse to growing them under glass. There is a daily tyranny of watering and tying up the fast-growing plants, but it is all worth it as soon as they start to ripen. Nothing compares to the intense flavour of a freshly picked tomato. The greenhouse has a warm, musty tomato smell that I love, and we also plant rows of basil in front of the tomato plants, making it even more aromatic.

The simplest way to eat them is on their own, whole, with a little salt and good bread. A large beefsteak tomato, the ribbed Costoluto Fiorentino, sitting on a plate is a main course for us. This is perhaps a bit minimal for most people, so they can be sliced and dressed with oil and balsamic vinegar with lots of torn basil leaves. Another way to serve them is with a vinaigrette dressing (page 309) and plenty of chopped chives, but the dressing has to be quite sweet to counteract the

acidity of the tomatoes. I also like to mix different varieties in one salad: it looks so colourful to have quarters of red, yellow and purple flesh with a scattering of lemon thyme over them. However, the salad we prepare the most has the perfect pairing of tomato and basil, and is the one we wait all those months for.

Serves 6
Ripe tomatoes – 6 large ones or about
*   600g cherry or baby plum tomatoes*
3 tablespoons extra virgin olive oil
1–2 tablespoons balsamic vinegar
Flaky sea salt and freshly ground
*   black pepper*
A large handful of basil leaves – about 24

Slice the tomatoes thickly if they are large, or simply halve smaller ones and lay them out on a large, flat plate or in a shallow bowl. Pour over the oil and then the vinegar. Season with some salt and lots of black pepper. Scatter the basil leaves over the tomatoes and the salad is ready.

Roast butternut squash salad with toasted seeds

Here is a lovely combination of sweet, roasted squash and salty feta mixed with peppery green rocket and toasted seeds to add some crunch. It is a very colourful dish and is substantial enough for a light lunch or supper on its own. A sweet pumpkin would also be delicious in this recipe. The seed mix can be varied, depending on what you have in the cupboard.

Serves 4

1 butternut squash, peeled, deseeded
 and cut into 2.5cm chunks
1 tablespoon olive oil
2 tablespoons sunflower seeds
1 tablespoon sesame seeds
1 tablespoon linseeds
1 scant tablespoon poppy seeds
A generous handful of rocket
200g feta cheese

For the dressing:
3 tablespoons olive oil
1 tablespoon balsamic vinegar

Preheat the oven to 200°C/Gas Mark 6.
    Put the cubes of squash in a roasting tin, trickle over the oil and toss to coat. Place in the oven and roast for about 25 minutes, until softened and starting to caramelise slightly around the edges.
    While the squash is roasting, toast the seeds. Warm a heavy-based frying pan over a medium heat, tip the sunflower, sesame and linseeds into the pan and cook for 1 minute, moving them around constantly so that they toast evenly and don't burn. Add the poppy seeds and continue to cook, rattling the pan, for a further minute until the seeds have taken on a little colour.
    To make the dressing, whisk together the olive oil and vinegar.
    Arrange the roasted squash on a plate with the rocket, sprinkle with the seeds, then crumble over the feta. Pour over the dressing and serve immediately.

Potato salad

When waxy new potatoes are plentiful, this salad is one of the many ways I like to prepare them.

I've never been keen on potato salads coated in mayonnaise, which is why I prefer this version, dressed in a mustardy vinaigrette while still warm so that it absorbs the flavours of the dressing. It's then mixed with lots of chopped chives. It is very good with summery foods, such as cold ham or poached fish.

Serves 6
1.5kg waxy small potatoes of even size, scrubbed but skins left on
A small bunch of chives, finely chopped

For the vinaigrette:
6 tablespoons extra virgin olive oil
2 tablespoons white wine vinegar
1 tablespoon Dijon mustard
1 teaspoon caster sugar

Cook the potatoes in a pan of boiling salted water until cooked through but still firm, about 12–20 minutes.

Meanwhile, whisk all the vinaigrette ingredients together to make a thick dressing.

Drain the potatoes well and put them in a serving bowl. Pour in the dressing and turn the potatoes to coat them evenly. Scatter over the chopped chives and serve warm or cold.

Lentils with yoghurt

On Saturdays we often have what we refer to as a 'picnic lunch', though it's usually eaten indoors as the weather is so unreliable. We make lots of different salads and assemble plates of cold meats and cheeses. Someone gets fresh bread and the meal is spread out on the table and everyone helps themselves. It will feed an expanding number of people and is very relaxed.

This lentil salad often appears. Use slate-green Puy lentils if you can get hold of them, and don't be tempted to omit the yoghurt dressing as it transforms the dish.

Serves 6–10
250g Puy lentils
Juice of 1 lemon
3 tablespoons extra virgin olive oil
A bunch of flat-leaf parsley (tough stalks discarded), finely chopped
A bunch of mint, leaves stripped off the stalks and roughly torn into small pieces
250g whole-milk yoghurt
Salt and freshly ground black pepper

Cook the lentils according to the packet instructions. Drain them and tip into a bowl. While they are still warm, dress them with the lemon juice and olive oil, salt and black pepper. Add the parsley and mint and mix together.

Lightly season the yoghurt with salt and pepper and serve the salad with a big dollop of yoghurt on each plate.

Salad dressings

We make salad in some form or another at least once a day, so I'm constantly mixing up one or other of these simple dressings. We tend to make them from scratch each time as they're so quick to whisk up by hand in a suitable jug.

The basic proportion of oil to vinegar we use is 3:1, so it's easy to remember. Taste them and increase the amount of oil if it's too sharp. Some vinegars are harsh and need more oil to soften them.

The simplest dressing of all, which doesn't even need mixing, is a trickle of extra virgin olive oil and vinegar or a squeeze of lemon over the salad, then a seasoning with salt and black pepper, which can be done individually at the table.

All these dressings make enough to dress a salad for 4 people.

Oil and balsamic

While we use an aged balsamic vinegar, the very costly versions that have been maturing for years and years are wasted on us. There is now a delicious English apple balsamic vinegar, which is inexpensive and makes a good dressing.

The dressing that follows is particularly good with grilled Mediterranean vegetables, such as aubergines and red peppers.

3 tablespoons extra virgin olive oil
1 tablespoon balsamic vinegar
*Flaky sea salt and freshly ground
    black pepper*

Whisk the oil and vinegar together. Dress the salad and season to taste. Serve immediately.

Dijon mustard dressing

This dressing is slightly thicker than a basic vinaigrette thanks to the addition of mustard. It is perfect with a crisp green salad or a tomato salad. I am not keen on raw garlic, but the flavour is gentle here and the clove can be removed before dressing the salad if you prefer.

1 tablespoon red wine vinegar
*1 small garlic clove, bashed but kept
    whole (optional)*
1 tablespoon Dijon mustard
½ teaspoon caster sugar
3 tablespoons extra virgin olive oil
A pinch of sea salt
Freshly ground black pepper

Put all the ingredients together in a jug, and give them a good whisk until the dressing thickens.

Salad cream

This summery, homemade dressing tastes rather like bottled salad cream, though it has a fresher, livelier taste. It is particularly good for dressing a simple green lettuce salad. I like to serve it with hard-boiled eggs, new potatoes, boiled little beetroots, spring onions and tomatoes as part of a cold lunch.

3 yolks of hard-boiled eggs, cooled
1 teaspoon sugar
½ teaspoon salt
3 tablespoons cider vinegar
½ teaspoon cayenne pepper
100ml double cream

Pound the egg yolks in a mortar, or in a small bowl with the end of a rolling pin, until smooth.

Dissolve the sugar and salt in the cider vinegar in a small bowl, then stir in the cayenne pepper.

Gradually add this mixture to the egg yolks, pounding them together to make a loose paste. Pour in the double cream and continue stirring for a few seconds until the ingredients have the consistency of a thickish pouring cream. Taste and add seasoning, adding a little more vinegar or cayenne pepper if you wish. Serve cold straight away, or cover and store in the fridge for no more than a day.

Herb dressing

Herbs give a freshness and complexity to the humble salad dressing. Use whatever is in season to vary the recipe. A few finely sliced spring onions are a tasty addition if fresh herbs are unavailable.

This dressing is best on a mixture of green leaves, including crisp cos or Little Gem lettuces and some watercress.

1 tablespoon cider vinegar
A pinch of sea salt
Freshly ground black pepper
2 tablespoons finely chopped herbs: chives,
*   mint, lemon thyme or chervil are all*
*   good, though you might want to use*
*   slightly less of the lemon thyme than*
*   you do of the other herbs as it has a*
*   stronger flavour*
4 tablespoons extra virgin olive oil

Mix all the ingredients in a jug and whisk them together until thickened before pouring over the salad.

Mayonnaise

Pale gold mayonnaise is a sauce we associate with fresh food such as cold poached trout or salmon, or as a dip for crudités. I usually make it in spring and summer, when there are many herbs at their best in the garden. I love to add a small handful of chopped tarragon, dill, chives or parsley, or even a small bunch of blanched and finely chopped watercress, which turns the mayonnaise an appetising green and is delicious with fish. It is also the basis for tartare sauce (page 180), one of my favourites.

Mayonnaise is not difficult to make, but it needs tip-top ingredients as you can taste them all. Extra virgin olive oil has too strong a flavour, so I use a combination of lighter oils. You can use a food processor to make a large amount, which speeds things up considerably, but for a smaller quantity, a hand-held electric whisk works well. As it's made with raw egg yolks, mayonnaise doesn't keep, so it should be eaten on the day it's made and kept in the fridge until you're ready to serve it.

Makes about 300ml
200ml lightly flavoured olive oil
100ml sunflower oil
2 very fresh organic egg yolks
1 teaspoon English mustard powder
A pinch of salt
1 tablespoon white wine vinegar
Squeeze of lemon juice

Pour the oils into a jug. Place the egg yolks in a large, high-sided bowl with the mustard powder, salt and vinegar. Using a hand-held electric whisk or mixer, start to beat everything together. Slowly trickle a few drops of oil at a time over the egg yolks as you continue to whisk. When it amalgamates and begins to thicken, trickle on the oil a little more quickly. Keep doing this patiently until the mixture thickens and gets paler. When all the oil is used up, add the lemon juice.

Taste and adjust the seasoning if necessary, give it a stir and the mayonnaise is ready. Keep refrigerated and use within 24 hours.

PICNICS

Some of the happiest memories from my early childhood involved picnics.
Occasionally, my mother would collect my sister and me from school and
the three of us would walk no more than a hundred yards up the lane
opposite the front gate of our house to the first field. We would then spread
a tartan rug and my mother would take jam sandwiches and fairy cakes or
jam tarts from the basket, along with a thermos of tea stopped with cork
and greaseproof paper. The grass was prickly and the tea spilt on the rough
ground, but no meal was ever better or more fun.

Other family picnics were bigger affairs and accompanied the annual
jaunt to the local point-to-point, or outings to a castle, preferably ruined.
This time the family extended to both my parents and all their five
children, as well as lots of cousins and friends. I never quite worked out
who had brought what food, but it was all shared. There would be great big
thermoses with homemade soup, as well as smaller ones with tea, Scotch
eggs, pork pies, Cornish pasties, ham sandwiches, cold sausages, salads,
fruit (both fresh and in pies) and, to complete the idyll, there would be
lashings of my father's homemade ginger beer. It usually rained, of course,
and there would have been a row in the car, and Granny couldn't get comfy,
but although everyone was rather glad that they only happened a couple
of times a year, such occasions were generally regarded with affection.

The moral of the story is that although picnics always have the potential
for farce, they have an innocence and adventure that would take a stony
heart not to relish, and which work their magic just as well at the bottom
of the garden as on a mountain side.

Sausage rolls

Sausage rolls are perfect picnic food, whether made with shortcrust pastry, as here, or with puff. Good ready-made varieties of both are now available.

And a further shortcut: if you can't get hold of sausage meat, buy your favourite sausages, take the meat out of the casings and use it to fill your sausage rolls.

Makes 8
15g unsalted butter
1 medium onion, finely diced
500g sausage meat, coarsely ground
  if possible
1 tablespoon finely chopped sage
Salt and freshly ground black pepper
A little milk for brushing
1 egg, lightly beaten, for glazing

For the pastry:
400g plain flour, plus extra for dusting
200g unsalted butter
A pinch of salt
2–3 tablespoons iced water

First make the pastry. Put the flour, butter and salt in a food processor and blitz until the mixture resembles coarse breadcrumbs. You can do this by hand by rubbing the butter into the flour and salt with your fingertips. Add the water a spoonful at a time – you might not need it all – and pulse or mix until a dough forms. Turn it onto a floured surface and shape it into a

ball. Wrap it in cling film and chill for at least 30 minutes.

Melt the butter in a frying pan over a medium-low heat and cook the onion until soft, stirring frequently. This should take about 10 minutes. Cool completely.

Place the sausage meat in a bowl. Add the sage, cooked onion and seasoning and mix well. Break off a walnut-sized piece of the mixture and fry until cooked. Taste and adjust the seasoning if necessary.

Preheat the oven to 180°C/Gas Mark 4.

Lightly flour a work surface and rolling pin, then roll the pastry into a rectangle, about 40 x 25cm and 3–4mm thick. Form the sausage meat into a long roll and place in the centre of the pastry. The meat will swell as it cooks, so don't make it too thick. Brush one long edge of the pastry with a little milk. Fold the dry side over the meat, then put the moistened side over that, pressing together to seal. Trim off any excess pastry with a floured knife, cutting the ends level with the meat, and slice into 8 equal-sized pieces.

Place the sausage rolls on a baking sheet, turning each one over so that the join is underneath. Brush with the beaten egg and slash the top of each one 2 or 3 times. Cook for about 40–45 minutes, until the meat is thoroughly cooked and the pastry golden. Cool on a rack, then wrap them in greaseproof paper, ready to take on your picnic.

Pork pies

When we ran away to Yorkshire over thirty years ago, we lived in a remote house on the edge of the moors.

Our nearest neighbours were a farming family who were very kind to us. We were young and poor and often hungry. Mrs Foord made us wonderful teas with cakes and scones. There was a tradition of baking on those remote farms that was an essential part of their way of life. It was so cold and harsh on the exposed edges of the moor that you needed to eat a lot just to keep going.

Robert Foord, the farmer, would take us on outings to the remote dales he had known all his life and tell stories of all the people who had once lived in the ruined villages before the war. On the way, we would stop at a butcher's shop in Danby to buy pork pies to eat on our journey. The shop was a stone building attached to a cottage, modest and plain, with a small sign outside. The pies were considered the best for miles around. Fresh out of the oven, the pastry was crisp and a dark golden colour. The meat in the pies was still warm and succulent and peppery. It was never pink, but a pale, cooked pork colour. They remain my benchmark for the ideal pork pie.

I use boned shoulder of pork that has some fat, and any left over can also be slow-roasted or used for sausages. Fresh hot-water crust pastry is so different from the flabby, stale stuff we are used to, and it's not difficult to make. It has to be worked while still warm and I use a small jam jar to mould the pastry around before filling it with meat, but it's not essential to mould them as the pies taste just as good if they're a bit wonky.

The pies will keep for a couple of days in the fridge, but we eat them up quickly as they are so delicious.

Makes 6 small pies or 1 large one
1kg pork shoulder
6 finely chopped sage leaves
Flaky sea salt and freshly ground
*   white pepper*

For the hot-water crust:
600g plain flour, plus extra for dusting
A pinch of salt
225g lard
1 egg, lightly beaten, for the glaze

Prepare the meat for the filling by cutting the lean bits into small chunks of about 1cm. Finely chop the rest, including the fat, or put it through a mincer, then mix them all together. Season the meat well and add the sage. Test for seasoning by frying a nugget of the filling, tasting and adjusting if necessary. I like lots of pepper.

If you are making the pastry by hand, sift the flour into a large mixing bowl and make a well in the centre. If you are making it in a food processor, place the sifted flour in the bowl.

Put the lard in a saucepan with 200ml water and a pinch of salt and bring to the boil to melt and amalgamate the lard. Pour the hot liquid over the flour, mixing by hand with a wooden spoon or pulsing in a food processor, to form a smooth dough. As soon as it's cool enough to handle, make the pies.

Preheat the oven to 200°C/Gas Mark 6.

To make 6 small pies:
Divide the dough into 6 equal balls. Working quickly, because the dough gets less pliable as it cools, remove a quarter from each ball. Generously flour a work surface and a rolling pin, then roll out the larger balls of dough into circles roughly 15cm in diameter. Put a sixth of the filling in the centre of each circle. Now roll the smaller balls of dough into circles and place on top of the filling as lids. Draw up the sides of the pastry to meet the lid and crimp them together.

Place the pies on a baking tray, brush the tops with the beaten egg and bake for about 35–40 minutes, until the meat is thoroughly cooked and the pastry golden. Cool on a wire rack and serve cold.

To make 1 large pie:
Using baking parchment, double-line the sides and base of an 18cm round, high-sided tin. This produces a spectacular raised pie, but you can make a shallower, looser-shaped pie without a tin if you prefer.

Set aside a quarter of the dough for the lid. Generously flour a work surface and a rolling pin, then roll out the larger ball of dough into a circle about 7cm in diameter.

Drape it over the rolling pin and use to line the tin, gently pushing it to the sides without stretching it, and allowing it to hang over the edge.

Fill the pastry case with the pork mixture, then roll out the smaller ball of dough to form the lid. Place on the top of the pie and crimp the edges together. Brush with the egg glaze and cover the top with a double layer of foil.

Bake the pie for 1½ hours, then remove the foil and cook for a further 10 minutes so the top turns golden brown. Allow to cool enough to handle, then carefully remove from the tin and peel off the baking parchment. Place on a wire rack to cool completely. Serve cold.

Scotch eggs

A homemade Scotch egg is so much nicer than the soggy orange version bought in shops. The crispness of the breadcrumbs contrasts pleasingly with the softness of the egg, and you can season the sausage meat with whatever herbs and spices you like. I like to use parsley and sometimes add some chopped chilli, though sage, thyme and dill, either alone or in combination, all work well.

The only drawback with Scotch eggs is that you have to prepare them in advance as they need to be chilled before cooking, so you have to be a bit organised, but I think they're certainly worth the wait.

Makes 6
800g sausage meat
A small handful of parsley (tough stalks discarded), finely chopped
1 small red chilli, deseeded and finely chopped (optional)
6 eggs
Salt and freshly ground black pepper

For the crumb coating:
3–4 tablespoons plain flour
2 eggs, lightly beaten
100g fresh white breadcrumbs
Sunflower oil, for deep-frying

Place the meat in a bowl and season with salt and pepper. Add the parsley and chilli, if using. Divide the mixture into 6 patties.

Place the eggs in a pan with enough cold water to cover them, bring to the boil and simmer for 5 minutes. Don't overcook them, as they will continue to cook when you fry them and you want the yolks to remain slightly soft. Drain and place in a bowl of iced water to cool completely. Shell the eggs.

Roll the eggs in the flour to coat them, shaking off any excess. Wrap a meat patty around each egg, squeezing gently into shape. Dip in the beaten egg and roll in the breadcrumbs until thoroughly coated. Place on a plate and chill in the fridge for several hours or overnight.

When you are ready to cook the eggs, pour the oil in a deep-fat fryer or a deep, heavy-based pan. You will need at least 10cm of oil, which should not come more than a third of the way up the pan. Heat until it reaches 160°C on a cooking thermometer, or until a cube of white bread dropped into the pan turns golden in just under a minute. Deep-fry the Scotch eggs in two batches for about 7–10 minutes, until crisp and golden brown. Drain on kitchen paper and serve warm or cold.

Grilled kebabs

Meat that has been cubed, marinated, speared on skewers and grilled has a flavour that is both primitive and complex. This method of cooking suits tender meats, such as chicken, lamb and pork. They taste best cooked outside over a wood fire or charcoal, but they can be grilled or roasted quickly in a hot oven too.

I first ate kebabs when I was 16, at a Greek restaurant in Rose Crescent, Cambridge. One of the cheapest items on the menu was homemade pitta bread filled with salad and fantastic lemony pieces of well-cooked grilled lamb. If we couldn't afford one each, we would share one, making sure we had equal helpings of the prized meat. The following year I went to Greece and ate real souvlaki, but it did not compare to my first awakening.

Serves 4
Zest and juice of 3 lemons
3 tablespoons olive oil
4 garlic cloves, crushed
2–3 bay leaves
1 tablespoon dried oregano
A small bunch of fresh oregano
800g lamb, leg or fillet, cut into 4cm cubes
Salt

To serve:
Pitta bread
Green salad

In a large bowl, mix together the lemon zest and juice, the olive oil, garlic, bay leaves and dried and fresh oregano. Stir in the meat and marinate for 2–4 hours.

If planning to use wooden skewers, soak them in water for at least 30 minutes: this will stop them burning on the grill.

Light the barbecue at least 30 minutes before you want to cook the kebabs. The coals should be glowing red and covered in pale grey ash before you start to cook.

Thread the cubes of lamb onto the skewers and grill for 3–5 minutes on each side, depending on whether you like the meat pink or well cooked. Rest the kebabs for 5 minutes and season with salt. Serve on the skewers or in warmed pitta bread with green salad.

Variation:
Pork can be cooked in a similar way, marinated in thyme rather than oregano. Thread onto skewers with sweet red onions and bay leaves and cook for about 10–12 minutes, turning frequently, until there is no trace of pink in the middle of the meat.

Barbecued chicken

I prefer not to buy boned chicken breasts as they are expensive. A whole chicken, jointed by you or the butcher, is always better value. This recipe is an exception as the marinated chicken breasts cook more evenly and grill faster over charcoal. I urge you not to use cheap, battery chicken as it is so much better to eat decently reared birds. At least do it as an occasional treat, even if it is more expensive.

I like to cook the chicken on a fired-clay coal pot I brought back from a market in Antigua. I was fascinated to see the hotel cooks frying the breakfast eggs in pans over the hot coals. Of course, you can make this chicken on any barbecue. Remember to light the fire at least half an hour before you need to start cooking as the charcoal has to get white hot before grilling.

Serves 4
2 chicken breasts, skinned
3–4 tablespoons olive oil
2 lemons
A small bunch of thyme
Salt and freshly ground black pepper

Put one of the chicken breasts on a chopping board, place your hand on top to steady it and make a horizontal cut through the centre, cutting to within 1cm of the other side. Open it out like a book and press it flat. Repeat with the second breast. Put them into a roomy plastic bag and bash them with a rolling pin to flatten them evenly. Remove them from the bag.

Place the flattened fillets in a wide bowl with the oil and the juice of one of the lemons. Add the thyme and season with salt and pepper. Make sure all the fillets are well coated with marinade and leave them for at least 30 minutes, preferably overnight. If you are marinating them for more than 30 minutes, cover and refrigerate them. Remove them from the fridge 30 minutes before you want to cook them so they lose some of their chill.

Once the charcoal is hot enough – the bright red coals should be covered with a layer of greyish ash – place the chicken breasts on the grill. Cook for at least 5 minutes on each side, depending on the thickness of the meat. Check that each one is thoroughly cooked by making a little cut in the centre of the meat to see that it is white rather than pink.

Rest the meat for a few minutes, then halve the fillets to make enough for 4. Serve simply, with lemon quarters, a green salad and bread. I also like to serve these with marinated aubergines (page 78) and roast red peppers (page 80).

Grilled fish

Our farmhouse is on the edge of a river and occasionally we eat the slightly muddy-tasting pike that we catch from it. The white fillets are good served with creamed horseradish (page 174), but it's not the same as the very fresh sea fish that we buy from Leominster, or Hereford Butter Market. I feel as if I am following in my grandmother's footsteps whenever I stand in the Victorian building at Hereford, as she fed her large family by shopping daily in the same market seventy years ago.

I buy the freshest fish recommended by the fishmonger that day, and when I get home I cook them as soon as possible with minimum effort. That usually means outside on a makeshift charcoal grill which is perfect for grilling fish.

We often eat oily fish such as mackerel and sardines, which cook in minutes, and they are fantastically good value. It always feels as if we are on holiday as we enjoy them served simply with lemon and salt.

Serves 3–4
1kg oily fish, such as sardines or mackerel,
gutted (ask the fishmonger to do this)
Sea salt and freshly ground black pepper
3 tablespoons olive oil
Bay leaves (optional)
2 lemons, halved

Light the barbecue about 40 minutes before you start grilling. The charcoal should be white hot with no flames. Let the grill rack get hot before you lay the fish on it.

Season the insides of the fish with salt and pepper and tuck a bay leaf inside each one if you like. Brush the fish with the olive oil before placing them on the grill. Cook for about 5 minutes on one side before carefully turning them over with a fish slice to cook the other side. It is impossible to be precise, as cooking times vary depending on the size of the fish, but 5 minutes should be enough. They are ready when the flesh is opaque and slightly flaky, and cooked to the bone. Keep an eye on them as they overcook quickly.

Serve immediately with the lemon halves and a little more salt and pepper. So simple and so good.

Elderflower cordial

Elderflowers grow along the edges of our garden in an old hawthorn hedge. They have been encouraged to grow tall, and every year I look forward to their sweet-scented creamy blossom. Elders love rich soil and will grow wherever you find nettles. It's important to make sure that you harvest your flowers away from roadsides or anywhere that might have been sprayed with chemicals.

As children we used to make elderflower 'champagne' and pretend to be drunk. We kept bottles hidden in our camp and occasionally one would explode, which added to the excitement. Nowadays I use the flowers to make a cordial that can be used for refreshing cold drinks and to add flavour to stewed fruit (page 16). It is especially good with gooseberries.

Makes about 2.5 litres
20 large elderflower heads
6 unwaxed lemons
50g citric acid (available from some chemists)
1.8kg caster sugar

Pick the flowerheads whole and give them a shake to get rid of any insects. Put them into a large bowl and grate the lemon zest over them, then slice the lemons and add them too, along with the citric acid.

Tip in the sugar then pour over 1.5 litres boiling water and stir until the sugar has dissolved. Cover and leave for at least 24 hours, stirring occasionally.

Sterilise some suitable bottles and lids (I use old apple juice bottles) in boiling water or in a dishwasher (page 37). Strain the cordial through a layer of muslin – I put the muslin in a sieve over a large bowl and strain the cordial through it before decanting it into the bottles using a jug and funnel.

I think this is the most refreshing of all summer drinks – diluted with still or sparkling water, poured over plenty of ice and served with slices of lemon. This makes a very syrupy, strong cordial, so you need to dilute it more than most commercial types. It will keep for at least 3 months in a cool place. Alternatively, you can freeze it as ice cubes or in plastic containers for up to 6 months.

SUNDAY LUNCH

Apart from Christmas dinner, no other meal has such a hold in the domestic imagination as Sunday lunch, although I suspect that it is honoured more in the breach than in the observance.

When Sarah and I were children, Sunday lunch was obligatory. It invariably followed church and was centred around a joint of meat. The menu rarely deviated from a rota of lamb, pork or gammon, beef and, as a special treat, chicken, followed by at least one pudding, always cooked, and often more. There was a sense of indulgence that no other meal in the week provided. You could eat more than usual and rest more than usual having done so. Although of course for our mothers it meant more preparation, cooking and clearing up than usual.

Sunday lunch is not the time or place for experimentation or culinary exhibitionism. The whole point is to do the expected very well indeed using the best possible ingredients. Other than the food, the essential characteristic of a proper Sunday lunch is that it is eaten by the whole household gathered together around a table as the main meal of the day. No one, unless gluttonous or double-booked, has dinner in any meaningful sense of the word having eaten a Sunday lunch. Nor have they snacked and grazed in the hours before it. It still retains the anticipation and respect of an important meal.

It is a social event shared primarily by those who know each other very well, so eased (and sometimes cursed) by familiarity. It is a meal that binds families. An invitation to have Sunday lunch with someone means more than just a personal act of hospitality – you are being invited to enter into the heart of the family.

Roast chicken

Roast chicken is one of our favourite family meals and our first choice when something soothing is needed. You'll have leftovers for lunch the next day, and a big pan of stock can be made from the carcass (page 58). Although it's more expensive, buy the best chicken you can afford. Avoid battery chickens at all costs. It is a cruel and inhumane way to rear poultry.

Easy peasy to cook, you just put the chicken in the oven after minimal preparation and out comes a fragrant, tender bird. For a simple feast, cook two birds side by side. They look impressive brought to the table on a big dish next to a bowl of crisp roast potatoes (page 326) and a watercress or lettuce salad. Pour the cooking juices into a little jug and serve with thick slices of the chicken. If you have time, bread sauce (page 176), is a very good addition, though it's not essential.

Serves 4
1.5kg organic or free-range chicken
1 lemon
4–5 tablespoons olive oil or 50g unsalted butter, softened
Salt and freshly ground black pepper

Preheat the oven to 220°C/Gas Mark 7.
Place the chicken in a roasting tin. Cut the lemon in half and squeeze one half over the chicken. Cut the other half into quarters and place in the cavity of the bird.

Pour some olive oil over the chicken or rub with butter and season with the salt and pepper.

Roast the bird for 15 minutes, then baste it and turn the heat down to 180°C/ Gas Mark 4. Continue cooking for about another 45 minutes to an hour – it is hard to be exact about cooking times because no two birds are the same. Baste the chicken from time to time. To check it is cooked, pierce the thickest part of the thigh with a knife; the juices should run clear. Alternatively, a meat thermometer should read 70°C.

Let the bird rest for 10–20 minutes before serving.

Parsley and lemon stuffing

I don't often stuff a chicken for roasting, as it takes more time to cook the bird, but this light, herb and lemon stuffing is definitely worth making, especially if you want the chicken to go further and feed more people. For the breadcrumbs I use a dense, white sandwich loaf rather than a more open-crumbed sourdough type. If you double the quantities, this recipe is also good for stuffing the Christmas turkey or goose.

The quantities below provide plenty of stuffing for a large chicken. Any left over can be put in a small, buttered roasting tin, dotted with more butter and cooked separately.

1 loaf of day-old white bread
A large bunch of flat-leaf parsley
A small bunch of marjoram,
 larger stalks removed
1 tablespoon fresh thyme leaves
1 large or 2 small lemons
1 large egg, lightly beaten
100g butter, softened and cut into chunks
Salt and freshly ground black pepper

Preheat the oven to 100°C/Gas Mark ½.

Cut the top off the loaf and scoop out the soft breadcrumbs with your hands, leaving the crust behind. Tear the bread into pieces and spread them out on a baking tray. Dry them out in the oven for about 20–30 minutes, making sure they do not colour. Take them out of the oven and break them up into fine crumbs in a food processor, or put them in a bag and bash them with a rolling pin.

Heat the oven again, this time to 190°C/Gas Mark 5.

Chop the herbs, including the parsley stalks. Tip them into a bowl with the crumbs, then grate over the lemon zest and add a good squeeze of the juice. Add the egg and butter and stir until combined. Season well with salt and pepper.

Use the mixture to lightly fill the cavity of the chicken, being careful not to over-stuff it as the stuffing should have room to swell and steam as it cooks. Make sure you add the weight of the stuffing to the weight of the chicken before working out cooking times. Allow 20 minutes per 500g, plus 15 minutes extra, and rest for 15 minutes or so before carving.

Roast shoulder
of lamb

Shoulder of lamb is an underrated cut of meat and is much cheaper – and I think as good as – the more popular leg of lamb (page 161). To get the best out of it, a lamb shoulder has to be cooked very slowly. This needs some planning, but it also means that it's an easy and forgiving roast. It can be shoved in the oven and forgotten about for 2–3 hours, or even longer if you have an Aga or the equivalent. I have cooked a shoulder in the low oven of an Aga all day and the meat was intensely flavoured in a way that is only possible with slow cooking. The aim is to have plenty of succulent meat with a crisp exterior, which will pull apart with two forks rather than needing to be carved.

If there is any left over, it makes an excellent shepherd's pie (page 116) the next day.

Serves 6–8
A large bunch of rosemary
1 x 2kg shoulder of lamb
1–2 tablespoons olive oil
Salt and freshly ground black pepper

Preheat the oven to 230°C/Gas Mark 8.

Spread the rosemary generously in the bottom of a roasting tin and place the joint of meat, skin-side up, on top of it. Pour a little olive oil over the meat; season with salt and pepper. Put in the oven and roast for 30 minutes, then lower the heat to

170°C/Gas Mark 3 and cook slowly for another 2–3 hours, until the outer layer is crisp and the succulent inner layer is falling from the bone.

Unlike with a leg of lamb, there will be few juices left in the roasting tin, although the meat itself is very juicy. Serve with potato gratin (page 321), damson cheese (page 184) and buttered Savoy cabbage. It doesn't need gravy as the meat is so tender.

Roast leg of lamb

This is something we look forward to in late summer when the Welsh lamb, which has grazed on the mountains surrounding us, is at its best. It's a fine but expensive joint of meat, and is good to share with those who really appreciate it.

While you can prepare the leg the French way – by making a dozen incisions in the skin with the tip of a sharp knife and pushing sprigs of rosemary and slivers of garlic into the slits for extra flavour – for me the salty taste of high-quality roasted meat is enough and needs no further embellishment. Serve it with a creamy potato gratin (page 321), damson cheese (page 184) and gravy, followed by a green salad, for a perfect lunch.

Serves 6–8
1 x 3kg leg of lamb
2–3 tablespoons olive oil
Salt and freshly ground black pepper

For the gravy:
170ml red wine
1 tablespoon damson cheese (page 184),
  or redcurrant jelly

Preheat the oven to 230°C/Gas Mark 8.

Place the meat in a roasting tin and pour over the olive oil. Season with salt and pepper and roast for 15 minutes, then reduce the heat to 180°C/Gas Mark 4 and cook for a further hour. It's impossible to be exact with roasting times, but I prefer lamb pink, not cooked to the uniform brown enjoyed by my father's generation. For pink lamb, allow 10 minutes per 500g after the first 15 minutes (a meat thermometer should read about 45°C). For medium lamb, allow 15 minutes per 500g after the first 15 minutes (a meat thermometer should read about 60°C).

Let the lamb rest on a warm plate in a warm place for 20–30 minutes after taking it out of the oven. While it's resting, make the gravy. Pour off any excess fat from the roasting tin, then add some hot water from the kettle to loosen all the delicious caramelised bits. Scrape them up with a wooden spatula, then add a glass of red wine and a tablespoon of damson cheese or redcurrant jelly. Pour the gravy into a small saucepan and let it simmer for a minute or two, whisking it all together. Taste for seasoning.

Carve the meat into thick slices and serve with the gravy.

Roast pork with crackling

We're very lucky in Herefordshire – every small town still has several good butchers. Nearby Leominster, Ledbury and Bromyard, and the slightly more distant Ludlow in Shropshire and Abergavenny and Talgarth on the Welsh borders, are all renowned for their independent butchers. They know which farms their meat comes from and I find them an inspiration. They make shopping and choosing what to eat a pleasure.

The farmers' markets, held several times a month, also sell poultry, pork and other organic meat. Their produce is often no more expensive than supermarket meat of unknown provenance. These shops and stall-holders are modest and hardworking. They are not faddish or fashionable, but they are vulnerable to the terrifying power of the supermarkets. They need to be supported, and if everyone who is able to spends a proportion of their food budget in local shops and markets, it will keep them alive. Use them or lose them.

We don't eat meat every day. When we do, roast pork is always popular. It's also great the following day – served cold with baked potatoes (page 320) and pickles, a favourite combination, or in rolls with apple sauce (page 175). We tend to eat pork more often in the autumn and winter, after the apples are harvested, because we use the fruit for making sauces or roasting with the pork.

The cooking method below is suitable for a leg or a more economical shoulder, which suits slow cooking, or a loin of pork, which is more elegant.

It's getting easier to buy rare-breed free-range pork, and I like Gloucester Old Spot, which is available where we live. Ask the butcher to closely score the skin for you to get good crackling. If cooking a loin, it needs to have the bones removed, but keep them to roast alongside the joint for flavour.

Serves 10
2.5–3kg free-range pork joint – leg,
*   shoulder or loin, skin scored*
2–3 tablespoons olive oil
1 tablespoon fennel seeds
A small bunch of bay leaves
2 onions
10 garlic cloves, unpeeled
Sea salt and freshly ground black pepper

For the gravy:
1 x 500ml bottle of organic cider
1 tablespoon quince jelly (page 185)

To serve:
Apple sauce (page 175) or roast apples,
*   roast potatoes (page 326) or mashed*
*   potato (page 322)*

As soon as you get home, take the pork out of its wrapper and rub it with olive oil.

Season it generously all over with salt and pepper, and scatter over the fennel seeds.

Place the joint in a roasting tin and tuck the bay leaves around and under it. It can stay like this for several hours, or even overnight, loosely covered with greaseproof paper and refrigerated. About an hour before it's due to go in the oven, take it out of the fridge to bring it up to room temperature. Remove the paper and add the onions and garlic to the tin.

Preheat the oven to 220°C/Gas Mark 7. Roast the pork for 20 minutes to puff up the crackling, then reduce the temperature to 170°C/Gas Mark 3 and continue to cook the pork at this temperature until the last 10 minutes of the cooking time. You should allow about 1¼ hours per kilo, so, depending on the size of the joint, it will take 3–3¾ hours.

Ten minutes before the end of the cooking time, when the meat is cooked but the crackling isn't yet crisp, strain off the juices for the gravy and give the joint another blast at 220°C/Gas Mark 7 for 10 minutes or so to crisp it up.

To make the gravy, skim the fat off the juices, then pour them into a small pan. Warm them through with a glass or two of cider, and sweeten the mixture with the quince jelly. It shouldn't need any salt if the meat was well seasoned. Strain into a warmed jug.

Serve with apple sauce or roast apples, roast potatoes or mashed potato, and simple greens, such as Savoy cabbage.

Roast rib of beef

A fore rib of beef is a magnificent thing. It's not something that many supermarkets sell, but a good butcher will always supply you, and in Herefordshire – which is famous for its high-quality beef – every butcher regularly displays it. Always buy and cook it on the bone as this gives it extra flavour.

My cousin has a herd of organically reared Hereford cattle, and the best roast beef I have ever eaten was a full fore rib from one of her animals. We roasted and served it very simply with Yorkshire pudding, spring greens, roast potatoes, gravy and creamed horseradish. It sounds plain, but it was one of those memorable meals when each part made a perfect whole.

Serves about 10
1 x 4.5kg fore rib of beef
3 tablespoons olive oil
Salt and freshly ground black pepper

Preheat the oven to 230°C/Gas Mark 8.

Rub the meat all over with the oil, then season well with salt and pepper. Place in a large roasting tin and roast for 15 minutes, then turn the oven down to 190°C/Gas Mark 5. Continue cooking for 12 minutes per 500g for rare beef (45°C on a meat thermometer), 15 minutes per 500g for medium rare (60°C on a meat thermometer), basting from time to time.

Put the meat on a warmed serving dish and let it rest, covered with foil, for 30 minutes, giving you time to make the Yorkshire pudding and gravy (both page 167). Serve with roast potatoes (page 326) and creamed horseradish (page 174).

Yorkshire pudding

Gravy

This is an essential addition to roast beef. I used to eat a version at a schoolfriend's farmhouse. Her mother was an instinctively good cook, and her secret was to pour the batter into the hot fat at the last minute, having just removed the joint from the tin to let it rest. What made it so remarkable was the way it puffed up magnificently around the edges and the batter soaked up the salty juices from the meat. Here is our version.

Serves 6
250g plain flour
A pinch of salt
3 large eggs
600ml whole milk
About 25g lard (you might not need this)

Sift the flour and salt into a bowl, make a well in the middle and beat in the eggs one at a time. Slowly add the milk, stirring until it has the consistency of thick cream. Rest the batter for 1 hour.

After removing the meat from the oven, reset the temperature to 220°C/Gas Mark 7. Pour the meat juices into a jug and skim off any fat, putting it back into the roasting tin. If there seems too little fat, add the lard, then put the tin back into the oven for 5 minutes, until the fat is smoking hot. Pour the batter into the tin and cook for 15 minutes until puffed up and golden. Serve straight away with the roast beef.

Good gravy is delicious and, as with all cooking, it's best to keep it as simple as possible. All we do at home is to make a sauce from the juices of the meat enlivened with a little alcohol, and sweetened with a fruit preserve.

We use more or less the same method for making gravy with various roasted meats. It's not an exact recipe, and we always make it at the last minute, while the meat is resting. Although my mother's generation thickened their gravy with a little flour cooked in the meat juices with some of the fat, our version is clearer and thinner with an intense flavour.

After we've poured off the excess fat from the roasting tin, we put the tin back on the stove on a low heat and loosen the juices with a splash of wine – usually red with brown meats, white wine or even dry sherry with chicken, and cider or perry with pork – taking care to incorporate every scrap of the delicious remnants stuck to the pan. Sometimes we add a little water if it's too thick and concentrated.

Then, for gravy to go with red meats, we add homemade damson cheese (page 184), or redcurrant jelly. It's the combination of a slightly sweet gravy with the naturally salty meat that is so good. For chicken, we add quince jelly, which gives a subtle, perfumed flavour. Finally, we season it with salt and pepper. That's it – good gravy.

SAUCES

There is a sloppy ease about sauces. Maybe this is a regression to baby foods, mashed up and easy to swallow and digest, yet the idea of an infantile slop is hardly seductive.

But sauces do much more than satisfy a regressive need to be comforted. In their very blandness they can add layers of subtlety to traditional dishes. So bread sauce with chicken or turkey, parsley sauce with ham, and onion (or, even better, leek) sauce with lamb add an important element of texture and taste that do not drown the meat. However, other sauces exist to add piquancy to slightly dull fare, or even to make bland food palatable. A lot of commonly used British sauces fall into this category, such as horseradish, caper and mustard, adding a sharp tang and falling somewhere between a sauce and a relish.

Pesto sauce is a foolproof favourite, and we always grow large quantities of basil for the purpose of making it, but there is also a long tradition of English green sauces made from a range of seasonal ingredients. We use wild garlic, parsley, rocket, marjoram and mint in various permutations – never planned or measured. There's little that it does not enhance.

One of the most distinctive traits of British cooking is the use of sweet sauces served with meat. Their origins are often medieval. Damson cheese or quince jelly is delicious as a foil to the rich, dark flavours of roasted meats and game birds. Cumberland sauce provides a perfect balance to ham or venison with its ingredients of redcurrant jelly, port and bitter orange zest. Mint sauce, sweetened with sugar, is a vinegary thin concoction to serve with slightly fatty lamb, which is a combination unique to the British.

The whole point about any sauce is that it is an accompaniment and counterbalance that can either be contrasting or subtly reinforcing the main ingredients, and should never overwhelm them.

Green sauce

Green sauce is our version of the Italian salsa verde. We make it with generous quantities of chopped, fresh herbs, sharpen it with mustard and capers, add anchovies for depth of flavour, then loosen it with olive oil.

All the ingredients are from the garden or store cupboard, and I vary the herbs according to the season. Mint and golden marjoram are prolific in early summer, and later on we use lots of basil, but I always use flat-leaf parsley as the basis of this sauce. It's fantastic with cold meats, as well as with roasts and the slow-cooked, boiled meats it traditionally accompanies.

Although it will keep for a day or two, the joy of this sauce is the freshness of the herbs, their aromatic scent filling the kitchen as they are chopped on an old wooden board. The texture created through chopping the herbs by hand is important, so resist using a food processor.

There is no need to be precise. I sometimes leave out the anchovies or capers if someone doesn't like them, and it still tastes good.

Serves 6–8

A large bunch of flat-leaf parsley
A large bunch of mint, marjoram or basil, or a combination of them
3 scant tablespoons capers, rinsed and chopped
8 anchovy fillets, finely chopped
1 small garlic clove, finely chopped
1 generous tablespoon Dijon mustard
2 tablespoons white wine vinegar
Extra virgin olive oil
Sea salt and freshly ground black pepper

Prepare the herbs by stripping off the leaves and discarding the thicker stalks. Place them on a board and start to chop. At first the herbs will scatter everywhere, but as they are cut up, the pile will diminish and become more manageable. I use an ancient mezzaluna that I bought in Venice. It has a rocking action that soon reduces the herbs to the coarsely chopped texture needed. A sharp knife will do just as well.

Place the herbs in a bowl and add the capers, anchovies and garlic. Add the mustard, vinegar and seasoning, and gently toss it all together. Pour over enough oil to loosen the sauce to a spoonable consistency. Serve freshly made, a large dollop of sauce per person.

Basil pesto

We pick our basil from July to September, having planted as much as we have room for. The main harvest takes place in September, when we pull up all the plants, pick off the leaves and set up a pesto production line. The kitchen table is covered with fragrant, brilliant green leaves that fill the room with their aromatic scent. I rope in anyone who's around to help make it, as we need to work quickly before the leaves wilt. Sometimes I use only Parmesan cheese, sometimes I use it half and half with pecorino.

Pesto freezes well, so if we have a good harvest, I fill lots of little plastic pots with it, which will last us all winter. However, I leave out the cheese in the batches I'm freezing and stir it into the sauce once it's defrosted and just before I want to use it.

Serves 4–6
85g freshly picked basil leaves,
  stalks removed
30g pine nuts
1 large garlic clove
A pinch of sea salt
100ml olive oil
75g Parmesan cheese, grated

Pesto can be made by hand with a large pestle and mortar, but I prefer to use a food processor, pulsing it rather than running it at full speed to ensure the sauce retains some texture. Put the basil, pine nuts, garlic and salt into a food processor and pulse for a few seconds until everything is roughly chopped. It's important not to over-process it at this point, or it will become an unappealing sludge. Add the olive oil in a thin stream through the top of the processor and pulse until just combined. Finally, stir in the cheese.

If you want to make the pesto by hand, use a pestle and mortar. Grind the leaves with a little salt, then add the garlic. When roughly mixed, work in the cheese and the oil until you have your preferred consistency.

If you are using the pesto for a pasta sauce, drain the pasta, retaining about a tablespoon of the cooking liquid. Add a knob of butter to the pan plus the spoonful of cooking water. Put the drained pasta in with it and mix in the fresh pesto. Add more oil if necessary and serve straight away with more cheese.

Mint sauce

For generations, roast lamb never appeared without mint sauce in tow. Certainly, the sweetness of the meat with the sourness of the sauce provides a sense of balance and inevitability that remains very satisfying. The very Englishness of it also appeals to me.

Makes about 160ml
1 tablespoon light muscovado sugar
2 heaped tablespoons chopped mint leaves
150ml cider vinegar

Put the sugar into a small bowl and pour over 2 tablespoons boiling water. Stir until the sugar dissolves. Add the mint and vinegar, stir together and leave for an hour or so to steep before serving.

Creamed horseradish

Horseradish can be a menace in gardens as its roots reach so deep that it's impossible to eradicate. It also grows wild on many grass verges. If you have access to fresh horseradish, it's definitely worth making your own sauce. It releases extremely pungent oils when grated, so whether you do it in a food processor or by hand, don't breathe deeply or your eyes will stream.

But don't let the prospect of streaming eyes put you off, as nothing compares to properly made horseradish sauce with roast beef (page 165). It's also excellent with fish, smoked or fresh. A fisherman once brought us a pike from the river at the bottom of our garden, which I baked and served with a warm version of this sauce. It was very good indeed. If you do heat it up, be careful not to boil it or the sauce will lose all its power.

Serves 6
2 tablespoons peeled and freshly grated
horseradish
150ml double cream, lightly whipped
A pinch of sugar
A pinch of salt
Juice of ½ a lemon

Mix the grated horseradish in a bowl with the cream. Season it with sugar and salt, and sharpen it with the lemon juice to taste.

Apple sauce

We make this sauce in the autumn to accompany pork chops, sausages or roast pork (page 162). It is also delicious with roast goose, in season from Michaelmas (29 September) until Christmas, coinciding with the apple harvest. Eating apples, such as the readily available Cox's Orange Pippin, are good to use, but they might need sharpening with lemon juice. Cookers, such as Bramleys, will do, but will need sweetening. Try out different varieties and find your favourites.

A quince is a lovely, aromatic addition to apple sauce, and raises it to a higher level. Quinces don't keep as well as apples and need to be cooked soon after they are picked. The sauce can be spiced up with a pinch of cinnamon or grated nutmeg for added richness. This recipe makes a generous amount, and I usually allow one eating apple per person if I am calculating for large numbers.

Serves 6
1kg apples
1 quince (optional)
50g caster sugar, or to taste, depending
  on the apple variety
Juice of ½ a lemon, if necessary to sharpen
  the sauce, and possibly a piece of lemon peel
50g unsalted butter
Freshly ground black pepper
A pinch of cinnamon or grated nutmeg
  (optional)

Peel, core and roughly chop the apples. If you are adding a quince, peel, core and chop it into much smaller pieces than the apples as it is harder and takes longer to soften.

Place the fruit in a saucepan with 150ml water and simmer until soft and pulpy, about 10–15 minutes, longer if you are using quince. Taste and add the lemon juice if the apples are bland. Add the butter and beat into the sauce until it has a smooth, glossy consistency. Stir in the pepper and spice, if using.

Serve warm. The sauce can be made several hours in advance and reheated.

Bread sauce

In our household we all love the succulence of bread sauce, eating it with roasted birds, such as chicken, pheasant or turkey. We also love to eat it with sausages, and it is an essential component of Christmas sandwiches made with leftovers. A bowl of bread sauce disappears quickly when everyone is at home.

It is useful to know how to make it, ready for a comforting meal on a cold winter's day. The amount of breadcrumbs depends on how thick you want the sauce to be. I prefer it with a bit of texture, so rather than use fine breadcrumbs, I tear the bread into pieces. Fresh bread works well, but a day-old white loaf from a proper baker's is my preference. Never use sliced white bread or you will get a gluey mess. The flavour is improved by being made in advance and then reheated.

Peel the onion and stud it with the cloves. Warm the milk in a saucepan over a medium-low heat, then add the onion, bay leaf, mace and a few gratings of nutmeg. Simmer gently for 20 minutes to allow the flavours to infuse. Remove the bay leaf and mace before stirring in the torn pieces of bread. Season to taste and allow it to stand for at least an hour so the bread can absorb the milk, then remove the onion.

Before serving, reheat carefully, taking care not to let the the sauce catch on the bottom of the pan. Stir in a knob of butter or a little cream to enrich the sauce at the last minute, and grate over some more fresh nutmeg. Serve hot.

Serves 6
1 small onion
6 cloves
450ml whole milk
1 bay leaf
1 blade of mace
Freshly grated nutmeg
100g white bread, torn into small pieces
A knob of unsalted butter or a splash
  of cream
Salt and freshly ground black pepper

White sauce

As white sauce forms the basis of several others, such as parsley sauce (opposite), cheese sauce and mushroom sauce, it is one of the most basic sauces to know how to make. It's also good in many other dishes, but I particularly like it plain, with broad beans or leeks.

I no longer make white sauce the way I was originally taught because I've speeded up the process. Before I simplified my method, I melted the butter in a saucepan, added flour to form a roux, then patiently stirred in warm milk with a wooden spoon until the sauce thickened. That's still a perfectly good way of making a white sauce, but this recipe is much easier and just as successful.

Makes about 540ml
450ml milk
45g unsalted butter, cut into cubes
45g plain flour
Freshly grated nutmeg
Salt and freshly ground white pepper

Warm the milk in a heavy-based saucepan over a gentle heat. As it warms, add the butter and sprinkle on the flour.

Stir or whisk continuously as it heats. It's important not to be distracted from this or it will get lumpy and burn on the bottom. The butter melts in the warm milk and amalgamates with the flour so that they cook as the liquid heats up.

You should not let it boil, but allow it to simmer gently, stirring for a few minutes until the mixture thickens into a sauce that coats the back of a spoon.

Grate over some fresh nutmeg and season to taste.

Parsley sauce

This green-flecked sauce is perfect with cooked ham (page 294) and bacon, and it's often served with white fish. Don't let its cod in parsley sauce, boil-in-a-bag reputation put you off – plain food, prepared with care and made with fresh ingredients often provides the most memorable meals. I have eaten slices of wild boar ham, which has a stronger flavour than the farmyard pig, served with parsley sauce and plain boiled potatoes. It felt like a feast and the sauce balanced the gaminess of the dark pink meat.

This sauce can lift boiled vegetables, such as broad beans, onions and little beetroots, up to a higher level. Note that raw chopped parsley is too coarse, so it needs to be blanched first, and that way the finer stalks can be used too for extra flavour.

Makes about 700ml
1 large bunch of parsley, flat-leaf or curly
600ml milk
30g unsalted butter
30g plain flour
Freshly grated nutmeg
Salt and freshly ground black pepper

Pick over the bunch of parsley, discarding the thicker stems. Bring a pan of water to the boil and blanch the stalks and leaves for a minute. Drain well, refresh under the cold tap and chop finely.

Pour the milk into a saucepan and as it warms over a low heat, add the butter and sprinkle on the flour. Stir or whisk vigorously and continuously. (This is where the sauce can go wrong, but as long as you keep stirring, the sauce will be smooth. If – despite all the whisking – it is lumpy, you can rescue it by blitzing with a hand-held blender or pushing it through a sieve.) Simmer on a low heat for about 5 minutes, stirring continuously until it thickens.

Season, stir in the parsley and grate a little nutmeg over it. Serve hot.

Tartare sauce

Caper sauce

Although fast and simple to make, this tartare sauce is far sharper and fresher than anything from a jar. When it comes to the mayonnaise, it should ideally be homemade (page 139), though if that's not possible, a good-quality ready-made one will do. A generous dollop of tartare sauce is the perfect accompaniment to fishcakes (page 114).

Makes about 370g
250g mayonnaise
60g capers, roughly chopped
60g gherkins, chopped
2 tablespoons finely chopped parsley leaves
½ a lemon
Salt and freshly ground black pepper

In a bowl, mix together the mayonnaise, capers, gherkins and parsley. Add a squeeze or two of lemon juice and season according to taste.

The tartare sauce is best eaten on the day you make it, though it will keep, sealed in a jar in the fridge, for a couple of days.

Caper sauce is essentially a white sauce sharpened with capers and vinegar and flavoured with chopped parsley. It is usually made to accompany boiled mutton, although nowadays it is more likely to partner a leg of lamb. For both, the sweetness of the meat balances well with the sharpness of the capers.

Makes about 500ml
450ml whole milk
45g unsalted butter
45g plain flour
Juices from a roast leg of lamb (page 161, optional)
2 tablespoons capers in vinegar, drained
Vinegar from the caper jar, to taste
2 tablespoons finely chopped flat-leaf parsley
Salt and freshly ground black pepper

Warm the milk in a heavy-based saucepan over a gentle heat. As it warms, add the butter and sprinkle on the flour. Stir or whisk continuously as it heats. You should not let it boil, but allow it to simmer gently, stirring constantly for a few minutes until the mixture thickens into a sauce that coats the back of a spoon. Stir in the strained meat juices, if using, to enrich the sauce.

Add the capers and a spoonful or two of the vinegar, taste and season. Stir in the parsley and serve hot with slices of boiled mutton or lamb.

Beurre blanc

This butter sauce is rich but light, with the consistency of double cream. We don't usually bother with fancy sauces, but this is not difficult to make and we usually have the ingredients to hand.

Beurre blanc is delicious with artichokes (page 264), asparagus or even poached fish, and it also makes a good dressing for a winter salad of bitter leaves and bacon. It must be made at the last minute, with really cold butter straight from the fridge. The shallot reduction can be prepared in advance, then warmed up and the butter added just before serving.

Serves 6
50g finely chopped shallots
100ml white wine vinegar
100ml dry white wine
225g unsalted butter, chilled and cubed
Juice of ½ a lemon
Salt

Place the shallots in a small saucepan with the vinegar, wine and 50ml water. Boil it down until it is reduced to just half of its original volume. I don't strain it as I like to leave the shallots in the sauce.

Lower the heat and add the butter to the reduction bit by bit, vigorously whisking it in to form a smooth, creamy sauce. Add the lemon juice and season with salt.

Serve immediately, or keep it warm over a bowl of hot water.

Mustard and cream sauce

This sauce is especially good with rare beef, though it also works very well with chicken, and is even better with the juices from a roast chicken added to it.

This is not an exact recipe, so adjust the quantities to taste. I like the sharpness of the lemon to cut through the richness of the cream.

Makes about 150ml
150g double cream
3 tablespoons Dijon mustard
Juice of ½ a lemon
Salt and freshly ground black pepper

Put the cream and mustard in a small pan, whisk together and gently warm through. Don't boil the sauce or you will lose the heat from the mustard. Squeeze in the lemon juice, then taste and add seasoning. The mustard is already salty, so you probably won't need to add much more salt. Serve warm.

Cumberland sauce

I always make Cumberland sauce at
Christmas to serve with the ham (page 294).
It's also a very good sauce to serve with
game during the autumn and winter. It is
a lovely, dark red colour flecked with little
strips of orange.

Makes about 200g
2 large unwaxed oranges
1 unwaxed lemon
4 tablespoons redcurrant jelly
1 teaspoon Dijon mustard
1 teaspoon ground ginger
120ml tawny port
A pinch of salt

Wash the oranges and lemon and pare off
the zest with a vegetable peeler or sharp
knife. Flatten the pieces of zest on a
chopping board and cut them into thin
matchsticks. Drop them into a pan of
boiling water and blanch for a couple of
minutes to remove any bitterness, then
strain them.

Squeeze the juice from the fruit and
pour it into a saucepan with the zest and
the rest of the ingredients. Heat gently,
stirring constantly, for about 5 minutes.
Serve hot or cold.

Damson cheese

Damsons are a feature of the hedgerows in Herefordshire and Worcestershire. They crop easily and can't be eaten raw, so we use them to make this cheese, as well as fruit crumbles and vodka. Despite the recipe name, this is not a cheese in the dairy sense, but a thick, fudgy preserve that keeps for several years. I like to think of it as a remnant of medieval cooking.

It's especially delicious served with lamb or game of any kind as the richness of the meat is balanced by the intensity of the fruit. In fact, of all preserves, none has so much depth of taste or colour as damson cheese.

Makes 4–5 x 300g jars
1kg damsons
Caster sugar

Put two saucers in the fridge to chill for testing setting point.

Wash the damsons, removing any stalks and leaves. Weigh the fruit, then place in a preserving pan or large, heavy-based stainless-steel pan with 350ml water per kilo of fruit. Bring the damsons to the boil and simmer until the fruits burst and soften, about 15 minutes.

Push the fruit through a sieve to remove the stones and skin, then measure the pulp in a jug in order to work out how much sugar to use. You need 1kg of sugar to 1 litre of pulp.

Pour the pulp and sugar back into the pan and stir over a low heat to dissolve the sugar. Once the sugar has dissolved, simmer gently and stir frequently to prevent the mixture from burning. The mixture should thicken to the point where a wooden spoon drawn across the bottom of the pan leaves a clear line for a few seconds.

To test if it has reached setting point, place a spoonful of the mixture on one of the chilled saucers. As it cools, it should wrinkle when you push it with your finger.

When ready, allow the mixture to cool for 15 minutes, then pour into warm, sterilised jars (page 37). Cover with wax discs and cellophane or lids.

The thick jelly can be spooned or sliced, and will keep for several years in a cool, dry place.

Quince jelly

Quinces are the most beautiful of all fruit. They have a strong perfume, and the exquisite, pear-shaped variety, with its deep ridges and perfect, downy yellow skin, is lovelier than almost anything made by man. Quinces might look like a glorious cross between an apple and a pear but, unlike those fruits, they are inedible when raw.

Unfortunately, they don't keep well, so must be cooked soon after picking. We use our windfalls to make this deep amber jelly. It's a good foil to rich meats and game, but it's also perfect on scones (page 225).

Makes 6 x 360g jars
About 2kg quinces
1kg golden granulated sugar

Using a sharp, heavy knife, chop up the quinces, cutting out any bad bits, but leaving the skins and cores. Put them in a saucepan and pour over just enough water to cover the fruit. Bring to the boil and simmer them for about 1 hour, until they are soft and easily pierced with a knife.

Strain the pulp through a jelly bag or a piece of muslin tied in four corners suspended over a large bowl. Leave it for several hours to drip slowly, and do not force the pulp through by squeezing or the jelly will be cloudy. You should end up with 1.8 litres of juice.

Put two saucers in the fridge to chill for testing setting point.

Preheat the oven to its lowest setting. Spread the sugar out on a baking tray and warm in the oven for about 10 minutes. This helps to speed up the cooking time of the jelly.

Pour the quince juice into a preserving pan or large stainless-steel saucepan and bring it slowly to the boil. Add the warmed sugar to the pan and bring it slowly to a simmer again, stirring to dissolve the sugar. When the sugar has dissolved (you can check this by testing to see if any granules of sugar remain on the spoon), boil rapidly without stirring until setting point is reached. This should happen quickly, within 10 minutes, as quinces are full of pectin. Test by placing a drop of the mixture on a chilled saucer. When cool, it should wrinkle when you push it with your fingertip.

Skim off any scum on the surface of the pan, then allow to cool for 15 minutes. Pour the jelly into warm, sterilised jars (page 37). Cover with waxed discs and cellophane or with lids. Store in a cool, dark place and use within 2 years.

PUDDING

Although like many of her generation my mother felt tyrannised by cooking for a large family, she loved a pudding. This meant that she became very good at making them. I have inherited my mother's taste, and adore pudding in almost all its forms. Indeed, I feel that there are few meals that cannot be improved, or indeed salvaged, by a pudding.

My favourite puddings are based upon cooked seasonal fruits, such as gooseberries, apples, pears, black- and redcurrants, quinces and rhubarb. (Cooking pears, by the way, implies a plentiful supply because when properly ripe and perhaps accompanied by a good blue cheese, the raw fruit cannot be improved.) The very British tradition of using cream, milk and eggs for puddings has lovely combinations too. All's well that ends with a good pudding.

The British love of cooked fruit stems from medieval times, when raw fruit was regarded in much the same way as we look upon shellfish – nice but potentially dodgy. Cooking it guaranteed safe digestion and made it easier to store. Cooked fruit does not have to be eaten hot in tarts, pies and crumbles – although damson crumble is worth clearing the diary for in September – it is just as good eaten cold in fools or ice cream. Even plain stewed fruit (page 16), despite its unglamorous image, is wonderfully soothing and refreshing. I never tire of it. While gooseberries, plums and rhubarb all stew very well, apples form the vast bulk of our stewed fruit, and we use windfalls for this as they will not store. Add a quince or two to a batch of stewed apples and it is subtly but immeasurably improved. As the apple season progresses we increasingly bake them, either treating large ones reverentially or cramming a number of small ones into a baking tray. It is the simplest of puddings, but still one of the best.

Rhubarb fool

Our rhubarb patch takes up a corner of the garden that is about three metres square. Some of the rhubarb is Timperley Early and some is an unknown variety that we dug up and brought with us from our last garden.

In the New Year we cover several crowns of rhubarb with terracotta cloches to force them into production. They came from a local pottery and have removable lids that I lift off every few days to see if there is enough to pick. Actually, you shouldn't pick rhubarb, but pull it so that the stalks separate from the crown just below ground level. I soon have an armful of slender, brilliant pink stalks, with acid green leaves.

I love fruit fools because they are so English and simple to make. The rhubarb is baked in its own juices and retains its beautiful colour. This recipe can be adapted by substituting cooked gooseberries or ripe strawberries for the rhubarb. It's very rich, so you need only a small portion. Serve it with shortbread biscuits (page 230).

Serves 6
1kg rhubarb stalks, trimmed and cut
  into 3cm lengths
200g caster sugar
Zest and juice of 1 unwaxed orange
280ml double cream

Preheat the oven to 180°C/Gas Mark 4.

Place the rhubarb in an ovenproof dish and sprinkle on the sugar, orange zest and juice. Give everything a good stir, then cover with a lid or greaseproof paper and bake until soft, about 30 minutes.

Cool, then strain off the juices into a jug. Reserve some whole pieces of rhubarb for decorating the fool. Purée the rest of the cooked rhubarb in a food processor.

Whip the cream until it forms soft peaks, then gently fold in the purée and a few tablespoons of the reserved juices, marbling the cream with colour rather than mixing it thoroughly. It should look rippled rather than a bright pink mush. Serve it in individual glasses, with a couple of pieces of whole rhubarb on the top.

Lemon sorbet

Sorbets provide an intense hit of fruit. Ice cold, they melt deliciously on the tongue. They are so refreshing on a hot day or whenever a light, clean taste is needed at the end of a meal.

As a young bride of nineteen in Papua New Guinea, I was an inexperienced and pretty hopeless cook, but I was able to make this lemon sorbet. (I also used to make it with limes if I couldn't get hold of lemons.) It was so hot and humid that all the familiar food of my childhood was inappropriate and, anyway, unobtainable. We lived mainly on tropical fruit and vegetables bought from the market, but also sampled food cooked by the other university staff recruited from all over the world – southern India, Nigeria, the West Indies – and also had wonderful Indonesian food cooked by the spies who ran the university club.

This cooling lemon sorbet includes beaten egg white, which is whipped into the half-frozen lemon syrup, giving it a frothy lightness. We eat this not only on hot English summer days, but also after a rich meal. It melts quickly, so I put little serving glasses in the freezer for an hour before spooning the sorbet into them.

Serves 4–6
100g caster sugar
Zest and juice of 2 large unwaxed lemons
1 egg white

Pour 450ml water into a saucepan, add the sugar and warm gently, stirring to dissolve the sugar. When that has happened, boil for about 5 minutes, then take off the heat. Allow to cool.

Add the lemon zest and juice to the syrup and let it infuse for 10 minutes. Strain the liquid through a sieve, then churn in an ice-cream machine according to the manufacturer's instructions.

Meanwhile, beat the egg white until it is stiff, adding it to the syrup in the ice-cream machine after about 15 minutes, as soon as the mixture starts to get slushy and before it is too frozen. Continue churning until it has thickened, another 15–30 minutes, depending on your machine. Scoop the sorbet into a plastic container and freeze for at least 2 hours.

For a simpler way without gadgets, as I first made it, freeze the lemon syrup in a shallow container until it is starting to freeze and get slushy. Beat the egg white until stiff, then gently stir it into the lemon mixture before refreezing until firm.

The sorbet will keep in the freezer for several days. When you are ready to serve it, spoon it straight from the freezer into small, ice-cold glasses.

Gooseberry ice cream

Gooseberry and elderflower fool

Gooseberries are the first of the soft fruits to ripen in summer, and they make a really good ice cream. I like to serve it with extra gooseberries poached in syrup, but the fruit should be simmered carefully so that it keeps its shape. Serve it with pieces of buttery shortbread (page 230) for balance.

Serves 4–6
500g gooseberries (no need to top or tail)
150g caster sugar
300g Greek yoghurt or 300ml double cream

Place the gooseberries in a saucepan with the sugar and 50ml water, and poach them over a medium heat until they are soft.

When they are a soft mush, push them through a sieve to remove the skin and pips and allow to cool. When frozen, their sweetness will be less pronounced, so taste and add more sugar now if necessary.

Mix the yoghurt or cream into the fruit purée and churn in an ice-cream machine according to the manufacturer's instructions. Spoon into a plastic tub and freeze for at least a couple of hours, though remember to remove from the freezer about 10 minutes before serving.

If you don't have an ice-cream machine, pour the mixture into a plastic container and place in the freezer. Every 30 minutes or so over the course of about 3 hours, whisk with a fork to break up the ice crystals and create a smooth ice cream.

If I have to make a quick pudding for lunch, I usually rush into the garden to get inspiration. Often a fruit fool is the answer, made with rich, whipped cream.

It's a good idea to recruit someone to help top and tail the berries as that is the only laborious part of this very simple recipe.

Serves 6–8
500g gooseberries, topped and tailed
2–4 tablespoons caster sugar, or slightly less if using elderflower cordial
2 elderflower heads or 1 tablespoon elderflower cordial
280ml double cream, the richest you can find
Sprigs of mint, to garnish

Put the fruit, sugar and elderflowers or cordial into a saucepan with 2 tablespoons of water. Cook over a medium heat until the gooseberries are soft, about 10 minutes. Remove the elderflower heads, then lightly mash the gooseberries with a fork so that they are broken but not puréed. Cool completely.

Whip the cream until it is just stiff enough to form soft peaks, then gently fold it into the fruit. The texture should be light and not too blended.

Serve in a big bowl or individual glasses decorated with mint, and with shortbread biscuits (page 230) on the side.

Eton mess

Strawberries in their season are a high point of the year. Unfortunately, the ubiquitous, polytunnel-reared Elsanta, with a good aroma but practically no flavour, dominates the commercial market, and a limited range of varieties have become available all year round, so strawberries are no longer a summer treat.

Out of season, the imported strawberries on offer in supermarkets are bred to withstand being knocked around during their journey, not for their flavour. The soft, English strawberry on the other hand – at its best in June and July – is has a short shelf life, but is worth waiting for.

I love to eat a bowl of strawberries and cream sprinkled with crunchy sugar while sitting in the sunshine at home. If I want to make something slightly more elaborate, Eton mess, that combination of strawberries, crushed meringues and whipped cream, is the easiest of puddings and seems to be loved by everyone. For a quick Eton mess, use the best-quality bought meringues. They shouldn't be too dry, so try to find some with chewy centres. This recipe makes enough for second helpings.

Serves 6
*600g strawberries, stalks removed
and quartered, with some left whole
for decoration, or a combination of
strawberries and raspberries*
600ml double cream

For the meringues:
3 egg whites
170g caster sugar

First, make the meringues. Preheat the oven to 140°C/Gas Mark 1. Line a baking tray with baking parchment.

Place the egg whites in a scrupulously clean bowl and whisk until they form soft peaks. Add the sugar a spoonful at a time, whisking constantly until the mixture is thick and glossy and forms stiff peaks.

Dab a little of the mixture beneath 4 corners of the baking parchment on the baking tray to keep it in place. Put dessertspoonfuls of the meringue on it. Bake for 1 hour, then turn off the oven, prop the door ajar and leave the meringues to cool inside for 45 minutes.

Assemble the pudding at the last minute as the meringue starts to dissolve very quickly in the cream. Place the fruit in the bottom of a serving bowl, mashing it slightly with a fork. Whip the cream lightly and add it to the bowl. Break the meringues into largish pieces over the cream and mix everything together gently. Scatter some whole berries over the pudding. Serve immediately in little glasses.

Summer pudding

For about two weeks in July, all the soft fruit is ready to pick – strawberries, raspberries, red- and blackcurrants – and this glorious pudding is a spectacular way to use them together. Each time I make it I vary the quantities of fruit, always including the base ingredients of redcurrants and raspberries, though if we have lots of strawberries I add them too.

It's better to use bread that is a day old rather than a very fresh, yeasty loaf, as older bread absorbs the juices better. Don't use a pre-sliced loaf, but buy a large white, unsliced one and leave it for a day or so.

The pudding freezes well and is a good way of using up a glut of fruit. One year I made 20 and we ate one on Christmas Day. Although this is against my principles of eating food only when it's in season, it did leave us with a lovely taste of the summer.

Serves 4–6
400g raspberries
250g strawberries, larger ones halved
300g redcurrants, or a combination of redcurrants and blackcurrants, topped and tailed
140g caster sugar
8 thick slices of day-old white bread, approximately 1 large loaf, crusts removed

To serve:
Double cream

Pick over the raspberries and strawberries and place them in a bowl. Put the currants and sugar in a saucepan with 1 tablespoon water and cook for a few minutes over a medium heat to release their juices. Add them to the bowl of berries and mix together.

Line a 1 litre bowl with the bread: start by cutting a circle for the base, then place the other slices around the sides, butting them up tightly together and making sure not to leave any gaps. Fill the bowl with the fruit and really pack it down, then put a final circle of bread on top. Cover the pudding with a plate that fits just inside the bowl and weigh it down with a couple of 400g tins. Leave overnight in the fridge so that the juices can saturate the bread.

When you are ready to serve it, turn the pudding out onto a plate. If any white patches remain in the bread, pour over some juice made with extra currants stewed with sugar. Serve with lots of double cream – and a little sugar, if you have a sweet tooth like me.

Redcurrant sorbet

When it's very hot, none of us has much of an appetite, only a thirst for cooling drinks and refreshing fruit. A sorbet is the perfect combination of both.

Redcurrants are one of the most beautiful fruits, their luscious red berries hanging like clusters of glass beads. They are very hardy and can be treated just like gooseberries, growing well in shade and tolerating almost any soil.

If you grow lots of soft fruit, it's worth investing in an ice-cream machine as they radically simplify the process of creating delicious sorbets and ice creams that taste so much fruitier and fresher than anything you can buy. This recipe, however, can also be made by hand.

You can, of course, use blackcurrants instead of redcurrants.

Serves 6
900g redcurrants, prepared weight
200g caster sugar

Put the redcurrants into a saucepan with 150ml water. Bring to the boil, reduce the heat and simmer for about 5 minutes, until the currants have broken down into a mush. Sieve them into a bowl, pressing down on the fruit to extract as much juice and pulp as possible.

Return the liquid to the pan with the sugar. Cook gently, stirring, until the sugar has completely dissolved. Cool and taste, adding a little more sugar if necessary. If you do this, stir thoroughly until the extra sugar has completely dissolved. You should have about 1 litre of juice.

If you're using an ice-cream machine, churn the fruit mixture according to the manufacturer's instructions, then spoon into a plastic container and put it into the freezer for 3 hours.

If you don't have an ice-cream machine, pour the juice into a plastic container and place in the freezer. Every 30 minutes or so over the course of about 3 hours, whisk the sorbet with a fork to break up the ice crystals.

Serve the sorbet directly from the freezer.

Blackcurrant meringues with cream

Almost all the blackcurrants in this country are grown in fields around us – they thrive in the rich, damp soil. We have a few bushes of our own in the garden, which, other than needing to be pruned back by a third every year, are no trouble to look after. If you prune when harvesting the fruit – cutting off the branches heavy with berries and stripping them in one go – it doesn't take long. They produce their fruit in July and August, and we use them in summer pudding (page 195), tarts and purées. They freeze well too.

The intense, sharp flavour of black-currants means that a little of the fruit goes a long way when added to fools and ice creams, or combined with meringue and whipped cream in this irresistible pudding.

Serves 6
300g blackcurrants, plus more
 for decorating
1–2 tablespoons caster sugar
300ml double cream

For the meringue:
4 large egg whites
220g caster sugar

First make the meringues. Preheat the oven to 140°C/Gas Mark 1. Line 2 baking sheets with baking parchment.

Place the egg whites in a scrupulously clean bowl and whisk them until they form soft peaks. Add the sugar a spoonful at a time, whisking constantly until the meringue is thick and glossy and forms stiff peaks.

Dab a little of the mixture beneath the 4 corners of each piece of baking parchment to keep them in place on the baking trays. Spread out the meringue mixture in two thick circles roughly 18cm diameter. Cook for 1 hour, then turn off the oven, prop the door open, and leave the meringues inside until they're completely cold.

Place the blackcurrants in a saucepan with the sugar and just enough water so the mixture doesn't stick to the bottom of the pan as it cooks – about 3 tablespoons should be enough. Simmer for a few minutes, until the fruit is soft and the juices running. Pass the fruit through a sieve and taste for sweetness. It should be slightly sharp.

Whip the cream until thickened and doubled in volume, taking care not to overbeat it or it will become grainy. Sandwich the two meringues together with half the cream, then spread the remaining cream on the top; dribble over the blackcurrant purée. Decorate with more fresh blackcurrants and serve immediately.

Blackcurrant fool

Fruit fools are lovely in summer for a light dessert, simple to assemble, and look pretty served in little glasses. This fool also makes a fabulous filling for a sponge cake, too.

Serves 6
250g blackcurrants
2–3 tablespoons caster sugar, to taste
300ml double cream or whipping cream
Sprigs of mint (optional)

Put the blackcurrants in a saucepan, keeping back about 18 good specimens for decoration. There is no need to top and tail them before cooking.

Add the sugar and 2–3 tablespoons water, bring to the boil and simmer until the fruit is soft and the juices running, which should take just over 5 minutes. Remove from the heat, cool and pass the cooked fruit through a sieve into a bowl. Discard the pulp left in the sieve.

In a separate bowl, lightly whip the cream until it thickens, being careful not to overbeat. Gently fold the cream into the fruit purée. I don't mix it in completely, preferring to see a ripple effect of purple-red blackcurrant through the pale cream.

Fill little glasses with the fool, then decorate with the whole blackcurrants and mint, if using. Any remaining fool will keep, covered, for a couple of days in the fridge. Serve chilled with shortbread biscuits (page 230), if you like.

Hazelnut meringues

These mountainous meringues are transformed by the addition of toasted hazelnuts. They look spectacular piled up together. Serve them on their own or with whipped cream and fresh fruit – my own favourite would be raspberries.

Sometimes we add a tablespoon of cocoa powder sifted over a scoop of the raw meringue, then stirred to blend before swirling the cocoa meringue in with the rest of the mixture at the last minute to create a marbled effect.

Makes 6 large meringues
100g skinned hazelnuts
6 egg whites
350g caster sugar

Preheat the oven to 180°C/Gas Mark 4.

Place the hazelnuts on a baking tray and toast in the oven for 8–10 minutes, until fragrant and golden. Allow to cool, then wrap half of them in a tea towel and roughly break them up by bashing with a rolling pin. Leave the rest whole.

Lower the oven temperature to 80°C/Gas Mark ¼. Line a large baking tray with baking parchment.

Place the egg whites in a scrupulously clean bowl and whisk them until they form soft peaks. Add the sugar a spoonful at a time, whisking constantly until the meringue is thick and glossy and forms stiff peaks. Dab a little of the mixture beneath the 4 corners of the baking parchment on the baking tray to keep it in place. Divide the meringue mixture into 6 equal mounds on the tray.

Scatter the toasted hazelnuts, both whole and broken ones, over the tops of the meringues, carefully pushing them down so the nuts won't fall off as they're cooking. Bake for 2–3 hours, until the base of the meringues is firm to the touch. When they are ready, cool on a wire rack and carefully peel off the baking parchment.

Baked apples

We often eat baked apples because we grow many suitable varieties in our small orchard, and we store as many as we can in a cool place over the winter. In fact, we eat apples in some form almost every day.

The largest of the apples we grow is Glory of England. It's a whopper and I love the way it seems to burst with pride as it cooks. We eat the early ones like Arthur Turner first, then move on to the better keepers such as Newton Wonder, William Crump and Hambledon Deux Ans. When they're gone, I use sweeter dessert apples, such as Rosemary Russett, Strawberry Pippin and Jupiter.

We grow far more than we can eat ourselves, so the windfalls are left for the birds, especially the fieldfares and redwings that arrive with the first of the cold weather in autumn. The fruit is an important food for them, and the apples lying on the ground disappear within a few weeks, so nothing is wasted.

Serves 6
6 large apples
150g sultanas or raisins
6 dessertspoons light muscovado sugar
150ml water, apple juice or cider

To serve:
Cream, pouring custard (page 215),
  crème fraîche, yoghurt (page 18) or
  vanilla ice cream (page 353)

Preheat the oven to 180°C/Gas Mark 4.

There is no mystery to baking apples, but if you make them frequently, an apple corer is really useful. To prepare an apple for baking, wash it and place, unpeeled, on a chopping board, then push the corer through the centre. A small, sharp knife will also do the job, but the core will have to be cut out from either end.

Place the apples closely together in a roasting tin so they're almost touching. You can make an incision in the skin around the middle of each apple to allow it to expand if you like, but I don't bother as a foaming, irregularly shaped apple tastes just as good. Stuff the hollow core of each one with the sultanas or raisins and a spoonful of sugar. Pour the water, apple juice or cider into the tin – this will become syrup by the end of cooking.

Bake for 45–60 minutes, depending on the size of the apples, until they are soft and puffed up. Place them in individual bowls, spoon over some syrup and serve with cream, custard, crème fraîche, yoghurt or vanilla ice cream.

Apple dumplings

I love everything about September, even though it means the end of summer, as the weather is often lovely with cool, misty mornings and hot, sunny days. The harvest is proof of all the hard work done during the year. It is also the month of a number of food festivals in this part of the world. They are filled with stalls where local producers show off their wares – from hams, cheeses, ice cream and honey to local wines, ciders and beers. But best of all to my mind are the apples. These come from gnarled orchards scattered across the hillsides of the Marches.

The orchard in our garden has 37 varieties, many of them local to a few miles around us. The best dessert apples are carefully picked from the trees and stored to be eaten over the winter, usually just with a hunk of local Cheddar. But the windfalls will not keep, so we try to find as many ways as possible of eating them up. This recipe makes a filling pudding, where one apple becomes almost a meal in itself.

Serves 4–6
500g plain flour
250g unsalted butter
125g caster sugar, plus more for filling the apples
2 eggs
1 tablespoon iced water
4 large or 6 medium-sized apples
Milk, to glaze

Combine the flour and butter in a food processor and pulse until the mixture resembles coarse breadcrumbs. Add the sugar and process just enough to blend. Add the eggs one at a time, pulsing until everything is combined. Add the water at the last minute to bind the dough. Take the dough out of the processor, gently pat into a ball, and rest it for 30 minutes, covered in cling film in the fridge.

If you prefer, you do this first stage by hand, rubbing the butter into the flour with your fingertips until it resembles coarse breadcrumbs. Mix in the sugar, then make a well in the middle and cut in the lightly beaten eggs with a knife. Add just enough iced water to bring it together into a dough, then pat into a ball, cover and rest as above.

Preheat the oven to 180°C/Gas Mark 4.

Peel and core the apples. Roll out the pastry on a lightly floured surface and cut into circles big enough to cover the apples completely – I use a side plate to cut around. Place an apple in the centre of a pastry circle, fill the empty core with sugar, then wrap the pastry right round it. Place it upside down in a baking dish and repeat with the rest of the apples. Brush them with milk and sprinkle with a little more sugar. Bake for 40 minutes until the pastry is golden and the juices are bursting through the cracks. Serve hot with cream or a dollop of crème fraîche.

Lemon surprise pudding

I like almost anything made from lemons, and this is one of my favourite, easy puddings. It's delicate and soothing, as nursery food should be, with the surprise of a lemony sauce beneath its sponge top. It can be simply baked in the oven, but I think it has a better texture if the baking dish is placed in a tray of boiling water as the pudding cooks.

Serves 6
2 unwaxed lemons
100g unsalted butter, softened and cut into
  cubes, plus a little more for greasing
180g caster sugar
4 eggs, separated
40g plain flour, sifted
500ml whole milk

Preheat the oven to 180°C/Gas Mark 4. Lightly butter an ovenproof dish about 25 x 20 x 6cm.

Grate the zest from one of the lemons, then squeeze the juice from them both.

In a bowl, cream the butter and half the sugar together with the lemon zest until light and fluffy. Add the egg yolks one at a time, beating well after each addition. Next stir in half the flour, then mix in half the milk. Add the remaining flour, then mix in the remaining milk. Add the lemon juice and mix again.

In a scrupulously clean bowl, beat the egg whites until stiff, then fold the rest of the sugar into them. Gently but thoroughly fold this into the flour mixture.

Spoon into the prepared dish and place in a roasting tin. Pour in enough boiling water to come about halfway up the sides of the dish. Cook for 40–45 minutes, until the sponge has risen and the top is golden.

Lemon tart

I have always liked the idea of the old-fashioned Paris bistro, with white tablecloths and inexpensive food: dish of the day, a green salad, bread and wine, a slice of lemon tart, coffee and possibly an untipped Gauloise. I wish. Those meals were affordable as an occasional treat when I was a student. I hope – for my children's sake – they still exist, so they can eat as well and as simply as I did.

You might need to adjust the quantity of lemons because they vary so much in size, from the huge, beautiful Amalfi lemons that arrive here in spring with their leaves still attached, to the little organic lemons I buy from the local wholefood shop. I don't bother with blow-torching the sugar-coated top – I leave that to the chefs.

Serves 10–12
9 eggs, lightly beaten
350g caster sugar
Zest and juice of 6–8 unwaxed lemons
300ml double cream

For the pastry:
300g plain flour, sifted, plus extra
  for dusting
A pinch of salt
150g unsalted butter, chilled and
  cut into small cubes
150g caster sugar
2 egg yolks
Iced water

First make the pastry. Put the sifted flour, salt, butter and sugar into the bowl of a food processor and pulse them until they resemble coarse breadcrumbs. Add the egg yolks and pulse briefly again to form a dough, adding a splash of iced water only if absolutely necessary. Take it out of the bowl and pat it gently into a ball.

Alternatively, if you want to make the pastry by hand, sift the flour and salt into a mixing bowl and rub in the butter with your fingertips until it resembles coarse breadcrumbs. Stir in the sugar, then cut in the egg yolks and a splash of iced water with a knife, before gently working it into a ball with your hands.

Wrap the dough in cling film and rest in the refrigerator for 30 minutes before using.

Flour a work surface and a rolling pin, then roll out the pastry thinly, to about a 4mm thickness. I use a 30cm metal tart tin with a removable base. Loosely drape the pastry over the tin, then gently nudge it into the corners without stretching it too much. I leave the pastry overhanging the edges, ready to trim off once cooked. (This is a good way of ensuring it doesn't shrink below the level of the tin.)

Place the pastry case on a baking tray and chill again in the fridge for at least 30 minutes.

Preheat the oven to 200°C/Gas Mark 6. Line the pastry case with a couple of layers of scrunched-up baking parchment and weigh them down with baking beans or uncooked rice. Bake blind for about 12–15 minutes, then carefully remove the baking parchment and beans or rice. Put the pastry case back in the oven for another 8 minutes, until the base is starting to turn golden brown. It must be cooked thoroughly or the base will be soggy, not crisp and biscuity as required.

Take the tin out of the oven and leave to cool a bit. As soon as it is cool enough to handle, trim off the excess pastry with a sharp knife. Let it cool completely before adding the filling.

Turn the oven down to 160°C/Gas Mark 2–3.

Make the filling by placing the eggs, sugar, lemon zest and juice in a large, heavy-based saucepan and whisking them together over a very low heat for a few minutes – as if you were making a custard – until the sugar dissolves and the filling starts to thicken. Add half the cream and continue whisking to ensure the mixture doesn't curdle, then whisk in the rest of the cream. Remove from the heat. If it hasn't thickened much, don't worry as it will set in the oven.

Transfer the mixture to a jug. Place the pastry-lined tart tin on a baking tray, then put it into the oven, leaving the door open. Slowly and carefully pour the filling into the pastry case. Bake for about 30 minutes, until the filling is just set. The tart will continue to firm up as it cools.

Serve on its own a few hours later or the following day, keeping it in a cool place overnight.

Fruit tarts

This summery homemade fruit tart is best assembled at the last minute.

Serves 6
For the sweet pastry:
225g unsalted butter, room temperature
115g caster sugar or vanilla caster sugar
2 eggs, lightly beaten
450g plain flour
Pinch of salt

For the filling:
1 vanilla pod
300ml whole milk
3 egg yolks
50g caster sugar
1 teaspoon icing sugar

To finish the tart:
180g fresh fruit: raspberries, strawberries,
    blackberries, stoned cherries or sliced figs
1 tablespoon icing sugar

In a food processor or mixer, cream the butter and sugar together. Add the eggs in a trickle while the machine is running. Scrape down the mixture from the sides of the bowl to make sure it is all thoroughly combined. Sift the flour and salt and add it a spoonful at a time, with the processor or mixer running. Pat the stiff dough into a ball, wrap in cling film and rest in the fridge for at least 2 hours. Remove from the fridge 15 minutes before you want to roll it out.

Preheat the oven to 200°C/Gas Mark 6.

On a lightly floured surface with a floured rolling pin, roll out the pastry and use it to line a 25cm tart tin with a removable base, allowing the excess pastry to hang over the sides. Line the case with baking parchment filled with baking beans or uncooked rice. Place on a baking tray and bake for about 12 minutes. Take it out of the oven, remove the parchment and beans, prick the base with a fork then put it back in the oven for about another 10 minutes until the pastry is just golden and the base looks dry and crisp. Trim off the excess pastry with a sharp knife. Allow to cool completely.

To make the custard, split the vanilla pod lengthways and scrape out the seeds with the tip of a sharp knife. Put the seeds and pod in a saucepan with the milk and warm over a medium heat to just below boiling point. Remove from the heat. Allow to infuse for 10 minutes, then remove the pod.

In a bowl, whisk the egg yolks with the sugar, then slowly pour over the scalded milk as you continue to whisk. Strain through a sieve into a clean saucepan and heat gently, stirring constantly with a wooden spoon until the custard is rich, thickened and smooth. Pour into a bowl, sprinkle with a fine dusting of icing sugar and cover it with greaseproof paper. As it cools it will thicken up more. When cold, fill the tart with the custard and smooth over the top. Decorate with fruit and dust with icing sugar.

Burnt cream

This rich but simple pudding is a delicious way to end a meal, although it is better eaten after a light main course for balance. It was often one of the courses served on the high table at my father's Cambridge college, where he was a don. He dined in once a week and would come home and tell us about the feast he had just eaten. (He had probably drunk quite a lot from their celebrated wine cellars too.) The burnt cream was served with a little silver hammer to break open the hard crust of burnt sugar. I imagined a magical world, where the silvery table glittered in the candlelight and every whim was catered for.

At Trinity College the cream was said not to be sweetened, but I add a little sugar. This recipe fits my favoured criteria of a few ingredients cooked simply, but it does need to be prepared in advance, as the custard has to be made the day before and chilled in the fridge. The custard should be barely set – almost liquid – but just thick enough for the sugar to sit on the surface.

Serves 4
600ml thick double cream
6 egg yolks
5 tablespoons caster sugar

Gently heat the cream and bring it to the boil; simmer until it has thickened and reduced a little.

In a bowl, mix the egg yolks with a tablespoon of the sugar, then pour on the reduced cream and stir together. Strain the mixture through a sieve into a clean saucepan and warm over a low heat, stirring constantly and being careful not to let it boil. When the custard coats the back of the spoon, it is ready. Pour it into 4 ramekins and cool in the fridge overnight.

An hour before serving, sprinkle a tablespoon of sugar in an even layer over each ramekin and blast under a hot grill (or with a blowtorch) to caramelise it. The sugar will darken to a golden brown, but take care not to blacken it, as although it's called burnt cream, it tastes bitter if it is too dark. The caramel hardens as it cools, and as I don't have any silver hammers, I break through to the cream below with a humble spoon.

Rice pudding

Rice pudding sounds as comforting as a woolly blanket. It is the most traditional of nursery puddings, easily digested and always welcomed. At school it was served in enormous bowls sprinkled with pink, crunchy sugar. We all loved it and would try to get second helpings, although afterwards we were so full that we could hardly keep awake in the afternoon. I like it now with dark muscovado sugar.

We sometimes leave a rice pudding cooking for hours in the simmering oven of the Aga, ready for when we come home. On the days when the old bread oven in the back kitchen is fired up, rice pudding and custards are the last to go in after the bread or roasts, making the most of the dying heat. It sounds nostalgic but it is actually an efficient way to cook as it uses the heat generated by a fire made from a pile of kindling and a few small logs. It was the main oven for the farm until the cast-iron range was installed at the end of the nineteenth century.

Serves 4–6
1 litre whole milk, the creamiest
    you can find
1 tablespoon double cream
110g short-grain pudding rice
3 tablespoons caster sugar
1 vanilla pod
Freshly grated nutmeg

Preheat the oven to 150°C/Gas Mark 2.

Pour the milk into a 2-litre pudding basin and add the rest of the ingredients except the nutmeg. Give it a stir and grate some nutmeg over the top. Place it on a baking tray and put it in the oven for 2 hours, by which time the top should be puffed up and golden brown and the creamy rice molten inside.

You can, if you like, leave the pudding undisturbed for the whole cooking time, or give it a stir halfway through. The skin that forms on the top keeps the pudding from drying out, so allow it to form.

Serve warm.

Ivington
custard pie

I love the traditional comfort of a custard pie, the spiced filling trembling and delicate in its pastry casing, speckled with nutmeg.

Serves 6
425ml single cream
1 stick of cinnamon
2 blades of mace
2 eggs and 2 egg yolks
50g caster sugar
Freshly grated nutmeg

For the shortcrust pastry:
225g flour, plus extra for dusting
A pinch of salt
110g unsalted butter, chilled and cut into cubes
1 tablespoon caster sugar
1 egg yolk
About 1 tablespoon iced water

First make the pastry. Put the flour, salt and butter into a food processor and pulse until it is the consistency of coarse breadcrumbs. Add the sugar and blend, then add the egg yolk and the iced water, just enough to bring it together into a dough. If you want to make it by hand, sift the flour and salt into a mixing bowl and rub in the butter with your fingertips until it resembles coarse breadcrumbs. Stir in the sugar, then cut in the egg yolk and a splash of iced water with a knife before working it gently into a ball with your hands.

Wrap the dough in cling film and rest in the refrigerator for 30 minutes before using.

Preheat the oven to 200°C/Gas Mark 6.

Lightly flour a work surface and rolling pin, then roll out the pastry and use it to line a 22cm tart tin with a removable base, letting the excess pastry hang over the sides. Cover the pastry with crumpled baking parchment and weigh it down with baking beans or uncooked rice. Place it on a baking sheet and bake for about 12 minutes. Take it out of the oven and remove the parchment and beans or rice. Prick the base with a fork and bake for a further 5–7 minutes. Remove from the oven, trim off the excess pastry with a sharp knife and allow to cool. Reduce the heat of the oven to 170°C/Gas Mark 3.

Pour the cream into a saucepan with the cinnamon and mace and gently bring to just below boiling point – small bubbles should appear around the edge of the pan. Remove from the heat and discard the spices.

In a separate bowl, beat the eggs, yolks and sugar together. Pour the scalded cream over the egg mixture, whisking constantly. Pour into the pastry case and grate some fresh nutmeg over the top. Bake for 35–40 minutes, until the custard is just set and the top golden. It will carry on setting as it cools, so when you take it out of the oven, it should still wobble a bit in the middle. When completely cold, carefully remove the pie from the tart tin.

Treacle tart

Treacle tart is definitely for those with a sweet tooth, but when it's served with custard or clotted cream to cut through the sweetness, it makes a great old-fashioned pudding.

My mother would make treacle tart on a tin plate and decorate it with pastry twists over the top. She is a very good pastry cook, as was my grandmother, which comes only with practice.

Serves 6
1 x 450g tin golden syrup
200g fresh breadcrumbs
A small handful of rolled oats
Zest of 1 unwaxed lemon
Juice of ½ a lemon
1 scant teaspoon dried ginger

For the pastry:
250g plain flour, plus extra for dusting
Pinch of salt
*125g unsalted butter, chilled and cut into
    small cubes, plus a little more for greasing*
*1 egg yolk, lightly beaten with 1 tablespoon
    iced water*

First make the pastry. Put the flour, salt and butter into a food processor and pulse until it is the consistency of coarse breadcrumbs. Add the egg yolk and iced water mixture, to bring it together into a dough. Alternatively, if you want to make it by hand, sift the flour and salt into a mixing bowl and rub in the butter with your fingertips until it resembles coarse breadcrumbs. Cut in the egg yolk and iced water with a knife before working it gently into a ball with your hands. Wrap the dough in cling film and rest in the refrigerator for 30 minutes before using.

Preheat the oven to 180°C/Gas Mark 4.

Lightly butter a 25cm tart tin with a removable base.

Lightly flour a work surface and rolling pin, then roll out the pastry and use it to line the tart tin. Trim off the excess pastry. Chill for 30 minutes in the fridge. Cover the base with crumpled baking parchment and weigh it down with baking beans or uncooked rice. Bake for 13 minutes, then remove the beans or rice and parchment, prick the base with a fork and pop it back in the oven for another 8 minutes. Allow it to cool completely before adding the filling. Lower the oven temperature to 160°C/ Gas Mark 2–3.

Make the filling by warming the golden syrup in a saucepan over a medium heat until it liquefies. Take off the heat and mix in all the other ingredients to form a soft paste. Spread it evenly over the pastry case and bake for about 50 minutes. Allow to cool enough to serve just warm, which should take about 30 minutes.

Pouring custard

Real custard, made with our own eggs laid the same day, is incomparably good and makes the perfect pudding when poured over baked apples (page 202) or crumble (page 364), poached fruit (page 16) or baked sponge (page 239). Even though fresh custard can be bought easily, I think it is too thick and can taste artificial compared to the real thing – although I confess that I was brought up on Bird's Custard and still have a soft spot for its nostalgic smell and colour.

If you want a really rich custard, use half milk and half cream.

Makes about 750ml
6 large egg yolks
50g caster sugar
½ vanilla pod, split
500ml whole milk
125ml double cream

Take a heatproof bowl that is large enough to hold all the ingredients and place it over a pan of simmering water. Put the egg yolks and sugar in the bowl and whisk them together.

Use the tip of a small, sharp knife to scrape out the seeds from the vanilla pod. Put both the seeds and pod into a saucepan with the milk and cream. Warm over a gentle heat, but do not boil – small bubbles should just appear around the edge of the pan.

Remove from the heat and allow the vanilla to continue to infuse for 5 minutes. Remove the vanilla pod and pour the liquid into the bowl with the eggs and sugar, whisking all the time.

Put a pan or double-boiler of water on to simmer. If you have a double-boiler, pour the custard into the top section. Otherwise place the bowl over the simmering water, making sure that the bottom of the bowl doesn't touch the water, and stir the custard for a few minutes with a wooden spoon until it thickens. This is an important and delicate stage and it is vital that the custard does not overheat or it will split and curdle.

The recognised test for the readiness of custard is when it coats the back of the spoon, although it's more intuitive than that. When it is ready, the custard will have a consistency of thick cream. Pour into a warmed jug, ready to serve over your chosen pudding.

Tea

TEA IS A CONFUSING and often confused meal. I was brought up with it representing, for adults at least, a minor refreshment in the afternoon, with anything to eat playing second fiddle to the eponymous cup of tea. Yet many people call their main evening meal 'tea'. If they have had a light lunch at work, this then becomes their main meal of the day. So the two meals, one almost incidental but specifically evolved to accompany tea drinking, the other really just another name for dinner, could not be more different. 'High tea' falls somewhere between these two extremes.

I remember experiencing the split personality of the meal when I would go to a friend's house for tea and be offered meat and two veg, compared to the appallingly stiff, anxious teas that we used to have with my Victorian grandparents, which were tyrannised by crumbs, social solecisms and awkward silences, with tiny pieces of cake balanced upon translucent plates and my grandmother sternly dispensing tea from a silver teapot.

But tea can be as genteel or hearty as you wish to make it. A cup of tea accompanied by fresh bread and homemade jam and a good slice of cake is the best way to fill the long gap between lunch and supper, especially if you are working outside. Writing this, I realise that a proper enjoyment of the delights of tea depends on resisting snacks. Constant grazing on cakes, sweets and biscuits makes tea as a meal with a set time and rituals of its own redundant. But then half the pleasure in all meals is in the anticipation followed by the gratification. To miss tea because you have already stuffed yourself with cakes and sweets throughout the day is to miss something more than calories at a certain hour.

Homemade jam and jellies transform tea. The quality of homemade jam that most commercial alternatives never quite capture is not its jammy sweetness but its intense fruitiness. The word 'jam' seems to appear only in the middle of the eighteenth century, coinciding with the arrival of sugar on an increasing scale from the West Indies. Jam was expensive until the end of the nineteenth century when, after sugar taxes were dropped, it became available to the population at large. My grandmother's family made a fortune in the nineteenth century from manufacturing jams of various kinds because it was a special treat that people were prepared to indulge in. So it has a history of being precious – something to be savoured in small quantities, preserving the essence of fruits whose season has passed.

The essential difference between a jelly and a jam is that one is sieved and clarified, thus making it more delicate both visually and to taste. Quinces, redcurrants and blackberries make my favourite teatime jellies. Jam has two seasons in our house – immediately after it is made, turning glut into a bright, jewel-like dollop on the plate, and then again on the other side of the year, stranded between memory and hope. Just a small jar of plum jam brought out at teatime in midwinter bridges last year's harvest with the promise of summer to come.

A cake – any cake – transformed tea into a special occasion. Baking cakes was a rite of passage when I was a child, something you did with your mother, an over-large apron tied around your waist, standing on a chair to stir the mix of a sponge cake, preferably chocolate with glossy icing to hide the flat or burnt bits, licking the spoon till it was shiny, opening the oven door too often, learning to cook by imitation and absurdly proud failure.

Cakes are always better shared, which is just as well because most cakes should be eaten up quickly if the basic ingredients of eggs, butter, sugar and flour are to be enjoyed at their best. However, the exceptions to this are amongst my favourites. A fruit cake packed so rich with raisins and sultanas that you could exist off a slice a day can be eked out to last for weeks. I recall being packed off to the south of France in the early 1970s with a large square Dundee cake in my suitcase to see me through the horrors of French cuisine. We often have one on the farm, and a good slab in the late afternoon provides fuel for another few hours on the hillside.

But that is cake in the guise of muscular frontier food. What I like best is the prettiness and delicacy of a beautifully made cake, fresh from the oven, playfully decorated and carried out on a tray with a pot of tea to be served in the garden and eaten surrounded by birdsong and flowers, or around the kitchen table in winter.

With it all is lovely tea, the best of all drinks. Whenever I am travelling I try to immerse myself in the food of the place I am visiting, but I never lose that deep yearning for a cup of tea towards the end of the afternoon. The truth is that half the time tea in this house consists of just that – a simple cup of tea – and jams, cakes and any other goodies are a bonus. However good the food, without tea to drink, teatime would be awry.

Sandwiches

Well-made sandwiches are always welcome, and worth the initial effort. These are my favourite fillings; although conservative, they're lovely for tea – a savoury foil to all those cakes.

Arrange the sandwiches on pretty plates and serve as soon as they are made because they dry out quite quickly.

The quantities given here serve 6 or more.

Egg and cress sandwiches

Butter, softened
12 slices of white bread
6 hard-boiled eggs
3 tablespoons good-quality mayonnaise
2 containers of mustard and cress
Salt and freshly ground black pepper

Butter the bread. Shell the eggs and mash them with a fork in a bowl. Mix in the mayonnaise and some salt and pepper. Put a dollop of the egg mayonnaise on 6 slices of the bread and spread evenly.

Use scissors to cut off the mustard and cress and sprinkle liberally over the egg. Top with the remaining bread slices.

Before cutting each into 3 rectangular sandwiches, carefully cut off the crusts. This will help to prevent the filling squeezing out.

Ham sandwiches

Butter, softened
12 slices of brown bread
English mustard, freshly made,
*   1 tablespoon of mustard powder to*
*   1 tablespoon of water*
9 slices of boiled ham

Butter the bread. Spread 6 slices with mustard, and place one and a half slices of ham over each of these slices. Top with the remaining bread. Cut off the crusts and slice each into 3 rectangular sandwiches.

Cucumber sandwiches

1 very fresh, crisp cucumber
Salt
Butter, softened
12 slices of white bread

Peel the cucumber lengthways using a potato peeler. Now slice it as finely as possible with a sharp knife or a mandolin. Put the sliced cucumber into a colander, sprinkle with a little salt, and leave it for 30 minutes.

Butter the bread. Lay the cucumber on 6 of the slices of bread, overlapping it, then top with the remaining bread. Cut off the crusts and slice each into 3 rectangular sandwiches.

Nanna's soda bread

I grew up in a small village dominated by a crumbling Georgian rectory. At teatime in summer, the rector's wife set out a table on the lawn for tea. We children, friends of her many grandchildren, would hover nearby in the hope of a getting a slice of her fantastic soda bread. She was Irish and I always associate the taste of this sweetish version of soda bread with her.

Buttered and chewy, a loaf is easily made in time for tea. It doesn't keep well, so enjoy it on the day it's baked.

450g wholemeal flour (or 250g wholemeal and 200g stoneground), plus a little more for dusting
1 teaspoon bicarbonate of soda
A large pinch of salt
1 teaspoon molasses sugar
25g unsalted butter
500ml buttermilk
A small handful of oats (optional)

Preheat the oven to 220°C/Gas Mark 7.

Mix the dry ingredients together in a bowl and rub in the butter. Make a well in the middle and gradually add the buttermilk, mixing everything into a sticky dough. It will be soft and won't have the elasticity of a yeast-based dough.

Turn it out onto a floured surface and form into a round about 2.5cm high. Place on a baking sheet dusted with flour. Cut a deep cross in the top with a serrated knife.

Sprinkle the extra oats, if using, into the cross.

Put the soda bread into the oven and bake for 10 minutes, then lower the heat to 180°C/Gas Mark 4 and bake for a further 30–35 minutes, until the loaf sounds hollow when tapped on the bottom. Leave to cool on a wire rack.

Scones

Scones are the epitome of teatime, and with clotted cream and homemade jam they are irresistible. Once you know the basic recipe, it can be adapted to be savoury as well as sweet. We all like cheese scones for elevenses (page 50), but they're as good in the afternoon too.

As with all baking, the lighter the touch in mixing the ingredients, the lighter and better the cooked result, which is why it is much better to make these by hand than in a food processor.

Makes 12–15 scones
450g plain flour, plus extra for dusting
2½ teaspoons baking powder
2 teaspoons caster sugar
A pinch of salt
100g butter, chilled and cut into small
*   cubes, plus a little more for greasing*
About 300ml whole milk

To serve:
Butter or jam and whipped or clotted cream

Preheat the oven to 220°C/Gas Mark 7. Lightly grease a baking sheet.

Sift the flour, baking powder, sugar and salt into a mixing bowl. Rub in the butter with your fingertips until the mixture resembles coarse breadcrumbs.

Stir in just enough milk to make a soft, sticky dough. You won't always need all the milk and it's important that you don't overwork the mixture or the scones will be tough.

On a lightly floured surface, gently roll out or pat the dough into a circle about 2cm thick. Using a round 8cm pastry cutter dipped in flour, cut the dough into smaller circles and place them on the prepared baking sheet. Brush the tops lightly with milk to glaze.

Bake the scones for 10–15 minutes, depending on their size, until lightly golden and well risen.

Cool on a wire rack and serve while they're still warm. Split them open and spread with butter or jam and cream.

Fruit scones

Add 100g of sultanas or similar dried fruit to the dry ingredients before you add the milk.

Drop scones

These light and meltingly soft pancakes can be quickly knocked up in time for tea. They need to be eaten as soon as they're cooked, spread generously with butter and jam. Because they're so straightforward to make, drop scones are a good recipe to try if you want to encourage children to cook.

Makes 12–14
125g self-raising flour
2 teaspoons caster sugar
1 egg
125ml whole milk
25g unsalted butter, melted and cooled
A *little softened butter or sunflower oil,*
    for griddling

To serve:
Butter and jam

Mix the flour and sugar together in a bowl, and make a well in the centre. Break the egg into the well and slowly mix the egg and enough milk into the flour to make a thick batter. Stir until smooth, then add the melted butter and the rest of the milk. It should be thicker than pancake batter – you want it to have the consistency of double cream.

Put a large, heavy-based frying pan or flat griddle over a medium heat to warm up. Take a thick wad of kitchen paper and dip it in the softened butter or sunflower oil. Rub the fat over the pan until it's lightly coated. Drop spoonfuls of the batter onto the pan (you should be able to make about 4 at a time) and cook for a couple of minutes until you see bubbles rising to the surface. Flip the scone over with a spatula and cook the other side until golden brown. This should take less than a minute.

The drop scones can be kept warm, wrapped in a folded tea towel, until they are all cooked. The pan should be regreased for each batch.

Serve hot with butter and jam.

Welsh cakes

We live on the Welsh borders and these little cakes pop up everywhere as a sign of hospitality. These are best served warm, sprinkled with caster sugar.

Makes 10
110g self-raising flour, plus a little more
  for dusting
A pinch of salt
40g unsalted butter, cut into small cubes
40g caster sugar, plus a little more for
  sprinkling
40g currants
1 egg, lightly beaten
A little softened butter or sunflower oil,
  for griddling

Sift the flour and salt into a bowl and add the butter. Rub it in with your fingertips until the mixture has the consistency of fine breadcrumbs. Mix in the sugar and currants, then stir in the egg to form a dough.

On a lightly floured surface, roll out the dough to a thickness of 1.5cm and cut into circles with a 6cm plain cutter dipped in flour.

Warm a flat griddle pan or heavy-based frying pan over a medium-high heat. Take a thick wad of kitchen paper and dip it in the softened butter or sunflower oil. Rub the fat over the pan until it's lightly coated.

Griddle each cake for about 4 minutes per side, checking frequently to make sure they are not burning. Sprinkle with caster sugar and serve immediately.

Shortbread

The crisp, buttery texture of shortbread is a lovely thing. Whether in the form of a thin biscuit or a more solid finger, it is good to eat at any time of day on its own. It also complements a fruity pudding of poached plums or a simple fool.

Here are two recipes. The second one has an additional ingredient, rice flour, which gives a lighter crumb.

Shortbread biscuits

These are delicious with fruit fools and can be made even more decorative if cut into heart or star shapes.

> Makes about 20 round biscuits
> *150g plain flour*
> *100g unsalted butter, cut into small cubes*
> *50g caster sugar*

Preheat the oven to 180°C/Gas Mark 4. Line a baking tray with baking parchment.

Sift the flour into a mixing bowl. Add the butter and rub it in with your fingertips until the mixture is the consistency of coarse breadcrumbs. Add the sugar and knead lightly into a dough. Wrap it in cling film and refrigerate for 30 minutes.

Roll out the dough on a floured surface to a thickness of about 5mm. Alternatively, roll it out between two sheets of cling film or parchment.

Cut the dough into 7cm circles with a plain biscuit cutter. Using a palette knife, transfer them to the lined baking sheet.

Place in the oven and bake for about 10–12 minutes, until still pale but turning slightly golden around the edges. Watch them carefully after the first 8 minutes as they must not overcook. Remove from the oven and leave them on the tray for 10 minutes to cool and firm up before placing on a wire rack to cool completely.

Scottish shortbread

These are wonderful with a cup of tea.

> Makes 12 rectangular fingers
> *100g plain flour*
> *50g ground rice flour*
> *100g unsalted butter, cut in cubes*
> *50g caster sugar*

Preheat the oven to 180°C/Gas Mark 4. Line a baking tray with baking parchment.

Sift the flours together into a bowl, then rub in the butter until the mixture resembles coarse breadcrumbs. Stir in the sugar and knead lightly into a dough. Wrap in cling film and refrigerate for 30 minutes.

Roll out the dough on a floured surface into a rectangle approximately 1.5cm thick. Alternatively, roll it out between two sheets of cling film or parchment.

Place on the prepared baking tray, then press down the edges with a fork. Mark out into 12 rectangular pieces with a knife, pressing about halfway through the dough. Prick each marked slice several times with a fork.

Place in the oven and bake for about an hour, but check frequently after the first 40 minutes to make sure that the shortbread does not overcook and remains pale golden. Cool on the tray for a few minutes until it firms up, then lift it – still on the baking parchment – onto a wire rack to cool completely. The pieces might not break exactly along the marked lines, but don't worry as they will taste just as good.

Alternatively, cut the shortbread slab into 12 individual rectangles. Prick with a fork before placing on the baking tray, then bake for 15 minutes. Carefully turn them over with a spatula and bake for another 10 minutes, keeping an eye on them to ensure they remain pale. Cool on a wire rack.

The shortbread will keep well in an airtight tin for about a week.

Variation:
To create different flavours of shortbread, you can add various items to the sugar before creaming it with the butter. For example, 1 teaspoon finely chopped, unsprayed lavender; 1½ teaspoons finely chopped rose geranium leaves; finely grated zest of 1 lemon.

Strawberry jam

Strawberry jam is not only perfect with scones (page 225) and clotted cream, it's also fantastic for sandwiching together a Victoria sponge (page 239). It is a little difficult to get strawberry jam to set as the fruit lacks pectin, but I don't mind if it's a bit runny. The lemon helps the set, but if you really like firmer jam, use jam sugar with added pectin instead of ordinary granulated sugar.

Makes 8 x 340g jars
1kg granulated sugar
2kg strawberries, hulled, large ones
  halved and small ones kept whole
Juice of 1 lemon

Put two saucers in the fridge to chill for testing setting point. Heat the oven to its lowest setting.

Spread the sugar over a baking tray and warm in the oven for 10 minutes.

Place the fruit in a preserving pan or heavy-based stainless-steel pan, add the lemon juice and simmer for a few minutes until the strawberry juices run. Mash the fruit with the back of a wooden spoon to help this along.

Add the warmed sugar and stir over a low heat until it dissolves, then bring to the boil and boil hard for about 5 minutes. Test for setting point by putting a spoonful of jam on a chilled saucer and letting it cool. If the surface wrinkles when pushed with your finger, the jam is ready. If not, boil for a few more minutes.

Skim off any scum. Allow the jam to cool for 15 minutes before potting in warm, sterilised jars (page 37). Cover with waxed discs and cellophane covers or lids.

The jam will keep for up to a year. Because of the low sugar content, store in the fridge once opened.

Gooseberry jam

Gooseberries are an easy fruit to grow. They even thrive in the hedgerows, their seeds sown by birds. The green or pink fruit ripens in early summer before most other fruit is ready. As well as fools, pies, tarts and ice cream (page 191), gooseberries make a delicious, pretty-coloured jam.

> Makes about 10 x 340g jars
> *2.4kg granulated sugar*
> *2kg gooseberries, topped and tailed*

Put two saucers in the fridge to chill for testing setting point. Heat the oven to its lowest temperature and warm the sugar on a baking tray for about 10 minutes.

Meanwhile, place the gooseberries in a preserving pan or heavy-based stainless-steel pan with 1 litre water. Bring to the boil, then simmer until the fruit is soft and pulpy, stirring to prevent it from sticking.

Add the warmed sugar to the fruit and stir over a low heat until the sugar has dissolved. Bring to the boil, then boil hard until it reaches setting point, about 20 minutes. Test by dropping a spoonful of jam onto one of the cold saucers: when it has cooled, the surface should wrinkle when pushed with your finger.

Skim off any scum. Allow the jam to cool for 15 minutes before potting in warm, sterilised jars (see page 37). Cover with waxed discs and cellophane or lids, and use within a year.

Raspberry jam

This is a lovely, deep pink jam, sometimes a little runny but absolutely delicious. It doesn't keep for long, so it's best to make it in small quantities and keep the jars in the fridge once opened.

> Makes 4 x 340g jars
> *1kg raspberries*
> *800g caster sugar*

Put two saucers in the fridge to chill. Heat the oven to its lowest temperature.

Pick over the fruit, removing any hulls, and place in a preserving pan or heavy-based stainless-steel pan. Place over a low heat for 5 minutes until the juices run, stirring gently. Bring to the boil, then simmer for about 12–15 minutes.

While the fruit is cooking, spread the sugar on a baking tray and warm in the oven for about 10 minutes. Add the sugar to the cooked fruit, stirring until it dissolves, then bring back to the boil and boil hard for a couple of minutes until the jam reaches setting point. Test by dropping a spoonful of jam onto one of the cold saucers: when it has cooled, the surface should wrinkle when pushed with your finger.

Skim off any scum, then cool for 15 minutes before pouring into warmed, sterilised jars (page 37). Cover with waxed discs and cellophane or lids, then store in a cool, dry place for up to a month. After opening, keep in the fridge.

Plum jam

We have several ancient plum trees still producing fruit, remnants of the farm's kitchen garden. I don't know what variety they are, but they produce enough fruit for plenty of jams and desserts. One of them, a yellow, egg-shaped plum, is a bit bland and woolly to eat fresh, but it makes fantastic jam. In all, our plums are plentiful for about 6 weeks.

I like to make this jam to remind me of late summer on a grey winter's day. When you're bottling the jam, reward yourself with a few spoonfuls on a thick slice of bread and butter. It will never again taste so good.

Makes about 10 x 340g jars
3kg plums
1.5kg granulated sugar

Halve the plums and remove the stones. Use a hammer or nutcracker to split open a few of the stones if you can. It's worth the effort as the kernels add a pleasing, bitter almond flavour to the jam.

Place the plums and kernels in a preserving pan or heavy-based stainless-steel pan and pour over 800ml water. Bring to the boil, then simmer, stirring from time to time, for about 20 minutes until the fruit softens.

While the plums are cooking, heat the oven to its lowest temperature. Spread out the sugar on a baking tray and warm in the oven for about 10 minutes.

Add the warmed sugar to the pan and stir over a low heat until the sugar has dissolved. Now bring to the boil and boil hard for about 20 minutes. Stir occasionally, checking that the jam isn't catching on the bottom of the pan or burning. The jam is ready when the fruit sinks to the bottom and no longer floats on the surface.

Skim off any scum, then cool for 15 minutes before pouring into warmed, sterilised jars (page 37), using a wide-necked funnel if you have one. Cover with waxed discs and cellophane or lids. The jam will keep for up to a year.

Bramble jelly

Lemon curd

Some years there are bumper harvests of free blackberries to pick to make this dark purple jelly. It's one of my favourites, and because it's so precious, I use small jars and consider it a special treat.

Makes 4 x 240g jars
1kg blackberries
Granulated sugar

Pick over and wash the fruit. Put a couple of saucers in the fridge to chill.

Place the blackberries in a pan with 250ml water and simmer until the fruit is soft, about 15 minutes, mashing it with the back of a wooden spoon to get out as much juice as possible.

Strain the fruit through a sieve into a measuring jug, reserving the juice; discard the pulp. For every 500ml juice, weigh out 500g sugar. Return the juice to the pan with the sugar. Warm over a low heat, stirring from time to time, until the sugar dissolves, then boil for about 10 minutes without stirring until the setting point is reached. Test for this by dropping a little of the jam on a chilled saucer: when it has cooled, the surface should wrinkle when pushed with your finger.

Skim off any scum. Allow the jam to cool for about 15 minutes before pouring into warm, sterilised jars (page 37). Cover with waxed discs and cellophane or lids. It will keep for up to a year.

This is my secret vice. I cannot spread it thickly enough on soft white bread, and I even eat it by the spoonful. It also makes an excellent filling for sponge cakes (page 239). Once I've made lemon curd, I make meringues (page 193) from the leftover egg whites, so there's absolutely no waste.

Makes 2 x 280g jars
100g unsalted butter
220g caster sugar
Zest and juice of 3 unwaxed lemons
3 egg yolks

Place a heatproof bowl over a pan of barely simmering water. Be careful not to let the water boil at any point or allow the bottom of the bowl to touch the water, or the curd will go grainy, like scrambled eggs.

Add the butter, sugar, lemon zest and juice to the bowl. As the butter melts, stir gently to mix everything together and dissolve the sugar.

When the sugar has dissolved, beat in the egg yolks one at a time, then stir the mixture until it thickens. This should take about 10 minutes.

Strain though a sieve into a wide-necked jug, then pour into warmed, sterilised jars (page 37). Cover with waxed discs and cellophane or lids. The curd will keep for a couple of weeks in the fridge, but we use it up quickly and make more when necessary.

Pound cake

There are countless old recipes for this cake, so called because it needed a pound of each ingredient to make it. It must have been an enormous cake. This recipe makes a pound of cake, which is a more manageable size. We bake one at the last minute if someone arrives unexpectedly and we don't even have a biscuit in the house. A slice warm from the oven and dusted with icing sugar is perfect with coffee or a cup of tea. It's also good served as a pudding with poached fruit (page 16).

Serves 8
125g unsalted butter, softened
125g sugar
2 eggs
125g self-raising flour, sifted
Icing sugar (optional)

Preheat the oven 180°C/Gas Mark 4.

Lightly butter a 25cm round cake tin and line the bottom and sides with baking parchment.

Cream together the butter and sugar until light and fluffy in food processor, mixer or by hand. Add the eggs one at a time, beating well after each addition. Lightly fold in the flour, being careful not to overmix. Pour into the prepared tin and bake for about 45 minutes, until the top feels firm and springs back when pressed with your fingertips or a toothpick comes out clean.

Allow the cake to cool in the tin for a few minutes, then turn out onto a wire rack to cool further. Peel off the baking parchment and dust with icing sugar, if you like, or serve as it is, warm or cold.

Victoria sponge

This cake is the one we bake most often. We can all make it practically blindfolded. I can't hold recipes in my head unless they're proportions of each other, so Victoria sponge is very easy because all you need to do is weigh the eggs, then weigh out equal weights of butter, sugar and flour. A teaspoon of baking powder and vanilla essence are the only other things to remember.

Our own fresh eggs make a bright yellow sponge with a golden crust, and I cannot emphasise enough the importance of good ingredients: fresh, organic or Fairtrade – it matters. This is not complicated baking but the freshness of the sponge, soft inside with a crisp exterior, and the cream and jam or fruit in the middle is a perfect marriage.

Serves 6
3 eggs
Self-raising flour
Unsalted butter, softened
Caster sugar
1 teaspoon baking powder
1 teaspoon vanilla essence

To serve:
200ml double cream (optional)
Raspberry or strawberry jam (page 232),
  or soft fruit such as raspberries or
  strawberries
Icing sugar

Preheat the oven to 180°C/Gas Mark 4. Lightly grease 2 x 20cm sandwich tins with butter and line their bases with baking parchment.

First weigh the eggs in their shells, then measure out equal weights of flour, butter and sugar.

Sift the flour and baking powder together into a bowl.

Cream the butter and sugar together in a food processor, mixer or by hand until fluffy and light. Add the eggs one at a time, beating well after each addition, and adding a little flour if it looks like it's going to curdle. Stir in the vanilla essence and gently fold in the remaining flour. Be careful not to overmix, as you need to keep air in the cake to make it light.

Divide the mixture between the tins and bake for 25 minutes, until a skewer or toothpick inserted into the middle comes out clean. Set aside until the tins are cool enough to handle, then remove from the tins, peel off the parchment and cool completely on a wire rack.

When they are cold, spread some jam over one of the cakes. Lightly whip the cream, if using, and cover the jam with a thick layer. For an extra fruity version, omit the jam and arrange a layer of fruit over the cream. Place the other sponge on top and dust with icing sugar. Display your masterpiece on a cake stand before it is demolished by admiring guests.

Lemon curd cake

Good lemon curd (page 236) is definitely a treat, and this lovely, moist cake, flavoured with lemon zest, really makes the most of it, with a generous amount spread inside it as a filling. For me, this is a perfect cake for a special tea.

Serves 6–8
225g plain flour
½ teaspoon baking powder
125g unsalted butter, plus a little
  more for greasing
125g caster sugar
3 eggs
1 tablespoon milk
Grated zest of 1 small, unwaxed lemon

For the filling:
5–6 tablespoons lemon curd, either
  homemade (page 236) or bought

To decorate:
Lemon icing (page 244)
Icing sugar (optional)

Preheat the oven to 180°C/Gas Mark 4. Lightly grease 2 x 20cm sandwich tins and line their bases with baking parchment.

In a bowl, sift together the flour and baking powder. In a food processor, mixer or by hand, cream together the butter and the sugar until light and fluffy. Add the eggs one at a time, beating well after each addition, and adding a little flour with the last one to stop the mixture curdling. Gently fold in the rest of the flour. Be careful not to overmix, or the cake will be heavy. Finally, stir in the milk and the lemon zest, reserving a few pieces for decoration.

Divide the mixture between the sandwich tins and place in the oven for 25 minutes, until the cakes have risen and a skewer or toothpick inserted in the middle comes out clean.

Set aside until the tins are cool enough to handle, then remove from the tins, peel off the parchment and cool completely on a wire rack.

When cold, spread one sponge with a generous amount of lemon curd and place the other sponge on top. The cake can be finished with either a lemon-flavoured icing and a sprinkling of lemon zest, or simply a dusting of icing sugar.

Lemon drizzle cake

This is a lovely light cake for teatime or pudding, and it slices up beautifully to take on picnics too.

Serves 8
110g unsalted butter, plus a little more for greasing
175g self-raising flour
1 teaspoon baking powder
175g caster sugar
2 eggs
Juice and zest of 1 unwaxed lemon
4 tablespoons milk

For the lemon drizzle:
Juice of 2 small lemons
75g caster sugar

Preheat the oven to 180°C/Gas Mark 4. Grease a 23 x 13 x 7cm loaf tin and line the bottom and sides with baking parchment, ensuring the parchment hangs over the sides of the tin – this will make the cake easier to remove later.

In a bowl, sift together the flour and baking powder. Cream the butter and sugar in a food processor, mixer or by hand until light and fluffy.

Add the eggs one at a time, beating well after each addition. Gently stir in the lemon juice, zest and milk.

Gently fold in the rest of the flour. Pour the mixture into the tin and bake for about 45 minutes, until a skewer or toothpick inserted into the middle comes out clean and the top feels firm and springs back if you press it with your fingertips.

To make the drizzle, combine the lemon juice and sugar in a small bowl. While the cake is still hot and in its tin, pour the drizzle over it, then allow to cool completely on a wire rack.

Fairy cakes with crystallised flowers

There are endless possibilities with these little cakes as they can be flavoured and decorated as you wish. I sometimes add a little vanilla extract, or orange or lemon zest. The cakes can be iced if you like, but edible flowers make pretty decorations too.

Makes 12
100g unsalted butter
100g caster sugar
2 medium eggs, lightly beaten
100g self-raising flour, sifted

For simple icing:
200g icing sugar
A squeeze of lemon juice

For crystallised flowers:
Edible, unsprayed flowers, such as violets
  or primroses, or small rose petals
1 egg white, lightly beaten
Caster sugar

Preheat the oven to 180°C/Gas Mark 4. Line a 12-hole bun tin with 12 paper cases.

To make the cakes, cream together the butter and sugar until light and fluffy in a food processor, mixer or by hand. Add the eggs one at a time, beating well after each addition, then gently fold in the flour.

Divide the mixture between the paper cases and bake for about 12 minutes, until the cakes are risen, golden and spring back into shape after being pressed lightly with your thumb. Cool completely on a wire rack before the next stage.

To make the icing, sift the icing sugar into a bowl. Mix in the lemon juice, then add just enough hot water – a tablespoon or so – to make a smooth paste.

Line a wire rack with baking parchment. Put the frothy egg white and the caster sugar in separate bowls. To crystallise the flowers, brush them with the egg white, then dip them into the caster sugar. Shake to remove any excess. Place them on the parchment-lined rack and leave in a warm place to dry out. This can be done in an airing cupboard overnight, or in a very low oven with the door open for about an hour.

Assemble the cakes by covering the tops with icing and placing a crystallised flower or petal on each one.

Icings

Fruit icings

Sweet little fairy cakes and larger sponges look and taste better when iced. In the recipe below, the sharp juice of raspberries or blackcurrants cuts through the sweetness of the icing sugar and stains it with the natural pinkness of the fruit. Strawberries or cherries also make a pretty coloured icing. If it's not the berry season, lemon juice is a good substitute.

I hate the modern obsession with garish, girly cupcakes, their lurid icing so artificial-looking I'm amazed they're even edible. Simple, homemade cakes are a lovely antidote to them. They look and taste wonderful, and are even better if a few of the berries used in the icing are placed on top.

Enough for 12 fairy cakes or
a 21cm sponge
200g icing sugar
*2 tablespoons freshly pressed fruit juice
or lemon juice*

Sift the icing sugar into a bowl. Push a handful of fruit through a sieve and catch the juice in a small bowl or jug. Stir 2 tablespoons of the fruit juice into the icing sugar with a spoon until it forms a smooth, loose paste. Spread it over the top of the cake/s in a thin layer with a flat knife or metal spatula.

Buttercream icing

This rich icing is a childhood favourite of mine, and is very useful for topping and filling all kinds of cakes. It can be flavoured with chocolate, coffee or vanilla – in fact, whatever you like. The quantity here makes enough to cover the top of a 21cm sponge; double the recipe if you want enough for the filling as well. The cake/s must be allowed to cool completely before icing them or the buttercream will melt and spoil the cake.

Enough for 12 fairy cakes or
a 21cm sponge
55g unsalted butter, softened
140g icing sugar, sifted
*2 teaspoons instant coffee or cocoa powder,
sifted, or the seeds scraped from the
inside of 1 vanilla pod*

Cream the butter, icing sugar and your preferred flavouring in a mixer, food processor or by hand until they are whipped up, light and smooth. Use a flat knife or metal spatula to spread the icing evenly over the cake/s. Take care that the buttercream isn't too chilled or it won't spread easily.

Candied orange peel

When we make oranges in brandy (page 368), there's always a huge amount of peel left over and I can't bear to throw it away. As it can't be put on the compost heap in large quantities because it affects the pH balance, I try to use up as much of it as possible in the kitchen.

It can be dried out in a low oven and used in homemade pot-pourri – I hate the overpowering smell of most ready-made mixtures, and it's so easy to make your own. It can also be candied and used to decorate cakes and puddings.

6 unwaxed oranges and/or lemons,
 washed and peeled
A pinch of salt
450g granulated sugar
Caster sugar, for coating

Cut the peel (the pith is left on) into strips approximately 1 x 7cm. Place them in a saucepan with the salt. Pour in just enough water to cover, bring to the boil and simmer for about 20 minutes, or until the peel is soft. Rinse in cold water and drain.

Put the granulated sugar and 300ml clean water into a saucepan and stir over a low heat until the sugar has dissolved. Bring to the boil and add the peel. Simmer for 30 minutes or so, until most of the syrup has been absorbed into the now-transparent pieces of peel. Keep an eye on it to ensure it does not burn.

Remove the peel with a slotted spoon and dip each piece into a bowl of caster sugar to coat, shaking off any excess.

Preheat the oven to 80°C/Gas Mark ¼. Line a large baking tray or two smaller trays with baking parchment. Place the strips of peel on the tray/s, ensuring they don't touch, and place in the oven to dry out for about 2–3 hours. Keep an eye on them to make sure they don't take on any colour.

Cool, then store in an airtight container sprinkled with caster sugar. The strips keep very well for up to 4 months.

Tea loaf

This is a simplified version of the Welsh bara brith. It's very easy to make, but the fruit has to be soaked in the tea for a few hours before you start.

Serves 6
500g mixed, dried fruit, a combination
    of raisins, currants and sultanas
250g soft brown sugar
170ml black tea
1 large egg, lightly beaten
275g self-raising flour, sifted
Butter, for greasing

In a mixing bowl, combine the dried fruit and sugar, then pour over the tea. Cover and leave for at least 4 hours, ideally overnight, stirring once or twice.

Preheat the oven to 180°C/Gas Mark 4. Grease a 23 x 13 x 7cm loaf tin with butter and line the bottom and sides with baking parchment.

Add the egg and flour to the soaked fruit and mix well. Fill the prepared tin with the mixture, smooth the top, and bake for about 1 hour. It's ready when a skewer inserted in the middle of the loaf comes out clean. Cool in the tin for a few minutes. When cool enough to handle, turn out of the tin, peel off the parchment and leave the cake to cool completely on a wire rack.

Serve sliced and spread with butter, and a cup of tea.

Chocolate cake

Nothing beats a good chocolate cake for tea, especially for a birthday treat. By using 5 eggs, this recipe makes a tall cake, which looks very special covered with a thick layer of dark chocolate icing.

Serves 6–8
325g unsalted butter, softened, plus more
    for greasing
325g caster sugar
5 large eggs
275g self-raising flour
50g cocoa powder
1 tablespoon whole milk

For the buttercream filling:
140g icing sugar
2 teaspoons cocoa powder
60g unsalted butter, softened

For the topping:
100g good-quality dark chocolate, about
    70 per cent cocoa solids
1 tablespoon double cream

To decorate:
Flowers, sweets, grated chocolate

Preheat the oven to 180°C/Gas Mark 4.

Grease 2 x 21cm sandwich tins; loose-bottomed ones make things easier, but are not essential. Line the bottom of each with baking parchment.

Cream together the butter and caster sugar in a mixer, food processor or by hand until light and fluffy. Add the eggs one at a time, beating well after each addition, and adding a little flour if the mixture looks like it is going to curdle. Sift together the flour and cocoa powder, then fold them into the mixture with a light touch, being careful not to overmix. (If you're using a food processor, just pulse it together until blended.) Add the milk last and briefly mix it in – this isn't essential but it makes for a lighter cake.

Divide the cake mixture equally between the prepared tins and bake for about 30 minutes. To test if the cakes are ready, press the tops with your finger. If they spring back, take them out of the oven and cool in the tins for a few minutes. As soon as they're cool enough to handle, remove them from the tins, peel off the baking parchment and place the cakes on a wire rack and allow to cool completely.

While the cakes are cooling, make the filling. Sift together the icing sugar and cocoa, then cream together with the softened butter. This can be done in a mixer, food processor or by hand.

To make the topping, break up the bar of chocolate and place in a small, heatproof bowl set over a pan of barely simmering water, making sure the bottom of the bowl doesn't touch the water. When the chocolate has melted, add the cream and whisk together until smooth.

Assemble the cake by spreading the chocolate buttercream over one of the sponges with a metal spatula or knife. Put the other sponge on top, then cover the whole cake with the melted chocolate, spreading it evenly over the top and sides.

Decorate the cake as you wish, with flowers from the garden for a grown-up, sweets for children, or simply some grated chocolate.

Chocolate fridge cake

Chocolate, sultanas and cherries combined with a biscuit crunch mean these more-ish treats disappear fast. They are delicious with a cup of tea anytime you need a hit of chocolate, or on a winter picnic. I use a good-quality 70 per cent dark chocolate, which adds a touch of bitterness to the very sweet base. The slices need to be kept cool, hence the name.

Makes 8–10 slices
225g digestive biscuits
100g unsalted butter
2 tablespoons golden syrup
2 tablespoons drinking chocolate
50g sultanas
3 tablespoons glacé cherries
150g dark chocolate, 70 per cent
  cocoa solids

Put the biscuits into a large bowl and break them into smallish pieces with the end of a rolling pin.

Melt the butter, golden syrup and drinking chocolate together in a pan over a low heat. Remove from the heat and mix in the sultanas and cherries.

Tip the chocolate mixture into the bowl of broken biscuits and stir together, taking care not to break up the biscuits much more in order to keep the crunchiness.

Line a Swiss roll tin, approximately 33 x 20 x 3cm, or a similar shallow dish with baking parchment. Spoon in the mixture, pressing it down in the tin to form a roughly even layer.

In a heatproof bowl over a pan of barely simmering water, carefully melt the chocolate, then spread it over the top of the biscuit mix. Place the tin in the fridge for a couple of hours until it's cold and hard. Cut into slices and keep them in a cool place or the fridge until you're ready to eat them.

Dundee cake

Montagu is descended from the Keillers of Dundee, renowned marmalade makers and also inventors of the Dundee cake, the rich, buttery, sultana cake decorated with concentric circles of golden almonds.

Unlike the marmalade recipe we've inherited (page 37), nothing has been handed down about the cake, but I have learnt that it was flavoured with candied orange peel (page 245), enriched with sultanas, ground almonds and muscovado sugar, and the top was decorated with whole almonds. No other dried fruit was used. These ingredients must have come from Spain with the Seville oranges, or so I like to think, and they have an integrity when used together.

Dundee cake is portable and keeps well, so is perfect on a picnic. On a cold winter's day a slice of this cake with a mug of tea keeps us going in the garden or on the farm.

Serves 10

175g lightly salted butter, softened,
   plus a little more for greasing
175g light muscovado sugar
4 eggs
100g plain flour, sifted
100g ground almonds
75g candied orange peel (page 245)
475g sultanas
Zest and juice of 1 unwaxed orange
50g whole almonds, blanched or
   unblanched (both work well)

Preheat the oven to 180°C/Gas Mark 4.

Butter a 22cm loose-bottomed cake tin and line the base and sides with buttered baking parchment.

Cream the butter and sugar together in a food processor, mixer or by hand. Add the eggs one at a time, beating well after each addition. If you are using a food processor, scrape the mixture into a large bowl. Fold in the flour, then mix in the ground almonds. Stir in the candied orange peel, sultanas and orange zest. Pour in the orange juice and stir the mixture well. Spoon into the prepared tin and smooth the surface with a spatula. Carefully arrange radiating circles of almonds on top.

Bake for about 90 minutes, or until a skewer pushed into the centre of the cake comes out clean. Cool completely in the tin on a wire rack, then remove the parchment and present the magnificent cake on a plate. It will keep for several weeks wrapped in greaseproof paper and foil in an airtight tin.

Coffee and walnut cake

If someone were to ask me what my favourite cake is, I would definitely say this one. I like the idea of it washed down with a cup of tea.

In local WI markets and more old-fashioned tea shops, the sponge is slightly oily, giving it a distinctive moistness. I don't use any vegetable oil in the recipe, preferring a more traditional sponge mix. It will keep for up to a week in a tin, but usually doesn't last that long in our house.

Serves 8–12
250g unsalted butter, plus a little more
  for greasing
250g caster sugar
4 large eggs
1 tablespoon instant coffee dissolved in
  1 tablespoon boiling water, or
  1 tablespoon coffee essence
250g self-raising flour, sifted

For the coffee butter icing:
55g unsalted butter, slightly softened
140g icing sugar, sifted to remove
  any lumps
2 teaspoons instant coffee diluted
  in 1 teaspoon boiling water, or
  1½ teaspoons coffee essence
100g halved walnuts

Preheat the oven to 180°C/Gas Mark 4. Lightly grease 2 x 21cm sandwich tins; loose-bottomed ones make things easier, but are not essential. Line the bottom of each with baking parchment.

Cream the butter and sugar together in a mixer, food processor or by hand. Add the eggs one at a time, beating well after each addition, until the mixture is pale and creamy, which is the secret of a light cake. Beat in the coffee and mix just to combine. Fold or pulse in the flour, being careful not to overmix.

Divide the batter between the prepared tins and bake for about 25 minutes, until the tops spring back if pressed lightly with a finger. Remove the cakes from the oven and allow to cool for a few minutes. As soon as the tins are cool enough to handle, turn the cakes out onto a wire rack, remove the baking parchment and leave to cool completely.

While the cakes are cooling, make the icing by creaming together the butter, icing sugar and coffee. When the cakes are completely cold, spread the icing over each sponge with a metal spatula or knife. Decorate what will be the top sponge with circles of walnut halves. Sandwich together with the bottom half.

Dinner

WHILST THE BRITISH CALIBRATE your economic and social class by the time of day that you eat it, dinner is the main meal of the day whenever you choose to consume it. In fact, the timing of the meal is a relatively modern agony. The early Tudor court sat down to dinner at 11 a.m., whilst by the time of George I in 1714, 2 p.m. was the norm, and in 1740 poor Alexander Pope was complaining bitterly that he could not hold out till the newly fashionable, and for him impossibly late, dining hour of 4 p.m.

The driving force behind the steady movement of dinner from morning to evening was the pattern of the working day. Increasingly, people were unwilling or unable to break up the day with the meal, which was almost universally eaten at home. Obviously, if you worked from home or within walking distance, this was not a problem, so manual workers tended to keep to the midday dinner, whilst clerical or professional people ate in the evening. By the middle of the Victorian era, trains meant that white-collar workers travelled further to work, so arrived back home later for dinner. But throughout all its peregrinations around the clock, dinner remained the day's main meal.

Going out to dinner adds further layers to the meal, all of them with their potential pitfalls. The food is often secondary or frankly disappointing. The truth is that it is rare to go out to dinner and eat as well as you can at home. The perfect homemade dinner combines a sense of occasion with none of the enforced formality or horrendous cost. Yet dinner parties in other people's houses often appear to bring out the worst in a certain type of Englishman and woman – the type that goes to dinner parties. As a nation, we seem to find it hard to enjoy the process of sharing a meal in a relaxed yet serious manner. Close friends do this without any trouble when holidaying together or at an impromptu meal at one of their homes, but the formal dinner party brings with it a brittleness that, in my experience, can be farcical. I have known drunkenness, tears, violent rows and excruciating boredom – let alone the behaviour of other guests – sweep away and wreck these meals like the rising tide. I now view them with deep suspicion.

But dinner, of all meals, should always have some formality and ritual to it. It must be eaten at a table that is properly laid. This might well be the kitchen table, and the settings might be just a knife, fork and glass at each place, but it is the symbolism that is as important as the choice of table dressing. I think that dinner is all the better with a glass or two of wine to accompany it, although this is as much to confirm the end of work for the day as anything else.

I am fully aware that this is increasingly rare. I know young adults to whom the concept of laying a table is unknown. But it is worth taking the trouble because beneath the slightly self-conscious formality of dinner is an enriching level of shared experience. And regardless of our backgrounds or our circumstances, there is a common vision of what comprises a really good dinner. This has little to do with space or style of living. I have visited Italian houses where whole families crowd round a small table in a packed kitchen with more relish and real manners than any Home Counties dinner party.

In general, the dishes we cook for dinner have the same ethos as all our food – simplicity based upon the best possible ingredients. However, when extra effort has been made to shop for a particular cut of meat, a whole fresh fish or a vegetable that is rarely in season, it is worthy of celebration. The beauty of doing this at home is that for the same money as a bad meal in any restaurant you can buy and prepare them without fuss to make something memorably delicious.

STARTERS

It is not often that our evening meal has three courses. It usually begins with the main dish and occasionally stops there. But there are times when the pace of the meal is best spread across more courses. 'Starters' is an ugly word, overly hearty and not suggesting that what follows will be refined. But it does successfully convey the awkwardness that many people feel upon entering into a meal at someone else's table, particularly if, for whatever reason, you are on your best behaviour. So the first course has to be accessible and set the tone for the meal.

It is certainly a mistake to start with something too ambitious. We always try to prepare something that has only to be assembled at the last moment and that does not need serving at the table. A salad of some sort is the easiest example of this, best served at the start of a meal on individual plates rather than from a communal bowl. A lettuce from the garden, walnuts and a local blue cheese is a delicious combination of salty, rich flavours and varied textures, and a great family favourite. Smoked salmon – wild rather than factory farmed – could not be simpler, and is another treat that can be prepared on individual plates in advance. Any of the soups that we have for lunch also make good starters.

There is something to be said for starting a meal with food that needs getting to grips with. Too much well-mannered reserve does not encourage the proper enjoyment of food or even each other's company. Artichokes, picked apart scale by scale, or asparagus dabbled in melted butter or oil will start to loosen the social stays. Soufflés are always fun and can be cooked in individual ramekins to make a celebratory starter – even if it is just the two of us sitting at the kitchen table.

Asparagus

We wait and wait for the asparagus to appear at the end of April, and then enjoy it as often as possible until its short season ends in June. I would eat asparagus every day if I could, either raw in salads if the spears are very small and tender, or simply steamed and served with melted butter.

Serves 2 as a starter
12 spears of asparagus, or 1 bundle, or a couple of handfuls of asparagus sprues

To serve:
Choose between: melted, unsalted butter; extra virgin olive oil, lemon juice and flaky sea salt; soft-boiled eggs

Preparation is easy. If you grow your own asparagus, don't collect the spears until the water is boiling in the pan. Wash them in cold water, then flex them until they snap in two, so you are left with only the tender, upper part of the spears. (Put aside the tougher ends for making asparagus soup.)

If you buy your asparagus, it's unlikely to be as fresh and will bend rather than snap, so trim the ends with a paring knife, then scrape off the hard, outer layer at the bottom of the spears back to the softer, edible part – sprues seldom need trimming. Alternatively, you could do what I do – eat down to the soft part and leave the rest.

The simplest way to cook asparagus spears is to tie them into a bundle and stand them upright in a tall, thin pan in about 6cm boiling water, put the lid on and cook for 5–7 minutes. The delicate tips will steam above the water as the stems soften. If you don't have a suitable pot, simply cook them in a steamer for 5–6 minutes. Alternatively, blanch them for a couple of minutes in boiling water, drain, then lightly oil them and grill or griddle on the stove or a barbecue – just 1 minute on each side. This gives them a sweeter, nuttier taste.

Serve the asparagus on warmed plates with melted butter in a jug, or dress them with extra virgin oil, a squeeze of lemon juice and a sprinkling of sea salt. I also like to dip them like green 'soldiers' into soft-boiled eggs, which makes a sensuous combination.

Stuffed courgette flowers

There are so many ways to cook courgettes that we never tire of them. If I'm in a hurry, I simply grate and fry them in a little butter, add salt and pepper, and eat them on their own or on hot toast. Young courgettes can be sliced thinly and eaten raw in salads or cooked whole in tomato sauce (page 102). I sometimes knock up a quick pasta sauce with diced courgettes cooked gently in olive oil with finely diced garlic and lemon zest, then finally sprinkled with chopped parsley. The mild flavour of courgettes is improved by herbs such as basil, parsley, mint, lemon thyme and chives.

If you grow your own courgettes, check them every day and pick them when they are no more than 16cm long. For this recipe, pick them when they are small enough to have the flowers still attached, or look out for them in farmers' markets in summer.

Serves 4
*8–12 courgette flowers, or small courgettes
with the flowers still attached*
*200g soft cheese (I use Perl Wen, a Welsh
cheese that's rather like Brie, or a soft
goats' cheese)*

For the batter:
200g self-raising flour
A pinch of salt
500ml iced water
Sunflower oil, for frying
Flaky sea salt, to serve

Carefully remove the stamens from inside the flowers. Place a walnut-sized piece of cheese inside each flower, gently twisting the ends of the petals to hold the stuffing in. The little courgettes look like handles, with the twirled flower on the end.

Pour the oil into a deep-fat fryer or a large, heavy-based saucepan. If using a saucepan, you will need to pour in about 10cm of oil and it should come no more than a third of the way up the pan. Heat the oil until it reads 180°C on a cooking thermometer, or until a cube of white bread dropped into the fat will brown in just less than a minute.

Prepare the batter while the oil heats up. Sift the flour and salt into a bowl, then stir in the iced water. Don't worry if the mixture is a bit lumpy – it will be all the better for that.

Dip the courgettes into the batter, then lower them carefully into the hot oil using tongs or a slotted spoon. Deep-fry in batches for 2–4 minutes, until they are crisp and light golden brown. Drain on a warmed plate lined with kitchen paper as you cook the rest. Serve immediately, sprinkled with flaky sea salt.

Globe artichokes

To me artichokes are everything that I like about food and cooking. They are easy to prepare, look fantastic and are a very sociable food, best eaten with family or friends sitting round a table.

Unlike the Italians, we do not eat artichokes when they are young, before the chokes develop, unless we have glut. We pick the fully grown globe artichokes in high summer and cook them whole. We grow Green Globe, which have a flattened top and practically no spikes, the purple Violetta di Chioggia, and Gros Vert de Laon, which is spikier, rounder and much bigger. All are delicious. They are large, dramatic plants and take up a lot of room in a cooking pot, so if you don't have one big enough, cook them in two batches. (You can keep the first batch warm in a colander, covered with a tea towel.)

I like to serve them simply, with extra virgin olive oil and sea salt, or just melted butter.

Serves 6 as a starter
6 large artichokes
½ a lemon
Extra virgin olive oil
Sea salt

Trim the stalks so the artichokes will stand flat on their bases, then tap them to dislodge any earwigs. Cook in boiling water for 25–35 minutes, depending on the size of the artichoke. They are ready when the outer leaves can be pulled away easily. Drain well and serve hot, one or more per person, with extra virgin olive oil and sea salt.

Pull away each scale, dip it into the oil and salt and bite off the fleshy base. It is a messy feast and I love it when everyone is sitting around the table enjoying the slow pleasure of eating them. The final treat is to cut off the fleshy bottom, removing the indigestible hairy choke. What is left is the delicacy, the heart, which has an earthy taste with a slight aniseed kick.

Variation:
Serve with beurre blanc (page 181) instead of olive oil and sea salt.

Cheese straws

On the precious times we sit down together for a drink in the evening, we like something savoury to nibble on. Cheese straws can be whipped up quickly and, like anything freshly baked, are crisper and more delicious than anything from a packet. They can be made with puff pastry and formed into cheesy twists, but this is my favoured recipe.

I think of them as a grown-up taste, but they frequently appeared at the children's parties of my childhood as part of the spread of bridge rolls with egg and cress, Twiglets and gaudy jellies in colourful paper bowls.

I often wonder what influence food will have on my own children's memories, as for me it is the trigger and stimulus to cook and eat. I hope that by learning how to cook, they will be able to feed themselves and have a lifelong interest in good food. Cooking a few basic things from scratch and avoiding processed food is something I have tried to drum into them. I am proud that they can shop and cook as well as me and could run the household. I hope I have taught them that it is a pleasure to cook, and even if they haven't got much time, simple foods such as these straws take only a few minutes to make, and taste so much better than anything you could buy.

Makes 12
100g plain flour, plus extra for dusting
A pinch of salt
A pinch of cayenne pepper
50g unsalted butter, chilled and cut into cubes
1 egg yolk
50g strong Cheddar cheese, grated
Iced water
1 tablespoon grated Parmesan cheese

Preheat the oven to 200°C/Gas Mark 6. Line a baking tray with baking parchment.

Sift the flour, salt and cayenne into a bowl. Add the butter and rub it in quickly with cool fingertips until the mixure resembles coarse breadcrumbs. With a knife, mix in the egg yolk and grated Cheddar, and add just enough iced water to form a stiff dough. Knead it briefly into a smooth ball, wrap in cling film and chill for 15 minutes.

Lightly flour a work surface and rolling pin, then roll the dough into a rectangle approximately 4mm thick. Cut into 12 equal lengths with a sharp knife. Carefully place them on the baking tray and bake for about 12 minutes, until they are a light golden colour. Sprinkle with the Parmesan, then cool slightly on a wire rack. Eat straight away.

Stilton and walnut salad

This simple but successful combination makes a lovely salad. Fast to assemble, it depends on really tip-top ingredients. If you have time and they are in season, fresh wet walnuts are a real treat. If not, check the walnuts are not rancid or stale as that would spoil the whole dish.

Serves 4
A couple of handfuls of very fresh, young lettuce leaves
100g Stilton, or similar salty, blue cheese, such as Shropshire Blue
70g walnut halves
2 tablespoons finely chopped chives

For the dressing:
2 tablespoons cider vinegar
2 teaspoons Dijon mustard
A pinch of sugar
Salt and freshly ground black pepper
6 tablespoons olive oil

First make the dressing. Whisk together the vinegar, mustard, sugar, salt and pepper, then whisk in the olive oil until it emulsifies.

Arrange the lettuce leaves on 4 plates, crumble over the cheese and scatter on the walnuts. Trickle some of the dressing over each plate (you may have some left over, in which case, keep it in the fridge). Sprinkle the salad with chives. Serve immediately.

Cheese soufflé

Cheese soufflé is a glamorous dish, really worth the effort it takes to make it. Serve as soon as you take it out of the oven, as it will sink before your eyes. It doesn't matter – in fact it is desirable – if it's still a little creamy in the centre.

Serves 4
50g unsalted butter, plus extra for
*   buttering the dish*
50g Parmesan cheese, grated
300ml whole milk
40g plain flour
½ teaspoon English mustard powder,
*   mixed with ½ teaspoon water*
A pinch of cayenne pepper
4 eggs, separated
100g good, strong farmhouse Cheddar
*   cheese, grated*
Salt and freshly ground black pepper

Preheat the oven to 200°C/Gas Mark 6 and put a roasting tin in the oven to heat up. Butter a 1 litre soufflé dish, then coat the inside with the Parmesan.

Warm the milk in a saucepan but do not let it boil. In a separate saucepan, melt the butter, then add the flour, mixing to a smooth paste. Gradually add the milk, stirring to prevent lumps. Simmer over a low heat, stirring constantly, until the mixture thickens enough to coat the back of a spoon, about 5 minutes. Stir in the mustard and cayenne pepper. Remove

from the heat, let the mixture cool a little, then whisk in the egg yolks, one at a time. Add the grated Cheddar, taste and season well. At this point, you can cover the mixture and refrigerate for several hours, adding the beaten egg whites just before you cook the soufflé.

Beat the egg whites until stiff and then gently fold into the cheese sauce with a metal spoon or spatula.

Spoon into the prepared dish and smooth over the top. Place the dish in the roasting tin in the oven and carefully pour about 5cm of hot water from the kettle into the tin. Cook for 25 minutes, or until puffed up and golden brown. Alternatively, the mixture can be divided between 4 x 200ml ramekins and cooked for about 12 minutes.

Pulled bread

This is an excellent way of adding interest to any dish requiring toasted bread. It was traditionally made in the days when households baked their own bread. A white loaf would be taken out of the oven just before it was cooked, then torn into rough pieces and put back in the oven until cooked and golden brown.

I find pulled bread particularly good with soup, salads and cheese, especially if you have no fresh bread or biscuits to hand. It looks really appetising piled up on a wooden board.

*1 large white loaf of bread
(it can be a day old)*

Preheat the oven to 200°C/Gas Mark 6.

If you wish, you can remove the crusts first, then tear the bread into rough pieces about the size of an egg. Don't worry if the pieces are odd shapes.

Place on a baking tray and bake until crisp and golden, about 10 minutes, depending on the size of the pieces. Serve immediately.

Hummus

We often have a bowl of hummus in the fridge ready to serve as a quick starter or as an instant meal with bread and salad. Tinned chickpeas are a good store-cupboard standby, but the flavour and texture is better if you have time to cook them from scratch yourself.

> Makes about 280g
> *100g dried chickpeas, which makes*
>   *about 200g cooked weight*
> *1 tablespoon tahini*
> *Juice of 1 lemon*
> *1 garlic clove, roughly chopped*
> *75ml olive oil*
> *¼ teaspoon cayenne pepper*
> *Salt*

Soak the chickpeas overnight in plenty of cold water. Drain and put them into a saucepan with enough fresh water to cover them by about 4cm. Bring to the boil and simmer for at least 1 hour, until the chickpeas are soft, skimming off any foam that rises to the surface. It's hard to be precise about the cooking time as it depends on the freshness of the chickpeas, but they are ready when you can mash them easily against the side of the pan with a wooden spoon. Drain, reserving some of the cooking liquid.

If you are using tinned chickpeas, drain and rinse them under the cold tap before making the hummus.

Put the chickpeas and 2–3 tablespoons of the cooking liquid (or a splash of hot water if you are using tinned chickpeas) into a food processor with the tahini, lemon juice and garlic. Whizz until you have a smooth paste. Slowly add the olive oil through the feed tube and pulse to blend as you go. Add salt to taste.

Just before serving, put the hummus into a bowl, trickle over a little olive oil and sprinkle with cayenne pepper.

Smoked salmon

As we do not yet smoke our own fish, this is not really a recipe, but I couldn't contemplate writing about my favourite foods without including smoked salmon. Whether eaten in Ireland with soda bread and a pint of Guinness, or with a glass of champagne as a birthday treat, it's one of my favourite indulgences. The beauty of the overlapping pinky-orange slices on a white plate with half a yellow lemon is all you need.

I try to get hold of really good smoked salmon from independent smokeries. It's worth trying out different cures as they vary so much in flavour. It is most important to buy the best wild salmon, where the fish swim freely and eat a natural diet, or at the very least try to source sustainably farmed salmon.

Treat this as a luxurious delicacy.

100g smoked salmon minimum per person
Slices of lemon

To serve:
Soda bread (page 222) and butter, or
   thinly sliced buttered brown bread

Simply plate the slices of smoked salmon and eat with a squeeze of lemon. Serve with champagne.

Good smoked salmon is delicious eaten like this, but if it is not of the very highest quality, I prefer to eat it on oatcakes with black pepper and lemon.

Potted salmon

This is a lovely way to start a meal, and it can usefully be made in advance. Pot either into small Kilner jars, which I really like, or make in one dish and divide up before serving. If dill is unavailable, I use fennel fronds, which have a similar but milder aniseed flavour. Try to source organic or wild salmon, and avoid the cheap farmed fish.

Serve the potted salmon with a sliced cucumber salad, dressed with a little vinegar and a pinch of sugar, and brown bread and butter.

Serves 6
Unsalted butter, for greasing
600g thick fillet of fresh organic
  or wild salmon
Juice of 1 lemon
1–2 tablespoons finely chopped dill
  or fennel fronds
1 tablespoon olive oil
Sea salt and freshly ground black pepper

To serve:
Cucumber salad (optional)
Brown bread and butter
1–2 extra lemons, cut into wedges

Preheat the oven to 200°C/Gas Mark 6.

Butter a piece of baking parchment and place the fish on it. Season well and pour over half the lemon juice. Wrap it up, folding in the ends of the paper to seal the parcel, and put it on a baking tray. Bake for about 10 minutes, until the fish is just cooked through – it should be opaque and firm to the touch.

Allow the fish to cool for a few minutes, then pour off the lemony juices into a jug. Flake the fish into a bowl, discarding the skin and bones. Add the rest of the lemon juice, the cooking juices and the dill or fennel and stir gently together. Season to taste and loosen with a little olive oil.

Divide the mixture between 6 x 200ml Kilner jars, press it down, then seal and chill for a couple of hours in the fridge.

To serve the salmon in a single dish, choose any container large enough for the mixture, fill with the salmon, press it down and cover the dish with cling film. Chill for a couple of hours or overnight.

Serve the potted salmon with a little cucumber salad, brown bread and butter and lemon wedges.

Kipper pâté

This pâté is a favourite of mine because it can be prepared in advance with few ingredients, and the combination of the smoky kippers and butter is delicious. Use only traditionally smoked kippers, not the fake dyed versions, because the flavour is better and you are supporting a superior method of production. I always buy them from a fishmonger rather than a supermarket.

Serves 6–8
1 pair of kippers
Unsalted butter, at room temperature
½ teaspoon cayenne pepper
½–1 lemon
Salt
Clarified butter, if not eating at once
  (see page 86 for method)

To serve:
Brown toast or melba toast (page 278)

Boil a large kettle of water. Place the kippers in a roasting tin or, if you have one big enough, a large jug. Pour over enough boiling water to submerge the fish. This plumps up the flesh and 'cooks' them. Leave for 10 minutes, then drain.

Now for the messy bit. Remove the skin and bones and discard them. Weigh the flesh and place in a food processor with the same weight of butter. As the fish is still warm, it will mix with the butter into a light paste as you pulse it.

Add the cayenne pepper, the juice of half a lemon and salt to taste. Depending on the size of the lemon, it might need a little more juice, but don't overdo it as too much lemon can overpower the delicate flavour of the smoked fish.

If you are eating the pâté immediately, place in a bowl and sprinkle with a little more cayenne pepper. If you are making it to eat later, cover with a layer of clarified butter to seal it. The pâté will keep for 2–3 days in the fridge, covered tightly with foil.

Eat with hot brown toast or melba toast (page 278).

Melba toast

Melba toast is surprisingly elegant. A basket of curled triangles of golden brown, thin toast wrapped up in a white napkin is a perfect accompaniment to pâtés, such as the kipper pâté on page 276, and even soup or soft cheese are good with its crisp texture.

When I was a child, the beautiful rector's wife would make these for us after choir practice, and it is without doubt an economical way of making basic bread into a more glamorous treat, and a frugal way of eking out a church income.

Serves 4
4 slices of white bread, about 1cm thick

Preheat the oven to 200°C/Gas Mark 6.

First, lightly toast the sliced bread in the usual way. While still hot, cut off the crusts and place each slice flat on a board. With a long, sharp knife, carefully slice the bread horizontally through its soft middle so you end up with two equal-sized slices of bread, one side toasted, the other still soft. Cut each slice in half diagonally and place on a baking tray in the oven. As they are so thin, they colour quickly, within minutes, so keep an eye on them.

Take them out of the oven when they have just started to turn golden – it doesn't matter if they are a bit blotchy. Keep them warm in a napkin until you are ready to serve them.

It is best to make them freshly each time, although they will keep in an airtight container for a couple of days.

Cider cup

I love our rackety house, where the young swallows fly in and out of the hall in July, and sometimes I have to rescue a dragonfly from a spider's web. It is 'old and cold', according to my youngest son. When it rains and the wind is strong, water pours down the walls in some of the rooms. We are used to it now and the lime plaster soon dries out, no damage done.

In summer all the doors are left open, and shafts of light stream through the oak-framed windows onto the indestructible stone floors. I love the light of summer and dread winter, but by then we have the great open fires burning, which provide a different kind of light. I can sit for hours in the darkness watching the flames. It is also the time when a warm, spiced drink is a comfort and pleasure.

We live in a cider area, as all around us were cider orchards, each farm making its own supply. There are still many cider-makers in Herefordshire, who are always winning prizes, so we have a great choice. It is more appropriate somehow to drink cider rather than wine here, although we don't stick to it.

Mulled cider and mulled wine (or 'mouldy' wine as the children called it) are delicious drinks in winter, and can be made in larger quantities for parties. As it heats up, the delicious spicy apple scent fills the kitchen. Cider is less strong than wine, which means you can sip it all evening without feeling completely intoxicated.

Serves 4

1 litre good cider, bottle fermented, preferably organic
10 cloves
2 cinnamon sticks
Freshly grated nutmeg
2 tablespoons light muscovado sugar
1 apple, sliced
1 orange or lemon, sliced
Juice of 1 orange
Splash of apple brandy, for extra fortification

Put all the ingredients into large pan and warm them up, but don't bring them to the boil. Serve immediately, ladled into glasses.

MAIN COURSE

Whenever I go to a restaurant and order something that the menu describes as, say, roast venison, mashed potato with celeriac, red cabbage and a redcurrant sauce, and then the plate arrives looking like a stack of coins in the centre of an enormous dish decorated with the said sauce smeared artfully around, I feel cheated, regardless of the taste. Food cooked and served at home should never sink to that level of pretension. Generosity is at the heart of good home cooking.

You cannot, of course, separate how you cook from what you cook. If you use ingredients that are in season, and as local and fresh as possible, the resulting dishes will be based on the long and glorious tradition of British cooking. Yet it is one of the curiosities of British society that when it tries to impress it invariably uses dishes from abroad. No other cuisine is so lacking in self-confidence.

Sarah and I live in the countryside and generally see what we put on our dinner table living and growing all around us for months before we eat it. That feels like a privilege. But it is not a kind of cosseted ghetto that has no relevance to any other kind of modern British life. When you carefully cook and sit down to eat boiled beef with carrots, wherever you are, it really matters what breed the animal was, how it was cared for and where it spent its life. It makes a difference if you can source the vegetables directly, and a big difference if you grow them yourself.

I forget who first observed that you are not just what you eat, but what what you eat eats, not to mention when it eats it. Season, place, soil and weather all find their way onto your plate, and never more tellingly than with these main courses that I feel are seldom heralded as they should be – amongst the great dishes of the world.

Fillet of beef
with rocket

This would be my last supper. I often make it for my birthday if I have to cook as it's very easy to prepare and it fulfils my criteria of using the best ingredients, simply cooked. Although expensive, it's an occasional luxury and it's certainly cheaper than going to a restaurant.

Ask your butcher to cut a whole piece of fillet from the thick end and get him to trim it for you. The best we ever had was from Dexter, a rare-breed specialist in Ludlow. I bought the whole fillet as it was smaller than one from a larger breed.

We grow two types of rocket in the garden, one with soft, peppery leaves, and the wild one with finely cut leaves. Both have a hot, mustardy bite to them. There's no need always to use these fashionable Italian leaves, though, when you can get watercress. It's one of the glories of English produce and has the same peppery kick.

Preheat the oven to 220°C/Gas Mark 7 and heat an ovenproof frying pan until very hot; you should be able to hold the palm of your hand 10cm from the surface for no more than a couple of seconds.

Rub the fillet with olive oil and season well with salt and pepper. Seal in the frying pan for 2 minutes on each side. Place the pan and fillet in the hot oven for 10 minutes. Remove from the oven, place the beef on a warm dish and rest for about 10 minutes.

To serve, arrange a handful of leaves on each plate. Slice the fillet thinly and place 3 or 4 slices beside the leaves. Serve with mustard and cream sauce and some more black pepper.

Serves 4
1 x 600g piece of beef fillet
1–2 tablespoons olive oil
Salt and freshly ground black pepper
A handful of rocket leaves per person,
*   or a large bunch of watercress*

To serve:
Mustard and cream sauce (page 181)

Boiled beef
with carrots

Boiled beef is a delicious way of cooking a cheaper cut of beef and, as a bonus, there should be a quantity of stock left over to make soup with later. Serve with parsley dumplings poached in the broth, and creamed horseradish.

Serves 4–6
1–1.5kg silverside of beef
2 bay leaves
10 black peppercorns
3–4 parsley stalks
A sprig of thyme
4 medium carrots, peeled
4 small onions, peeled
4 small turnips, peeled, or 1 large
    turnip, peeled and quartered
A small handful of chopped parsley
Parsley dumplings (page 287)

To serve:
Creamed horseradish (page 174)

Put the beef in a deep, heavy-based pan or casserole and cover with cold water. Add the bay leaves, peppercorns, parsley stalks and thyme and bring to the boil. Skim off any scum that rises to the surface, then simmer, partially covered.

After the first 1 hour 20 minutes, add the vegetables. Simmer for a further 20 minutes, then add the dumplings. If there isn't enough room in the pot for the dumplings, pour some of the cooking liquid into a separate pan and poach them on their own for about 20 minutes. The total cooking time for the dish should be around 2 hours, depending on the toughness of the beef. It should be tender and soft enough to insert a fork or skewer easily, but not so tender that it falls apart.

When the beef is ready to serve, carefully remove the dumplings with a slotted spoon as they are quite fragile, and divide them between warmed plates. Take out the beef, carve it into slices and arrange them on the plates with the dumplings and some of the vegetables.

Spoon over a little of the hot stock, scatter over the parsley and serve with the creamed horseradish.

Beef stew

Good old stew, nourishing and dependable and none the worse for that. This is a thick, meaty stew and contains no vegetables other than the onion.

We serve it with whole carrots, cooked separately and with a little crunch left in them, and baked or mashed potatoes (page 320 or 322) to soak up the delicious gravy. The stew can be made in advance and improves with reheating, so is even better the next day.

Serves 4
2 tablespoons olive oil
1 large onion, roughly chopped
3–4 tablespoons plain flour
1kg stewing steak, chuck or skirt,
trimmed and cut into 3cm cubes
300ml beef stock or water
2 tablespoons Worcestershire sauce
1 tablespoon Dijon mustard
2 teaspoons redcurrant jelly or
damson cheese (page 184)
A small handful of finely chopped parsley
Salt and freshly ground black pepper

Pour the olive oil into a large, heavy-based saucepan. Tip in the onion and cook over a medium heat for 5 minutes. While it is cooking, season the flour well with salt and pepper, then coat the meat with it, making sure each piece is covered in a dusty layer but shaking off any excess. This will thicken the gravy as the meat cooks.

Remove the onions from the pan with a slotted spoon and set aside. Raise the heat a little and brown the meat on all sides. You might need to do this in batches, as you don't want to crowd the pan or the meat will steam instead of brown.

Tip the onions back into the pan with the meat, pour in the stock or water and bring to the boil, stirring to mix everything together. Simmer, partially covered, on top of the cooker for 1½ hours. Alternatively, you can cook it in the oven at 170°C/Gas Mark 3.

The stew is ready when the meat is tender. Add the Worcestershire sauce, Dijon mustard and redcurrant jelly or damson cheese and cook for a further 5 minutes to blend the flavours. Serve sprinkled with chopped parsley.

Parsley dumplings

It is very useful to know a basic dumpling recipe as they are so good added to a stew or soup towards the end of cooking. You can also poach them in the liquor from boiled beef (page 285).

Although they're meant to be filling, dumplings shouldn't be stodgy, and they can be whatever size you choose. They were traditionally made with suet, although you can substitute butter if you prefer.

As they no longer need to be simply a filling addition to eke out a thin stew, avoid blandness by seasoning them well and be generous with the chopped herbs. Parsley, thyme, chives and a little sage or rosemary all work well. Grated nutmeg, fresh horseradish or powdered English mustard are good additions too.

Makes about 8 large dumplings or
   16 small ones
250g plain flour, plus a little extra
   for dusting your hands
2 teaspoons baking powder
100g shredded suet, or chilled unsalted
   butter, cut into small pieces
3 tablespoons finely chopped parsley
A pinch of freshly grated nutmeg
About 100ml milk or water
Salt and freshly ground black pepper

Sift the flour and baking powder into a bowl, then rub in the suet or butter with your fingertips. Mix in the parsley and nutmeg and season well. Add enough milk or water to make a sticky dough (you might not need all the milk). With floured hands, form the dough into balls: for stew, they should be the size of tangerines; for soup, they are better walnut-sized.

With a spoon, gently lower each dumpling onto the surface of the stew, then partially cover the pan. Cook large dumplings for 20 minutes, small ones for 10 minutes. They are ready when they are puffed up and light.

Dumplings are prone to losing their shape during cooking, but don't worry as they will still taste good.

Steak and kidney pie

Steak and kidney pie is one of the great British dishes – a welcoming taste after a cold winter's day spent outside.

Serves 6
350g lambs' kidneys
650g stewing steak, trimmed and cut
into 2.5cm cubes
5 tablespoons plain flour
2 tablespoons olive oil
1 onion, halved and thinly sliced
600ml good-quality beef stock
2 bay leaves
¼ teaspoon fresh thyme leaves
Salt and freshly ground black pepper
1 egg, beaten with a splash of milk, to glaze

For the shortcrust pastry:
400g plain flour
A pinch of salt
200g unsalted butter, chilled and cubed
1 egg, lightly beaten

First make the pastry. Place the flour, salt and butter in a food processor and pulse until the mixture is the consistency of fine breadcrumbs. Add the egg and, if necessary, a few drops of cold water, then pulse until the mixture forms a ball of dough. Wrap in cling film and chill in the fridge for at least 30 minutes.

To make the filling, slice the kidneys in half, remove the white, gristly parts, then cut them into slightly smaller pieces than the steak. Season the flour with salt and pepper, then toss the meat in it. Shake to remove any excess.

Heat the oil in a large, heavy-based pan over a medium-high heat and brown the meat in batches on all sides. Return all the meat to the pan, add the onion and stir for 3–4 minutes. Pour in the beef stock and bring gently to the boil, scraping all the brown bits from the bottom of the pan. Add the bay leaves and thyme, then simmer gently, partially covered, for about 1½ hours. Check occasionally, and top up with water if necessary. The gravy should be rich, thick and savoury, and the meat tender. Taste and adjust the seasoning if necessary. Pour the filling into a deep pie dish with a wide lip and cool completely before covering with pastry.

Preheat the oven to 180°C/Gas Mark 4.

Lightly flour a work surface and rolling pin, then roll out the pastry to a thickness of 5mm. Cut some thin strips from the edges, dab the lip of the pie dish with cold water and press the pastry strips on them. Place a pie funnel, if you have one, in the centre of the dish, then drape the rest of the pastry over the pie. Trim off the excess and crimp the edges. Brush the top of the pie with the egg wash, then cut around the funnel or make a few slashes in the pastry.

Place the pie dish on a baking tray and cook for 45 minutes, until the top is golden and the filling piping hot.

Slow-roasted pork belly

Pork belly is an inexpensive cut that is best cooked very slowly, leaving the meat meltingly tender. A breed like Gloucester Old Spot, which traditionally grazes on orchard windfalls, is ideal, although any free-range, well-kept breed is good. Ask your butcher to score the skin of the pork for you as it needs a very sharp knife. Serve simply, with potatoes and/or celeriac, either mashed or boiled, and other winter vegetables.

Serves 4
1.5kg belly pork, on the bone,
*   skin scored*
2–3 tablespoons olive oil
4–8 small apples, whole and
*   unpeeled (optional)*
Salt and freshly ground black pepper

Preheat the oven to 160°C/Gas Mark 2–3 and boil a kettle of water.

Place the pork, skin-side up, in a roasting tin and pour over the boiling water to open up the slashes. Drain off the water and pat the skin dry with kitchen paper or a clean tea towel. Rub some salt and pepper into the skin, splash over the olive oil and place in the oven.

Roast for 2 hours, then, if you are using apples, place them around the pork. Cook for about a further 30–40 minutes, until the apples and meat are tender. If the crackling isn't crisp enough, transfer the apples to a warmed serving dish, then turn up the oven and roast the meat a little longer, or place under the grill for a few minutes, taking care not to burn the crackling. Put the meat on the serving dish with the apples and keep warm.

Pour off any excess fat from the roasting tin, then deglaze it with a little water. Heat through and pour the juices into a jug.

Remove the crackling and cut the pork into thick slices. Serve the slices with the pan juices poured over, a generous piece of crackling, and the apples.

Pork chops
with apples

At moments of indecision when I am standing in the butcher's trying to choose something easy to cook, I often buy pork chops. I usually ask for loin chops with the kidney still attached. These are perfect for a quick meal, requiring minimal cooking skills, a frying pan and a source of heat.

Apples are the best accompaniment to pork in any form, and in this recipe they caramelise in the pan and cook with the meat. A small onion, peeled, cut in half and added for the last 10 minutes of the cooking time, can be substituted for the apples if you prefer.

Add some good bread and a green salad and you have a feast. Serve with some mustard on the side, and cider to drink.

Serves 2
25g unsalted butter or 2 tablespoons
  olive oil
2 loin chops
4 sage leaves
2 dessert apples, peeled, quartered
  and cored
250ml dry cider
Salt and freshly ground black pepper

Heat the butter or oil in a frying pan over a medium-high heat. You might want to score the fat on the loin chops, as it helps to keep them flat when they are cooked. Season the chops well and press a couple of sage leaves onto each one. Fry for about

8–10 minutes per side until golden brown, depending on the thickness of the meat. The chops must be cooked thoroughly without a hint of pink in the centre. Place the apples around the chops for the last 5 minutes and cook until they are soft and slightly caramelised. Transfer the chops to a warm plate with the apples.

Deglaze the pan with the cider, scraping up all the caramelised bits, and let it bubble away until the sauce is reduced by half. Place the chops and apples on two warmed plates, pour over the sauce and serve immediately.

Ham on the bone

At Christmas we always order a dry-cured ham on the bone from a local butcher. I buy it on the bone because not only does it look more decorative and appetising on the table, I think the flavour is better too. It feeds lots of people and lasts for days covered in greaseproof paper in the fridge, although it is usually eaten within a week. It forms the basis of many meals. We eat it at breakfast with eggs and with pickles for supper.

A ham is very easy to prepare but requires time and a large pot that can take the whole joint covered in water. I use a cheap, stainless-steel cooking pot that looks like something from an army field kitchen. It's important to know the weight of the ham to estimate cooking times. I confess, I have often forgotten and have had to take it out of the pot to reweigh it.

I sometimes glaze the ham with runny honey, or even marmalade with the bits of peel sieved out, instead of brown sugar.

Serves 12 generously
1 cured ham, weighing 3–3.5kg
1 tablespoon black peppercorns
A handful of bay leaves
1 large onion, cut in half

For the glaze:
Whole cloves
3–4 tablespoons dark muscovado sugar

To serve:
Cumberland sauce (page 182)
Baked potatoes (page 320)

First, wash the ham thoroughly and soak it in lots of cold water overnight. I should point out that the cooking pot containing the ham filled with water is very heavy, so you will probably need help carrying it or tipping out the water later.

Pour off the soaking water, then put the ham, skin-side down, back into the pot with the peppercorns, bay leaves and onion and cover it with fresh, cold water. Bring it to the boil, then simmer for 40–45 minutes per kilo, making sure the ham is always covered with water by topping it up with boiling water from the kettle if necessary. It takes about 2½ hours to cook, but it also takes a while for the water to come to the boil, so allow for that too.

If you don't have a pot large enough, it's possible to cook the ham in a deep roasting tin in the oven at 180°C/Gas Mark 4. Place the ham skin-side down in the tin surrounded by the peppercorns, bay leaves and onion. Pour water halfway up the sides of the tin, taking care that it's not too heavy for you to manoeuvre into the oven. Cover tightly with a tent of foil. It will cook in the steam in a similar time to a ham simmered on the hob.

Preheat the oven to 220°C/Gas Mark 7. When the ham is cooked, take it out of the cooking pot or roasting tin and allow it to cool for 30 minutes as it will be too hot to handle immediately. Carefully remove the skin with a large knife while the ham is still warm, leaving a layer of fat still attached to the meat. Discard the slippery skin.

Put the ham in a large roasting tin and decorate it by scoring the covering of fat in a diamond pattern with a sharp knife. Dot the fat with whole cloves, pushing them into the centre of each diamond. Finally,

cover the fat with a thin layer of the muscovado sugar, sprinkling it all over the upper surface and patting it down to get an even covering. Roast for about 15 minutes, until an attractive brown crust has formed. This gives a contrasting dark edge to the pretty pink ham when it is carved.

Serve the ham as the centrepiece of the meal, carved into thin slices and eaten with Cumberland sauce and baked potatoes.

Rabbit in cider and mustard

Wild rabbits are slightly gamier than farmed ones and, as far as we're concerned, all the better for that. As an added bonus, they're so prolific in the countryside that they're very cheap too. I buy rabbits ready for cooking, dressed and cut into joints, from the butcher when there is an 'R' in the month. Since you can't age wild rabbits when you buy them, they're often better cooked slowly to ensure that they are tender. This also means that they reheat very well.

This is an adaptable recipe and can be made without the carrot and celery, but I prefer it with them.

Serves 4–6
4 tablespoons plain flour
2 wild rabbits, jointed
15g butter
1 tablespoon olive oil
4 carrots, finely diced
4 sticks of celery, finely diced
2 onions, finely diced
2 bay leaves
A sprig of thyme
1 x 500ml bottle organic cider
300ml chicken stock or water
2 tablespoons Dijon mustard
2 tablespoons double cream
A small handful of parsley, finely chopped
Salt and freshly ground black pepper

Season the flour well with salt and pepper, then toss the rabbit joints in the flour, shaking to remove any excess. Melt the butter and oil in a large heavy-based casserole over a medium heat. Fry the rabbit pieces until they are browned on all sides. You might need to do this in batches as you don't want to crowd the pan, adding more butter and oil if necessary. Transfer the rabbit pieces to a plate and reserve.

Add the carrots, celery and onions to the pan, stirring them around in the oil. Return the rabbit to the pan, add the herbs and pour on the cider and stock. Bring to the boil, then simmer, partially covered, for at least 45 minutes, until the rabbit is tender and the liquid reduced. Stir in the mustard and cream to enrich the sauce and let it bubble away in the pan for a few minutes for the flavours to develop.

Arrange the rabbit on warmed plates and scatter over the parsley. This is delicious served with little, crisp fried potatoes and a salad, or simply with mashed potato (page 322).

Lambs' liver

Until the 1980s everybody ate liver pretty regularly, but over the past twenty years or so it seems to have gone out of fashion. This is a pity as it is excellent value, delicious and nutritious, but it does have to be cooked with care to get the best from it.

Lambs' liver has a more delicate flavour than pigs' liver and has to be eaten very fresh, so it's not always easy to get hold of. Butchers tend to pre-slice livers, but I buy them whole so I can slice them to whatever thickness I want before cooking. This recipe is best with the liver sliced very thinly indeed. Serve with plenty of mashed potato (page 322).

Serves 4
500g lambs' liver
20g unsalted butter
1 tablespoon olive oil
2 tablespoons wine vinegar or cider vinegar
A generous tablespoon of finely
*   chopped flat-leaf parsley*
Salt and freshly ground black pepper

Remove any gristly bits from the liver, then cut into thin slices about 8mm thick. Season with salt and pepper.

Heat the butter and olive oil in a frying pan over a high heat until it's very hot, and flash fry the liver for 1 minute per side. It should be browned on the outside but still pink and creamy in the middle. Transfer the slices of liver to 4 warmed plates.

Add the vinegar to the pan, let it bubble for a minute, then pour the sauce over the liver. Sprinkle with chopped parsley and serve immediately with the mashed potato.

Roast brace of pheasant

Pheasants are in season from 1 October to 1 February, and you often see them hanging outside good butchers' shops in a Dickensian display. Sold as a brace, that is to say a cock and a hen side by side, they are easy to prepare, as the butcher will dress them ready for roasting.

Sometimes we are given pheasants from a local shoot and, after a few days' hanging, I pluck, draw and truss them myself, although they never look as appetising as the ones I buy. It takes me ages and there are feathers everywhere. It doesn't, however, dampen my love for them, as they make a grand feast served with fried breadcrumbs, bread sauce (page 176) and game chips (page 325).

Serves 4
2 pheasants
50g unsalted butter
2 sprigs of thyme
1 small onion, finely chopped
6 slices of streaky bacon
4 bay leaves
Salt and freshly ground black pepper

For the fried breadcrumbs:
75g unsalted butter
75g fresh white breadcrumbs, made from thick slices of bread, crusts removed and pulsed in a food processor into coarse crumbs

Preheat the oven to 180°C/Gas Mark 4.

Rub the pheasants all over with the butter, then put some thyme and chopped onion in the cavity of each bird. Season with salt and pepper and cover the breasts of the birds with slices of bacon. Place the pheasants breast-side down in a roasting tin, tuck the bay leaves under them and place in the oven.

After 50 minutes, turn the pheasants breast-side up to let them brown. This should take a further 10 minutes. Make sure that the birds are cooked by tipping up one of them and checking that the juices run clear. Transfer the birds to a warm plate and let them rest for 20 minutes before carving.

While the birds are resting, make a simple gravy by loosening the juices in the pan with a splash of hot water and scraping all the delicious bits into a small saucepan. Taste for seasoning, bring to a simmer, then strain the gravy into a warmed jug just before serving.

To make the fried breadcrumbs, melt the butter in a frying pan over a medium-high heat until it foams. Tip in the fresh breadcrumbs and fry for a few minutes until they are crisp. Keep stirring to prevent them from burning. Serve the fried breadcrumbs piping hot in a little pile next to slices of pheasant on each plate.

Roast goose

One of our most memorable Christmas dinners was when the children were very small and we were coming to the end of a particularly difficult year. We had no work and little money, but we managed to raise enough to buy a small goose from a neighbouring farm. Stuffed with windfall apples from the orchard and accompanied by a cabbage and potatoes roasted in the goose fat, it was delicious and we enjoyed every mouthful. We drank a bottle of local cider and felt happy with our lot. Since then, we have fared better, but no Christmas dinner has ever improved on that one for all its utter simplicity.

While the apples work very well with goose, sage and chopped onions also make a good, simple stuffing if you prefer.

Don't discard the goose's liver. Fry it separately in butter with some apple quarters and, when cooked, remove them and deglaze the pan with a splash of brandy. Season and serve on toast as a savoury.

Serves 6
1 x 4.5kg goose
4–6 apples, peeled, quartered and cored
Salt and freshly ground black pepper

For the gravy:
450ml good chicken stock (page 58)
150ml cider
1 tablespoon quince jelly (page 185) or
  other fruit jelly

Preheat the oven to 200°C/Gas Mark 6.

Prick the fatty parts of the goose and rub the skin with salt. Season the cavity with salt and pepper and loosely stuff it with the apples.

Weigh the goose and calculate the cooking time: 30 minutes per 500g. Place the bird on a rack over a roasting tin and put it in the oven for the required time, but keep an eye on it as the fat may have to be tipped out of the roasting tin during cooking if it gets too full. You can use the fat for roast potatoes (page 326).

When it's cooked, take it out of the oven and let it rest for 30 minutes.

While the bird is resting, make the gravy. Skim the fat from the juices and combine them with the stock in a saucepan. Add the cider and a spoonful of quince jelly and simmer for a few minutes to reduce it. Taste, add salt and pepper if necessary, and strain into a warmed jug. Carve the goose into slices and serve with the apple stuffing and gravy.

Coq au vin

When I was eighteen I spent the summer on an archaeological dig in Burgundy, looking for the camp of Augustus's 8th Legion in some fields near Dijon.

We started the excavations early in the morning after a breakfast of fresh bread and milky coffee. At 11.45 a.m. we put down our pick-axes and walked through the village back to our camp. A barn was used for meals, and we sat on benches at trestle tables, waiting to be served our midday lunch. What a feast it was – four courses cooked by a motherly Burgundian in a flowery pinafore.

First came soup or pâté followed by meat or poultry steaming aromatically with garlic and herbs. Then jewel-like fruit tarts, salad and cheeses. There were bottles of the local wine to drink. We had a little rest before returning to work on the excavations until early evening.

After washing off the dust of the day we sat down again, this time to a dinner of five courses cooked on a basic stove. There were about thirty of us, students and academics, privileged to have our food prepared by such a wonderful cook. I returned home a little plumper but so

fortunate to have eaten such memorable French regional dishes.

This coq au vin is my version of one of those courses. It is a useful dish as it can be made in advance and reheated, tasting the better for it. One year we let a broody hen sit on her eggs until they hatched, which resulted in too many cockerels. This is how seventeen of them ended up.

Serves 4–6
1 x 1.8kg chicken (traditionally a cockerel), jointed into 6 pieces
3–4 tablespoons plain flour
50g unsalted butter
1 tablespoon olive oil
100g streaky bacon, cut into thin strips
250g shallots or small onions, peeled and left whole
2–3 garlic cloves
3 bay leaves
4 sprigs of thyme
500ml red wine
300g button mushrooms
A small handful of parsley, finely chopped
Salt and freshly ground black pepper

Dust the chicken pieces with the flour, shaking off any excess. Heat half the butter and the oil in a large, heavy-based saucepan or casserole – a cast-iron one is perfect – and cook the chicken pieces until golden all over. You might need to do this in batches.

Transfer the chicken to a plate and set aside. Add the bacon to the pan and fry until crisp. Add the shallots or onions and stir them around until they're a rich golden brown, then add the garlic and herbs. Place the chicken back in the pan. Pour over the wine, season well and bring to a simmer. This can be done on the hob over a low heat, or in the oven at 180°C/Gas Mark 4.

While the coq au vin is bubbling away, melt the rest of the butter and sauté the mushrooms until they are softened and lightly coloured. Add them to the stew for the last 10 minutes of the cooking time.

It's not possible to give exact cooking times as it depends on the size and age of the chicken, but it should take about an hour. Check to see how tender the pieces of chicken are before serving. The dish will also improve if cooled down, then refrigerated and reheated the next day.

Sprinkle with parsley and serve with boiled potatoes and, if you're in a celebratory mood, a glass of good Burgundy.

Chicken and leek pie

A homemade pie is always very special, and this one is no exception. As with any dish, the quality of the ingredients defines it, so buy the very best free-range, organic roasting bird you can find. Next time you're roasting a chicken, think about roasting two: one to enjoy straight away and another to transform into this pie the next day – it saves time and fuel.

Serves 6
1 x 2kg chicken, roasted (page 156) and
    cooled, with the cooking juices retained
250ml double cream
250ml whole milk
50g unsalted butter
1 onion, finely sliced
6 leeks, trimmed, white and pale green
    parts only, finely sliced
2 tablespoons plain flour
2 bay leaves
A pinch of freshly grated nutmeg
Salt and freshly ground black pepper
1 egg, beaten

For the shortcrust pastry:
500g plain flour
A pinch of salt
250g unsalted butter, chilled and
    cut into small cubes
1 egg, beaten

First make the pastry. Sift the flour into a bowl with the salt. Add the butter and rub it into the flour with your fingers until the mixture resembles coarse breadcrumbs. Alternatively, you can pulse to blend in a food processor.

Form the dough by adding the beaten egg and up to 100ml cold water – just enough to bind the flour mixture. Work gently into a ball, wrap in cling film and refrigerate for at least 30 minutes, or while you make and cool the filling.

Preheat the oven to 170°C/Gas Mark 3 and butter a pie dish. I use an oval dish, approximately 30 x 20cm.

Strip the meat off the chicken and cut it into large pieces. Keep the carcass and bones to make stock later (page 58).

Pour the cooking juices from the chicken into a saucepan and add the cream and milk (you might not need them all if there are lots of juices). Heat them all up together.

In a separate large saucepan, melt the butter over a medium-low heat and sweat the onion for 5 minutes, then add the leeks and cook gently for a few more minutes until they soften. Sprinkle over the flour and stir for a couple of minutes. Pour the warmed cream and juices a ladleful at a time over the onions and leeks, then simmer, stirring continuously, until you have a thickened sauce. Add the chicken pieces and bay leaves to the sauce, season, add a few gratings of nutmeg and mix together. Set aside to cool.

Remove the pastry from the fridge and divide it in two. Flour a work surface and a rolling pin, then roll out the first half thinly and use it to line the pie dish. Allow the pastry to hang loosely over the sides and be careful not to stretch it to fit or it will be tough. Fill the pie with the cooled chicken mixture. Brush some of the beaten egg around the edge of the pie.

Roll out the second half of the pastry, cover the pie with it, then trim off the excess with a sharp knife and crimp the edges together. Cut 3 small slashes in the top to let out the steam. Brush the pastry lid with the remaining beaten egg and place on a baking sheet in the oven for 40 minutes until the filling is bubbling and the pastry is golden brown.

VEGETABLES

We grow a lot of vegetables. It is a fallible, slightly random and constantly changing process. Nevertheless, our kitchen revolves around it.

The main purpose is to give us a supply of fresh, seasonal vegetables as and when we want them. Our primary concern is taste, followed by considerations of seasonality, ease of growth and suitability to our particular conditions. Some things – lettuce, tomatoes, rocket, carrots, potatoes, onions, beetroot, beans, courgettes, cabbage, chard – are essentials. Some – chillies, pumpkins, peas, sweetcorn, melons – are a bit variable in performance. But whatever we grow I try to ensure we have in sufficient quantity so that we can use it with freedom and generosity. There is usually something we can harvest that will either add an important element to a dish or upon which an entire meal can be based, whether it is parsley to make all the difference to a chicken or spaghetti carbonara, or a cauliflower to become cauliflower cheese.

By far and away the best aspect of having a well-stocked garden a few yards from the kitchen door is what Sarah calls 'marketing'. She loves to wander round the garden with a basket and choose her vegetables based upon what looks, feels and smells good at that moment, just as one might in a French or Italian market. Having selected the best vegetables that the garden can offer on that day, then and only then does she think about what to do with them. In other words, the ingredients are driving the choice of dish rather than the dish dictating the choice of ingredients.

Buttered spinach

As a child we ate a lot of spinach but it was always served simply boiled, whereas the secret to really good spinach lies in the addition of lots of butter and nutmeg, which transform this rather puritanical vegetable into something deliciously rich and creamy. This goes wonderfully well with any meat dish and is also excellent served with poached eggs on top.

Serves 4
1kg spinach
80–100g unsalted butter
Freshly grated nutmeg
Salt and freshly ground black pepper

Wash the spinach, removing any very large, tough stalks. Drain roughly and immediately place in a large saucepan with no extra water. The liquid still clinging to the leaves will be enough to cook the spinach. Place over a medium heat, stirring once or twice as it reduces – which it will do very dramatically. Cook until all the leaves have wilted, about 2–3 minutes.

Drain the spinach, putting a plate over the colander and compressing it to remove as much liquid as possible. Set aside.

Meanwhile, melt the butter in the pan. Spinach will absorb almost any amount of butter, so the quantity you use is a matter of personal taste, but I allow a walnut-sized knob per person. Mix in the spinach and heat gently, stirring well, grating a generous amount of nutmeg over it. The idea is not to fry the spinach, but simply to let it absorb the butter. Season well. When the spinach is cooked, you can put it to one side for a while until it's needed and then reheat it with a little more butter. Serve very hot.

Spinach frittata

A frittata is a type of omelette enriched with cheese and sometimes cream. This is not an exact recipe and you can successfully use a wide variety of herbs, such as parsley, chives, dill or basil, or leaves such as spinach, sorrel or wild garlic in spring, in any balanced combination and according to the season. Blanched asparagus sprues, sold off in great bunches as they're too thin for expensive restaurants, are delicious in frittatas.

For cooking this I use a large, cast-iron frying pan I bought in a Chinese food shop for £7. It's perfect for making frittatas, as it has a metal handle, which means it can go in the oven or under the grill, though I do have to remember to grab a thick oven cloth to hold it with.

Serves 4–6
750g young spinach or other greens,
roughly chopped
6 large eggs
2 tablespoons double cream
150g strong, hard cheese, such as
good Cheddar or Parmesan, grated
4–6 tablespoons olive oil
Salt and freshly ground black pepper

Preheat the oven to 200°C/Gas Mark 6, or heat up the grill.

If you are using tough greens, such as chard, you will need to blanch them first in boiling water for 4–5 minutes. Drain them well in a colander, refresh under the cold tap, then squeeze out the excess moisture before chopping them roughly. Tender greens, such as young spinach, can be used raw, roughly chopped.

In a large bowl, mix together the eggs, cream and cheese. Season, but go steady on the salt as the cheese is already quite salty.

Heat the oil in a metal-handled frying pan, approximately 20cm diameter, over a medium heat.

Add the greens to the egg mixture and stir them together before pouring it all into the hot pan. It will set on the bottom after 5–7 minutes. Finish the cooking by placing the pan in the oven or under the grill until the top is puffed up and golden, about 5 minutes. Be careful to use an oven glove to remove it from the oven or grill.

Cut into wedges and serve straight away, with a salad or some chutney.

Leeks vinaigrette

This is a simple, economical, but really good dish that's best in winter and early spring when leeks are plentiful. Choose thin, equal-sized leeks rather than the very thick ones. The dish is good in its own right as a starter, or served as a side course as part of a more substantial meal.

Serves 4

8 leeks, about 3–4cm diameter, trimmed
and thoroughly washed, white and a
little of the pale green part only

For the dressing:
3 tablespoons extra virgin olive oil
1 tablespoon white wine vinegar
2 teaspoons Dijon mustard
A pinch of sugar
Salt and freshly ground black pepper
2 tablespoons finely chopped flat-leaf
parsley

Poach the whole leeks by placing them horizontally in a shallow pan, covering them with water, bringing to the boil and simmering, partially covered, for about 10 minutes, until soft enough to pierce easily with a knife.

Make the dressing by whisking the oil, vinegar and mustard together until thick. Season to taste with the sugar, salt and pepper.

Drain the leeks well as they will be very watery. Lay them on a warm serving dish and pour over the dressing while they are still hot.

Sprinkle over the chopped parsley and serve warm or cold.

Baked onions

Glazed carrots

Onions are the cornerstone of many savoury recipes. This one pares them down to their essence and, despite the simplicity of the process, the result is as delicious as any complicated dish. They look primitively beautiful as they come out of the oven. The onion flesh tastes sweet and meltingly soft, and needs nothing more than a little butter and seasoning.

Serve them on their own as a first course, or as a side dish with a roast.

Serves 4
4 medium onions
60g unsalted butter
Salt and freshly ground black pepper

Preheat the oven to 220°C/Gas Mark 7.

Trim the tops off the onions and cut the bases level so they will sit steady. Leave the skins intact. Place them in a baking dish and bake for about 1 hour, until tender when pierced with the blade of a thin, sharp knife.

Cut the tops open and peel back the skin to reveal the silky flesh within. Add a knob of butter, salt and pepper and serve immediately.

Lovely orange carrots cheer up any plate, especially in winter. They can be a bit boring if simply boiled, but this way of cooking them brings out their sweetness and colour. It's worth using the freshest, organic carrots and avoiding the flabby or prewashed bagged ones as those have little flavour and a mass of pesticide residues.

Finely chopped parsley is usually added at the end of cooking, but in season we often use a generous sprinkling of mint instead. These carrots are particularly good with roast chicken (page 156).

Serves 4
500g carrots
50g unsalted butter
A pinch of salt
A large pinch of caster sugar
1 heaped tablespoon of very finely
  chopped parsley or mint

Peel the carrots and slice them diagonally into 2cm pieces. Place them in a pan with just enough water to cover them, add the butter, salt and sugar, and bring gently to the boil. Carefully stir everything together and simmer until the carrots are cooked and the liquid has reduced just enough to coat them, about 12 minutes.

Sprinkle on the parsley or mint and serve immediately.

Baked Florence fennel with Parmesan cheese

We usually eat Florence fennel raw (page 127). Finely sliced and simply dressed with salt, pepper and olive oil, it is deliciously crisp and fresh. The green fronds can be saved to cook with fish. In this recipe, however, the fennel bulbs are baked, which transforms them into a succulent savoury dish, ideal for a cold autumn night.

Serves 4
2 large Florence fennel bulbs
4 tablespoons double cream
50g Parmesan cheese, freshly grated
Freshly ground black pepper

Preheat the oven to 220°C/Gas Mark 7, or heat the grill until very hot.

Cut the feathery tops from each bulb, trim the bases and remove any tough outer layers, then cut each bulb into quarters. Bring a pan of water to the boil and simmer the bulbs until tender but not disintegrating, about 20 minutes.

Drain well and place the fennel in a shallow baking dish. Pour over the cream, season generously with pepper and sprinkle with a good layer of Parmesan. Bake in the oven or place under the grill for 10–15 minutes, until the Parmesan is browned.

Serve very hot, although this is a dish that Montagu also loves to eat cold the next day.

Celeriac purée

We usually make this purée at Christmas time, but we enjoy it right through the winter until early spring, serving it with roasted meats.

Celeriac is a useful vegetable, delicate and filling. It's good cooked with equal parts of potato and mashed with lots of butter and a couple of spoonfuls of cream. It can also be eaten raw, grated and dressed in a classic rémoulade sauce. If there's any purée left over – which there usually isn't, as it is very more-ish – you can make a lovely soup simply by thinning it with some stock.

Don't waste the peelings. Spread them out in a dry place or thread them and hang them up to dry as the French do. You can make your own celery salt by finely chopping a few dry peelings with some sea salt in a food processor. Celery salt is good in a bloody Mary or added to soups.

Serves 6–8
2–3 celeriac, about 1.5kg peeled weight
Juice of ½ a lemon
50g unsalted butter
Salt and freshly ground black pepper

Scrub the celeriac well to remove any soil. Cut off the leafy tops and peel them carefully with a knife, removing the skin and little roots. Cut them into 3cm chunks. To stop the celeriac oxidising, put the chunks into a bowl of water acidulated with the lemon juice until you are ready to cook them.

Put the celeriac in a saucepan with enough cold water to cover and add a little salt. Bring to the boil and simmer until soft, about 20 minutes. Drain and retain the cooking water.

Blend in a food processor or mash by hand, adding a little of the cooking water to make a light, smooth purée.

Return it to the pan, stirring in the butter and seasoning with a little salt and lots of freshly ground black pepper. Serve immediately.

Braised red cabbage

We make a big pot of braised red cabbage just before Christmas as its flavour improves after a couple of days, in time for Christmas lunch. This is a beautiful dish to prepare as the sliced cabbage, apples and onion look like a still life piled up on the chopping board.

One of the reasons I like this dish so much is because, as it simmers slowly on top of the cooker in an enamelled cast-iron pot, the house is filled with the sharp aroma of vinegar and spices. It is first served with the Christmas meal, then – hot or cold – into the New Year until it is finished. It is good with cold ham (page 294) and in sandwiches made from leftovers. It is also excellent with any wintry rich food, such as game and roast pork (page 162).

Serves 6–8

1 red cabbage
30g unsalted butter
1 large onion, finely chopped
2 dessert apples, peeled, cored and
  roughly chopped
170ml red wine
4 tablespoons red wine vinegar
3 tablespoons light muscovado sugar
5 juniper berries, crushed
3 bay leaves
1 stick of cinnamon
A good pinch of freshly grated nutmeg
Salt and freshly ground black pepper

Remove any tough or damaged outer leaves from the cabbage, then cut it into quarters, removing the hard core. Slice the cabbage as thinly as possible, no more than 5mm thick.

In a large saucepan over a medium-low heat, melt the butter and sauté the onion until soft, about 10 minutes. Tip the cabbage and apples into the pan, along with the wine, vinegar, sugar, juniper berries, bay leaves, cinnamon and nutmeg. Season with salt and pepper and stir.

Cover the top of the cabbage with a circle of greaseproof paper cut to fit and put a tight-fitting lid on the pan so that as little moisture as possible escapes. Simmer on a very low heat for a couple of hours, occasionally checking that it hasn't dried out. If it is a little dry, add some water. Towards the end of the cooking time, check for seasoning and adjust it as you wish.

If you prefer, the cabbage can be cooked in a moderate oven, 170°C/Gas Mark 3, for about 2 hours, but cooking it on top of the stove makes it easier to keep an eye on.

Mashed swede

I am always surprised when someone says they hate swede as it is one of our favourite vegetables – and the children have always loved it. I buy swedes from a neighbouring farmer who puts up a hand-painted sign advertising his crop by the side of the road every year. Irresistible. The pale, yellowy-orange flesh has an unusually earthy taste and, once cooked, reheats well. When buying swede, look for smallish roots, as anything heavier than 2kg will be coarse and fit only for animals.

Swede is cubed and cooked inside Cornish pasties, and served with haggis in Scotland, simply boiled and mashed with lots of butter, salt and pepper. A splash of double cream improves it even more. We like it with sausages and roasts.

Serves 4–6
*1 swede, about 1–2kg, peeled and cut into
    equal-sized chunks*
A good knob of unsalted butter
1–2 tablespoons double cream
Salt and freshly ground black pepper

Put the prepared swede in a saucepan with enough water to cover, bring to the boil and cook until soft, about 15–20 minutes.

Drain through a colander and leave to steam for a couple of minutes, then mash with a large knob of a butter and the cream. Season with salt and plenty of pepper.

Winter vegetables

I love roasted root vegetables. They're so simple to make, and roasting keeps their full flavours locked into the flesh.

The easiest way to prepare them is to cut them up roughly, spread them on a baking tray, splosh some olive oil over them and pop them into a hot oven for 30–60 minutes, depending on their size. But this can become a little predictable after a while, and when it does I use this slightly more adventurous cooking method.

I think cooking the vegetables in parchment parcels intensifies the flavours even more than simply roasting them, and it somehow keeps all the individual tastes separate. The buttery juices and herbs are all sealed in and the whole thing becomes a treat. The ingredients are infinitely variable – I hope you will try your own mixtures, perhaps including bay leaves or other favourite herbs. The parcels are delicious on their own or with sausages.

Preheat the oven to 200°C/Gas Mark 6.

Cut some baking parchment into 40cm squares – they need to be large enough wrap around a pile of vegetables – one square for each serving. Arrange a mound of prepared vegetables in the centre of a parchment square and add a sprig of thyme and the lemon zest. Season well and place a generous knob of butter on the top.

Gather up the corners of the paper, twist the top to seal everything in and tie it with a piece of cotton string. Place in a roasting tin large enough to take as many parcels as you are making without crowding. They need room to puff up a bit as they cook.

Place them in the oven for 30 minutes. Don't worry if the edges of the parchment char as this improves the flavour. Cut them open and serve each parcel individually, tipping them out onto warmed plates.

For each parcel:
1 medium potato, cut into 3cm cubes
*1 wedge of pumpkin or squash, peeled and
    cut into 3cm cubes*
2 small carrots, quartered lengthways
2 small parsnips, quartered lengthways
¼ of a medium-sized red onion, halved
1 sprig lemon thyme
Finely grated zest of ½ a lemon
Salt and freshly ground black pepper
A large knob of butter

Roast parsnips

Crisp roast parsnips are synonymous with roasted meat and Christmas dinner. Their unique, sweet earthiness is an important part of any old-fashioned Sunday lunch in winter. They are an ancient root vegetable, considered a food for the poor in the past, but they are fit for a king if made into soups or mash, or – best of all – roasted. Buy the firmest roots you can, avoiding any flabby specimens.

Serves 6
1.3kg parsnips, trimmed and peeled
3–4 tablespoons sunflower oil
Salt and freshly ground black pepper

Preheat the oven to 220°C/Gas Mark 7.

If the parsnips are small, leave them whole, but quarter larger ones lengthways. As parsnips get older and bigger – and some can be enormous – they develop a woody core, so remove this when you quarter them. Aim to end up with pieces of more or less the same size.

Put them into a saucepan with enough cold water to cover, bring to the boil and parboil them for about 5 minutes. Don't let them get too soft.

Drain the parsnips well and transfer them to a roasting tin. Add the oil and season with salt and pepper. Shake them around in the tin so that all the parsnips are coated in the oil and seasoning. Place in the oven and roast for about 30 minutes.

Check after 15 minutes and turn them over if they are starting to brown.

Serve as soon as possible, when they are hot and crisp.

Minted new
potatoes

Nothing compares to the flavour of freshly dug new potatoes straight from the garden. I refuse to buy air-freighted new potatoes early in the season, coated in imported peat in a phoney attempt to make them look earthy and fresh. It is worth waiting for the real thing.

Here on the Welsh border, we expect to make our first harvest of first earlies, such as Swift or Red Duke of York, in the first week of July, and to continue harvesting them for another six weeks before the second earlies, such as Charlotte, take over. To taste them at their very best, cook them as soon as they are dug from the garden.

Serves 4
1kg new potatoes
Sprigs of apple mint or other mint
Unsalted butter
Flaky sea salt

Gently scrub the potatoes to remove any dirt, but leave their skins on. Bring a pan of water to the boil and add the potatoes. Simmer them for 10–15 minutes, testing whether they are cooked through with the point of a sharp, thin knife.

Drain in a colander, add the mint sprigs, cover with a clean tea towel and leave for a few minutes so the mint flavour is absorbed. Toss in a generous knob of butter and serve sprinkled with sea salt.

Baked potatoes

It might seem a bit of a cheek giving a recipe for baked potatoes, but we had to include them as they are such an important winter food for us. We can't grow main crop potatoes organically in the garden here, as there is a tendency for the whole crop to be affected with blight by late summer. We enjoy our own new potatoes in summer, but in winter I buy a sack of large, floury potatoes from a local farm. They are incredibly cheap, costing only a few pounds, and last for ages stored in a cool, dark place.

We don't do anything fancy to them, just bake them in the oven. Eaten with cold meats and chutney, they are a perfect combination. I secretly like them best straight out of the oven, split open with lots of butter and salt and pepper. The children prefer them with cheese and beans. Anything with tomatoes, or even ratatouille, alongside them is also delicious. They make for a good single, solitary meal, or dinner for fifty. They are certainly an easy way to cater for a lot of people.

Serves 6
6 large, thick-skinned baking potatoes
*   of roughly equal size*
2–3 tablespoons olive oil
Flaky sea salt
Butter
Freshly ground black pepper

Preheat the oven to 200°C/Gas Mark 6.

Scrub the potatoes to remove any dirt, then coat them in oil – this will result in a crisper skin. The easiest way to do this is to pour some oil into the palm of your hand and rub it all over them. Alternatively, place them in a roasting tin, making sure they do not touch, then trickle a little oil over each one.

Cut two diagonal slashes in the top of each potato, forming a cross, then sprinkle with sea salt. Put them into the oven and bake for 1–1½ hours. They are ready when soft all the way through.

The potatoes are best eaten straight out of the oven, as they start to shrivel and loose their crisp outside if kept warm for too long. Serve with plenty of butter, some more salt and freshly ground black pepper.

Potato gratin

This recipe transforms the ordinary potato into a rich and comforting dish. It can be eaten on its own with a green salad, or as an accompaniment to roast chicken (page 156) or a roast leg of lamb (page 161).

Potato gratin is one of those simple dishes that everyone likes, and it looks very appetising with its golden crust bubbling away over the creamy potatoes as it is served. It does take a little more preparation than, say, mashed potatoes, but if the rest of the meal is straight-forward and easy, and all I have to do is wash and dress some salad or roast some meat, it is definitely worth it.

Serves 6
1kg potatoes, such as Desirée
* or King Edward*
500ml double cream
100ml milk
2 garlic cloves, peeled
Freshly grated nutmeg
Knob of butter, for greasing
300g good, strong Cheddar cheese, grated
Salt and freshly ground black pepper

Preheat the oven to 170°C/Gas Mark 3.

Peel the potatoes and slice them as thinly as you can, ideally about 3mm thick.

Pour the cream and milk into a large saucepan, add the garlic and a few gratings of nutmeg and warm over a gentle heat until bubbles begin to appear around the edge of the pan. Put the potatoes into the pan, season and stir gently so the slices remain intact. Simmer for 5 minutes, until they start to soften.

Butter a large, ovenproof dish, about 30 x 25 x 5cm, and arrange a layer of potatoes over the bottom of it. Reserve a third of the cheese for the top of the gratin, then scatter some of the rest over the first layer of potatoes. Continue layering potatoes and cheese until you have used them both up, ending with a layer of potatoes. Pour over any remaining cream and sprinkle the reserved cheese over the top.

Bake for about 1 hour, or longer if the dish is deep. Keep an eye on it to ensure the oven isn't becoming too hot, as the cream will split and become greasy.

Mashed potato

The secret of perfect mash is to use a floury variety of potato such as Romano, which makes a particularly creamy mash, King Edward, Wilja or Maris Piper, and plenty of butter. It should have a smooth, almost whipped texture, and definitely no lumps.

It takes a bit of effort but the result is so good that it's worth making properly. Never be tempted to use a food processor as it will reduce the potatoes to wallpaper paste. Some people recommend using a potato ricer, but to me that is just another gadget gathering dust in the kitchen drawer. I always use a simple, old-fashioned masher.

Soothing and easily digestible, mashed potato is best as a contrast to strong-textured meats, and to mop up delicious gravy. Or just enjoy a little bowl of it on its own.

Serves 4
1kg floury potatoes, such as Romano,
* King Edward, Wilja or Maris Piper,*
* peeled and cut into equal-sized pieces*
50g unsalted butter, plus more to taste
200ml whole milk
Salt and freshly ground black pepper

Put the potatoes in a pan, cover with cold water and bring to the boil. Cook them on a gentle boil as anything more vigorous will make them break up. When you can slide a knife or skewer through them easily, remove from the heat, drain in a colander and leave to steam for a couple of minutes.

Put the pan back on the stove, add the butter and milk and heat until the butter has melted. Return the potatoes to the pan and break them up with the masher, gently at first so that they absorb the butter and milk, then increasingly vigorously until they have a smooth texture, adding more butter if necessary.

Salt to taste but offer the freshly ground black pepper separately. Serve immediately.

Potato cakes

Potato cakes are a favourite way of using up leftover mashed potato (page 322), but they're certainly worth making from scratch. If you're boiling potatoes, cook double the amount so you have some left to make these little savoury cakes.

They are good fried with bacon for breakfast, or flavoured with chives or thyme to serve with roast game. I like them the Irish way, split and spread with butter.

Makes 16
*450g floury, cooked potatoes, mashed
   and cooled*
50g plain flour, plus more for dusting
25g butter, softened, plus more for frying
1 egg, lightly beaten
Salt

Put the mashed potato, flour, butter and egg into a bowl, season with salt and mix together to form a dough. Divide the dough into 2 balls.

Lightly flour a work surface and rolling pin, then roll each ball into a circle about 1.5–2cm thick. Cut each circle into 8 wedges.

Warm a generous knob of butter over a medium-high heat and fry the potato cakes in batches, for 3 minutes on each side, until golden. Eat them while they are hot.

Game chips

Alternative chips

These are really homemade crisps, but properly called chips because they are fried in batches. They are a traditional accompaniment to roast pheasant (page 298). One large potato makes a generous amount for four, which just goes to show the profit in the average packet of crisps. Fry them just before the meal is served so that they are as hot as possible.

Serves 4–8
1–2 potatoes, Desirée or King Edward
Sunflower oil for frying
Flaky sea salt

Peel the potatoes and slice them as finely as possible in a food processor or with a potato peeler or mandolin. Soak the slices in cold water for a few minutes to remove the starch. Dry thoroughly on a clean tea towel.

Heat the oil in a deep-fat fryer or in a large, deep, heavy-based pan (ensure the oil doesn't come more than a third of the way up the pan) until it's hot enough for a cube of white bread to turn golden in about a minute. Fry the potato slices in batches until they float to the surface. Remove with a slotted spoon. Drain on kitchen paper.

Bring the oil up to temperature again, and refry the chips in batches until golden brown. Drain on kitchen paper and keep them warm in a low oven, uncovered, until they are all ready. Season with a little salt just before serving hot with roast game.

The best chips I have ever eaten were from the traditional fish and chip shop at the Black Country Museum. They were deep-fried in dripping, and on a cold December day, the hot chips with salt and vinegar were perfection.

I seldom cook conventional chips at home because the deep-fryer makes a mess and it takes so much oil to make a serving of chips that, unless you use the fryer regularly, it's not worth it. Instead, I have a simpler method, which uses far less fat and produces very good chips, even if not quite in Black Country class.

Serves 4
4 medium potatoes, unpeeled
4–6 tablespoons olive oil
Salt and freshly ground black pepper

Preheat the oven to 200°C/Gas Mark 6.

Cut the potatoes lengthways into wedge-shaped chips – you should be able to get six wedges from each potato. Put them in a bowl and trickle over the olive oil, stirring until each wedge is coated. Season well with salt and pepper, spread out on a roasting tray (don't crowd them; if necessary use 2 trays) and roast for at least 30 minutes, turning halfway through, until crisp on the outside and soft in the middle. Sprinkle with salt if desired and serve immediately.

Roast potatoes

Perfect roast potatoes are a fine thing. You would think that it should be impossible to cook them badly, yet they so often are. At their best, they are crisp and golden on the outside, puffy and light on the inside.

The choice of potato is important. Choose a floury variety, such as Maris Piper, King Edward or Desirée. A very hot oven is also essential, and the potatoes should be parboiled before roasting in the hot oil or fat for a surprisingly long time.

Goose fat produces fantastic crisp potatoes, or you can use ordinary olive oil (not extra virgin, as it burns at high temperatures and would be a waste) or sunflower oil.

Serves 6
2kg floury, medium-sized potatoes, peeled
    and quartered into even-sized pieces
4–6 tablespoons goose fat, olive oil or
    sunflower oil
Sea salt

Preheat the oven to 200°C/Gas Mark 6.

Put the potatoes into a saucepan and cover them with cold water. Bring to the boil and cook them for 5 minutes. Drain well in a colander, leave to steam for a few minutes, then return to the pan and shake to rough up the surface of each potato.

While the potatoes are parboiling, heat the fat or oil in a roasting tin in the oven for 5 minutes. Remove the roasting tin from the oven and add the parboiled potatoes, rolling them around to coat them in the fat or oil. Return to the oven and roast for at least 45 minutes, turning them occasionally, until they are crisp and golden brown.

Take them out of the oven, transfer to a warmed dish using a slotted spoon and sprinkle with sea salt. Serve immediately.

Herb butters

Herbs are magical ingredients that can make the simplest foods into aromatic, enticing dishes. Think of the heavenly marriages of tarragon and chicken or rosemary and lamb. Herb butters are a brilliant way of encapsulating their depth of flavour. A little round pat of herb-flavoured butter, melting on new potatoes or grilled meat, is certainly an appetising sight.

Most soft herbs work well, and I have even used watercress. Although not actually a herb, it makes a bright green, peppery butter that is delicious with fish. If you decide to use watercress, double the herb quantity suggested here as its flavour is not as intense as a herb. I like to experiment with different combinations, but bright green herbs that don't bruise easily are best.

Makes about 140g
*3 tablespoons finely chopped herbs, such
    as French tarragon, flat-leaf parsley,
    chervil or chives*
125g unsalted butter, at room temperature
A squeeze of lemon juice

Tip the finely chopped herbs into a bowl, add the butter and mash together with a fork. It takes a bit of work and can be done much more quickly in a food processor, but when I'm making a fairly small amount I prefer to do it by hand.

Form the herb butter into a roll then wrap it in cling film or greaseproof paper and chill in the fridge for an hour before serving, cut into slices.

Herb butters keep well in the fridge for a few days. They freeze wonderfully too, so it's a good idea to make some in the summer when you have an abundance of herbs. Use within 2 months.

SUPPER

Supper is a lighter, and often later, meal than dinner. It carries an air of informality. We treat its timing in a cavalier manner. Here at Ivington we often don't eat till well after nine in summer, staying outside for as long as possible, whereas in winter we tend to eat much earlier. Flexibility is built into the very idea of supper.

In the light of this, supper dishes are usually quick and easy to prepare. Inevitably, certain standbys are returned to again and again. Pasta with a sauce has been the mainstay for years. A glut of tomatoes and basil can be made into sauce and frozen, which in turn can be thawed and heated up in the time it takes for the pasta to boil. Having fresh eggs and salad crops growing outside round the year means that an omelette and salad can be put together in the same time that you could dial for a pizza. Risottos and simple cuts of meat, such as chops or spatchcocked chickens, all fit the bill.

A great virtue of supper is that it can usually be enjoyed with a glass or two of wine, which is rarely the case with lunch. For most of us, supper is the one time of day when you can wholly relax over a meal and enjoy it unconditionally.

Baked eggs

From Easter onwards, our hens start to lay prolifically, and their eggs are the perfect fast food. I love the simplicity of baked eggs. They are a soothing dish, ready in minutes, and delicious eaten at any time of day. They make an excellent, quick supper as they cook virtually in the time it takes to toast the bread – especially if, as we do, you have a stove that runs constantly, meaning that there is no need to preheat the oven. You can make baked eggs for just one, or to feed the whole family. It's important to use the freshest eggs, organic preferably, and good bread.

Serves 2
Unsalted butter, for greasing
  and spreading
4 eggs
2 tablespoons Jersey cream or
  other good double cream
2 large slices of bread
Salt and freshly ground black pepper

Preheat the oven to 200°C/Gas Mark 6.

Generously butter the insides of 2 large ramekins and break 2 eggs into each one. Pour over the cream, place on a baking sheet and put in the oven for 8–10 minutes. When the egg whites are set but the yolks still runny and the cream brown and bubbling, take them out of the oven and season with salt and pepper.

While the eggs are cooking, toast the bread, butter it and cut it into soldiers. Dip the soldiers into the eggs yolks and eat the rest with a teaspoon.

Herb omelette

If I had to choose a single group of plants to grow in a garden, it would have to be herbs. I use them in almost everything we eat. My favourite cooking herbs are lemon thyme, bay, sage and rosemary, but when other herbs are abundant I use them too in generous quantities. I mix them into salads, strew them over roast vegetables and stir them into sauces.

In summer I try to spend less and less time in the kitchen, escaping to the garden for hours on end, so food has to be simple and quick. A favourite meal is a herb omelette, often cooked just as it is getting dark, as we work outside until we can't see what we're doing. Every moment is precious. It might seem ridiculous to give a recipe for an omelette, but the secret of this is the absolute freshness of the eggs and masses of herbs.

One of the most useful herbs is flat-leaf parsley, which we sow in long rows to provide a steady supply for months. Chives are part of the edging to the vegetable garden, and proved so structural that when we dug some up, the brick path butting up to them collapsed because the roots had held it in place. Another prolific herb seeding itself everywhere is golden oregano, which looks fantastic in spring as it forms an acid yellow mat with aromatic leaves. There are well established mounds of this, and the bees love them when the flowers develop in summer.

Serves 1

2–3 eggs
15g unsalted butter or 1 tablespoon
  olive oil
A generous handful of fresh herbs, such as
  flat-leaf parsley, chives and oregano
  (tough stalks discarded), roughly
  chopped
Salt and freshly ground black pepper

Beat the eggs together in a bowl. Heat the oil or butter in a small, heavy-based frying pan over a medium heat and pour in the eggs. Cook for a couple of minutes, until the underside is set and the top is still a little runny. Strew the chopped herbs over the omelette, season with salt and pepper, fold in half with a spatula and slide onto a heated plate.

Eat with a big hunk of bread and butter and a glass of wine.

Spaghetti carbonara

This has been our standby supper for a long time, and it has been perfected by Montagu over the years. It is made with the sort of ingredients we always have in the cupboard or fridge. We prefer to use smoked bacon for its stronger flavour, although after Christmas we make it with ham, which is also delicious.

This is a very rich dish – more bacon and eggs with pasta – with a high ratio of sauce. We never add cream, as served in Soho restaurants in the 1980s. We worked nearby then and would often wander down for a bowl of pasta when it was late and we were too tired to cook. Their versions of carbonara were swimming in cream with bits of ham floating in it. Horrible. Ours has pieces of crisp bacon enriched with eggs and cheese. We also add a generous handful of parsley at the end for balance. It's a good idea to have the warmed plates ready, as it should be eaten whilst piping hot.

Heat the oil in a large frying pan over a medium-high heat, add the bacon and fry the strips until they are crisp.

Bring a large pan of salted water to the boil. Add the pasta and cook for about 10 minutes, or according to the packet instructions. It should still have some bite to it. Drain well and return it to the pan.

Working fast, tip the bacon and hot fat into the pasta and mix well. Then pour in the beaten eggs and stir, just coating the pasta, but being careful not to cook the eggs. This should take no more than 30 seconds. Add two-thirds of the cheese and mix well, then add lots of black pepper.

Sprinkle over most of the parsley, give the pasta a quick stir, then dish it out straight away on hot plates, adding the rest of the cheese, a little more parsley and some black pepper scattered over each serving.

Serves 4–6
1 tablespoon olive oil
500g smoked bacon, pancetta or ham,
  cut into thick matchsticks
500g pasta, penne or spaghetti
5 organic eggs, beaten
240g Parmesan, pecorino or
  Cheddar cheese, finely grated
Freshly ground black pepper
A small bunch of parsley (tough stalks
  discarded), finely chopped

Welsh rarebit

Welsh rarebit was a popular Victorian savoury, served at the end of a formal dinner so that wine could continue to be drunk. I suppose it was the equivalent of the modern cheese course.

At home, we eat Welsh rarebit if we want a quick supper, as we usually have all the ingredients to hand. It's a variation of cheese on toast, but more intensely flavoured with ale and mustard, and the sauce soaks into the toast, so the texture is creamy and rich rather than crisp and dry. Sometimes we make buck rarebit, which is Welsh rarebit with a poached egg on top.

Serves 2
125g strong English cheese, such as Cheddar, Gloucester or Lancashire, grated
3 tablespoons ale or milk
30g unsalted butter
1 teaspoon English mustard
2 slices of toasted bread

Put the cheese and ale or milk into a heavy pan and stir over a low heat until it has melted into a cream. Add the butter and mustard and heat gently but do not boil.

Put the toast in a heatproof dish and pour over the cheese mixture. Place it briefly under a hot grill, until it's brown and bubbling – don't worry if it splits, it will taste just as good. The molten cheese tends to spill over the edges of the toast, so if you toast only one side of the bread, it will absorb more sauce, but I prefer it toasted on both sides.

If there are a lot of people to feed, give everyone a slice of toast and pour some sauce over each one. It won't be bubbling from the grill, but it will be just as savoury and is still very good.

Cauliflower cheese

The best cauliflower cheese we have ever had was made using Cheddar sent to us from Glastonbury by Michael Eavis, founder of the festival there. Although this is a very rich dish, it's always better to be generous with the sauce so that it can be mopped up with crusty bread. This is a wintry dish that we serve with crisp bacon.

Serves 4
1 large cauliflower or 3 small ones
750ml whole milk
100g unsalted butter
100g plain flour
1 tablespoon English mustard powder,
  mixed into a loose paste with
  1 teaspoon water
250–350g strong Cheddar cheese, grated
Salt and freshly ground black pepper
100g fresh breadcrumbs

Preheat oven to 180°C/Gas Mark 4.

Trim any unappetising leaves from the cauliflower and cut a deep cross in the base of the stalk to help it cook evenly.

Bring a large pan of water to the boil. Add the cauliflower and simmer until just tender, as you still want it to have some 'bite' – 10 minutes for large ones, about 7 minutes for small ones. Drain and cut it into quarters lengthways (leave small ones whole) and place in an ovenproof dish.

Next make the cheese sauce. Pour the milk into a saucepan and add the butter and flour. Gently heat the mixture, stirring constantly, until it amalgamates into a smooth sauce. If it remains lumpy, whisk it vigorously until smooth.

Beat in the mustard paste and mix in most of the grated cheese, keeping a little back for finishing the dish. Taste the sauce and adjust the seasoning if necessary.

Pour the mixture evenly over the cauliflower and sprinkle the remaining cheese over the top, and scatter over the breadcrumbs. Place the dish on a baking sheet in the oven for 20 minutes, until the sauce is bubbling and the cheese is golden brown. Cool slightly before serving.

Macaroni cheese

This is another family staple, often prepared a few hours in advance so it's ready to pop in the oven when we're tired and hungry. The secret is to use strong Cheddar cheese and add mustard as it can otherwise be disappointingly bland. We prefer to use penne rather than the smaller macaroni.

One of my strongest memories of macaroni cheese isn't one of cosy domesticity, however. On the night of the Brixton riots in 1981 we were having a rather surreal dinner at the Ritz in Piccadilly, listening to the distant police sirens outside the deserted dining room, when one of our guests ordered macaroni cheese. Despite the luxurious menu of lobster and other extravagances, his choice, not on the menu, was specially made for him and served with a flourish from under a huge silver cover.

Serves 4
250g pasta, penne or similar
*   small pasta shape*
1 litre milk
100g unsalted butter
100g plain flour
250g strong farmhouse Cheddar cheese,
*   grated*
3 teaspoons Dijon mustard
4 tablespoons fresh breadcrumbs (about
*   2 small slices of bread, crusts removed,*
*   whizzed in a food processor)*
Salt and freshly ground black pepper

Preheat the oven to 180°C/Gas Mark 4.

Bring a large pan of water to the boil, add a generous amount of salt and cook the pasta for 7–8 minutes, or until slightly undercooked as it will continue to cook in the oven. Drain and put to one side.

Gently warm the milk in a heavy-based saucepan over a gentle heat. As it warms, add the butter and sprinkle on the flour. Stir or whisk continuously as it heats. Allow it to simmer gently, without boiling, stirring continuously for a few minutes until the sauce has the consistency of thick cream. Add the cheese to the warm sauce and stir until it melts into the mixture. Stir in the mustard and taste for seasoning before adding the salt and pepper.

Put the cooked pasta into an ovenproof dish, pour over the sauce and stir until the pasta is thoroughly coated. Scatter the breadcrumbs over the surface. Place the dish on a baking sheet and bake in the oven for about 30 minutes, until the top is golden brown and the sauce bubbling through. Cool slightly before serving, with tomato ketchup if desired.

Mushroom savoury

There are rare, memorable years when field mushrooms are abundant. One September, when we were still living in our old house, The Hanburies, the fields around us were carpeted in them, their white caps pushing through the grass. We tried out lots of recipes – fried them for breakfast, added cream, made pasta sauces and I dried strings of them hanging above the Aga, ready to use in the winter. I hope we soon have another year like that one.

This savoury is our favourite mushroom recipe, delicious on toast for supper. It can be made with a mixture of different types of mushroom, and the portions should be generous. It is also best served in small quantities.

Serves 2 as a main course,
    4 as a starter
75g unsalted butter
100g finely chopped shallots,
    or 1 small red onion, finely chopped
500g mushrooms, finely sliced
100ml dry sherry
200ml double or whipping cream
3 tablespoons grainy mustard
½ a lemon
2 large slices of toast made from good
    bread, such as a sourdough, kept hot
1 tablespoon finely chopped flat-leaf
    parsley (optional)
Salt and freshly ground black pepper

Melt half the butter in a large frying pan over a low heat and gently fry the shallots until they soften, adding a splash of water to stop them burning if necessary.

With the shallots still in the pan, add the rest of the butter, increase the heat and fry the mushrooms quickly for a few minutes, until they are soft and cooked through. Season with salt.

Deglaze the pan with the sherry and let it bubble for a minute to reduce the liquid and cook off most of the alcohol. Add the cream and simmer for a minute or so. Stir in the grainy mustard and a squeeze of lemon, taste and season with black pepper.

Put the hot toast on 2 warmed plates and spoon half the mushroom mixture onto each piece. (If serving as a starter, halve the toast slices and place a quarter of the mushroom mixture onto each piece.) Sprinkle on the parsley, if using, and serve immediately.

Potatoes with bacon, onion and sage

When the clocks go back and it is dark and cold, gathering ingredients from the garden has none of the fun of a high summer day. This is when stored vegetables come into their own. If we've had a good harvest, we keep our potatoes in the tool shed in large plastic pots covered in sacking, and they store quite happily like this right through winter. Charlotte is our favourite. It has a waxy texture that is perfect for boiling and it keeps well. Also, being a second early means it can be harvested before the risk of blight.

I use up our red onions (Red Baron and a long red Florence variety, grown from seed) before the white ones as they do not keep so well, but they tend to be sweeter and look lovely.

Even the best potatoes and onions can be a little uninspiring, however, and need something to transform them. Luckily, the autumn herb garden still has plenty of fresh sage, and the combination of sage, onions and potatoes is really delicious. Add some bacon, a little cheese and cream, and you have a satisfying dish that is quick and easy to prepare. It can be a meal in itself, served with a fresh green salad, or simply a way of making a special side dish from humble potatoes.

Serves 6 as a side dish
1.5kg small- to medium-sized waxy potatoes, such as Charlotte
500g back bacon, cut into 1.5cm strips
2 red onions, halved and finely sliced
6 garlic cloves, finely chopped
A big bunch of fresh sage, about 25 leaves, stalks removed
150ml double cream
50g Parmesan cheese, or any strong, hard cheese, grated
1 tablespoon olive oil
Freshly ground black pepper

Preheat the oven to 180°C/Gas Mark 4.

Wash but do not peel the potatoes, then quarter lengthways so that they look like very fat chips. Put them into a roasting tin with the bacon, onions, garlic and sage leaves, then mix in the cream, cheese, olive oil and some black pepper. I use my hands to mix them together to make sure everything is well coated.

Cover the tin with foil and cook for 45 minutes. Remove the foil and cook for a further 15 minutes, until the potatoes turn a beautiful, golden brown. Serve immediately.

Hamburger

In the 1960s my father taught at Berkeley University in California for a year. Normally rather square, he bought a gigantic 1950s Pontiac Star Chief to drive around in. At weekends, we piled into the car and headed to the beach, collecting a picnic lunch on the way.

I have never forgotten the first time we stopped at a roadside hamburger van, where I ordered a cheeseburger and a bottle of Coke. The 10-year-old me, my parents and two younger sisters carried our order away in thick brown paper bags. We drove on in blazing sun along sandy roads and past the wooden house where Alfred Hitchcock filmed *The Birds*.

As soon as we reached the deserted beach, we couldn't wait a moment longer to eat our hamburgers, so we unwrapped their waxy paper covers and took a bite. I had never known such a sensation. The toasted sesame bun enclosed a grilled beef patty layered with cheese, gherkin, tomato, lettuce, ketchup and also the squirty mild mustard you then found only in America. The combination of juicy meat, slightly charred, and the crunch of the sweet gherkin topped with the other ingredients was perfect. It was a revelation.

Hamburgers are now not only commonplace but also seem to epitomise junk food. These days I would never eat a fast-food hamburger as they have come to represent so much of what is depressing about the way we eat, and they taste and smell horrible. But a well-made hamburger is a fabulous thing, and I do make them at home.

It's best to avoid cheap, anonymous mince and buy the best cut of beef you can afford – rump, chuck or topside all make good burgers. Consider them a special treat and assemble all the ingredients with care. Either finely chop or mince the beef yourself at home or get the butcher to do it for you, asking him to grind your chosen cut quite coarsely as it makes for a better texture. If the meat is very lean with little fat, we add an egg yolk to the mix to help bind it.

Makes 4

450g rump steak, chuck or topside
1 small onion, finely chopped or grated
1 egg yolk (optional)
1 tablespoon sunflower oil
Salt and freshly ground black pepper
4 soft baker's baps, split in half
1 cos lettuce, leaves roughly torn
1 or 2 large beefsteak tomatoes, sliced
Gherkins, sliced lengthways
Ketchup
Mustard
Mayonnaise
4 slices mild Cheddar cheese (optional)

If you haven't had the butcher grind the beef for you, finely chop the steak with

Steak tartare

a sharp knife or cut it into large pieces and put it through a mincer. Place the minced beef in a bowl with the onion and season well. Mix everything together with your hands, adding the egg yolk if necessary to bind the mixture. Divide into 4 equal-sized balls, then flatten them into thick patties.

Heat a ridged griddle pan or a frying pan until very hot. Pour the oil over a thick wad of kitchen paper and lightly rub the pan with it.

Fry the hamburgers for about 4 minutes on one side before turning over and cooking the other side for about 3 minutes. They take a surprisingly long time to cook. You want them quite well done on the outside but still pink in the centre.

Leave them to rest for a couple of minutes, then assemble the hamburgers by placing each one in a bun and adding the additional ingredients as desired. Plain, salted crisps are the perfect accompaniment.

I love the clean taste of steak tartare. It is essentially a patty made from raw steak with none of the heaviness of cooked beef. It's simple to make, though it takes time, so it's not suitable for preparing in large quantities. Use the best-quality steak you can find, and serve it on a pure, white plate with a few dressed salad leaves and really good chips.

Per person:
125g fillet steak
1 teaspoon finely chopped flat-leaf parsley
Extra virgin olive oil
1 organic, very fresh egg yolk
A small handful of watercress or
 lambs' lettuce
1 lemon
Worcestershire sauce (optional)
Sea salt and freshly ground black pepper

Trim the steak of any fat or sinews, then slice and chop it up on a board with a very sharp knife until it is finely textured or minced. Put it in a bowl with the parsley, add seasoning and a dash of oil and mix together. Form into a small mound on a plate, make an indentation in the centre and place the egg yolk in it.

Dress the leaves with a little olive oil and a squeeze of lemon juice and arrange them on the plate. Serve with Worcestershire sauce and season to taste.

Toad in the hole

This is definitely a winter meal. When feeling homesick in New Guinea thirty years ago, I made the mistake of cooking toad in the hole in the tropical heat. It was inedible. It taught me that food has to be appropriate to the place, the time and the temperature.

Nevertheless, it hasn't put me off cooking it when the weather is cold outside. I still marvel at the miracle of the puffed up toad in the hole as it comes out of the oven – plump butcher's sausages nestling in the golden, pillowy batter. Although I think that proper sausages are best, chipolatas are more popular with children and go further, so adapt it as you wish. It needs something to moisten it as there are no juices, so make an onion gravy (page 346) to go with it.

Serves 4
250g plain flour
A pinch of salt
3 large eggs
600ml milk
4 large sausages or 8–12 chipolatas
3–4 tablespoons olive oil

Make the batter 30 minutes in advance. Sift the flour and salt into a bowl, then make a well in the centre. Add the eggs, one at a time, mixing between each addition, then pour in the milk, whisking until the batter has the consistency of single cream. Rest the batter in the fridge while you prepare everything else.

Preheat the oven to 220°C/Gas Mark 7.

Pour the oil into a heatproof dish, approximately 28 x 22cm in size, and add the sausages. Put it in the oven and cook the sausages for about 15 minutes; chipolatas need only 10. Turn the sausages over and arrange them evenly apart in the dish. Gently stir the rested batter, then pour it over the sausages. As with Yorkshire pudding, the oil must be very hot or the batter won't rise. Cook for about 25–30 minutes, until the batter is puffed up and golden. Serve immediately with onion gravy.

Onion gravy

This is useful if you need gravy but there are no juices from a roast to use as a base. It's ideal for toad in the hole (page 345) and good with bangers and mash too. This is my basic recipe, which can be enriched by deglazing the pan with balsamic vinegar before adding the stock, and/or sweetened with a spoonful of sugar to taste.

Makes about 400ml
2 large onions, halved and finely sliced
A large knob of unsalted butter
250ml good-quality beef stock (an organic
*   stock cube is fine)*
Salt and freshly ground black pepper

Fry the onions in the butter over a low heat, stirring from time to time, until they start to caramelise. This can take a long time, up to 30 minutes, but it's worth the wait as the caramelised onions add so much flavour. If they start to catch, add a couple of tablespoons of water.

When the onions are nicely browned, add the stock and simmer for a few minutes to reduce the gravy. Taste and season with salt and pepper.

Devilled chicken

I often buy a large, free-range chicken in the market, which is too big for a single meal. It looks a bit sad the next day, but stripping off all the meat and devilling it provides an appetising meal of spiced chicken with crisp, brown edges.

It's a really easy recipe and, although made from leftovers, it's one of our favourite meals. This is also a useful way of using up the remains of the Christmas turkey. If there's less meat, the sauce is looser; if there's lots of meat, the result is crisper. This isn't an exact sort of recipe, but is made mainly from store-cupboard ingredients and is fast to knock up.

Serves 2–4, depending on how much
    chicken you have
Leftover chicken, white and dark meat
4 tablespoons yoghurt or double cream
2 tablespoons Dijon mustard
2 tablespoons mango chutney
1 tablespoon olive oil
1 tablespoon Worcestershire sauce
1 teaspoon cayenne pepper
Juice of ½ a lemon
Salt and freshly ground black pepper
3–4 tablespoons finely chopped flat-leaf
    parsley

For the rice:
250g brown basmati rice
Knob of butter (optional)

Preheat the oven to 200°C/Gas Mark 6.

Strip the meat off the chicken, tearing it into bite-sized pieces. (Use the skin and carcass to make ever-useful stock, page 58.)

In a large bowl, thoroughly combine the yoghurt, mustard, chutney, olive oil, Worcestershire sauce, cayenne pepper and lemon juice. Season well with salt and pepper. Add the chicken and mix it well so that all the pieces are coated in the sauce.

Spread them out in a baking tin or gratin dish and place in the oven for about 20 minutes. The cooking time depends on how much meat there is, so keep an eye on it. It's ready when the pieces have browned a little and the edges are crisping up. (If you prefer, the chicken can be spread out in a shallow heatproof dish and browned under the grill until piping hot.)

While the chicken is cooking, rinse the rice in a sieve, then place in a pan with 600ml cold water and some salt. Stir, bring to the boil, lower the heat and put a lid on the pan. After 20 minutes, remove from the heat but do not take off the lid. Let it sit for 5 minutes, then add some butter if you like and fluff up the rice with a fork.

Put the rice in the centre of a warmed serving dish, surround it with the devilled chicken and sprinkle over the parsley. Serve it with mango chutney and a green salad.

Devilled kidneys

Once, on an expedition to the Trobriand Islands off the coast of Papua New Guinea, I was stranded because the weekly plane could not land due to bad weather. Rescue came in the form of an Australian naval boat. The captain gallantly gave up his cabin for me, and the following morning my companion and I were served an unexpectedly grand breakfast of kidneys cooked in sherry. I am a good sailor, so I tucked in, trying them for the first time.

We now make them for a leisurely breakfast or an easy supper in less-adventurous Herefordshire whenever I can get hold of fresh lambs' kidneys. They are a grown-up taste, so we tend to make enough for just the two of us, and I am always surprised at how inexpensive they are for such a delicacy.

Serves 2
6 lambs' kidneys
3 tablespoons plain flour
1 teaspoon English mustard powder
1 teaspoon cayenne pepper
2 tablespoons unsalted butter
A splash of Worcestershire sauce
A squeeze of lemon juice or a splash
of dry sherry
2 tablespoons double cream
2 thick slices of good white bread,
toasted, and kept hot
1 tablespoon finely chopped flat-leaf parsley
Salt and freshly ground black pepper

Remove any membranes from the kidneys, then slice in half and cut out the white core.

Mix the flour, mustard and cayenne pepper in a bowl and toss the kidneys in the seasoned flour, shaking off any excess.

Melt the butter in a frying pan over a medium-high heat and, when it's foaming, cook the kidneys for a couple of minutes on each side. Add the Worcestershire sauce and lemon juice or sherry and let it bubble for a minute, adding a little water if the juices in the pan need loosening. Add the cream, stirring it for another minute. Season to taste.

Place the hot toast on warmed plates, spoon over the kidneys, scatter with parsley and serve immediately.

PUDDING

Because my mother had a sweet tooth she lavished as much care on pudding as on the main course; it was not unusual for there to be three quite different dishes for the dessert course. So I grew up with the scale of a meal as an event measured as much by the quantity and quality of puddings as by the main course, table setting or guest list.

Puddings had their own hierarchy. The poshest always involved some degree of complexity of preparation – or at least time. So summer pudding, queen of puddings, baked Alaska, chocolate or lemon mousse, fruit salad, meringues, éclairs or brandy snaps appeared only on high days and holidays. Any great occasion would have three puddings, one hot and seasonal, one prepared well in advance, and one that was almost playful. This was 1950s and 1960s provincial Home Counties after all.

Next in the pecking order were puddings that had seasonality, skill and time put into them, but that had – to my mother at least – less status. These were the ones that I loved best and included fruit pies, apple Charlotte, rhubarb, gooseberry or apple crumble, bread and butter pudding, steamed apple pudding, treacle tart, fruit fools, poached pears, and fresh raspberries and strawberries in season. Lastly, there were the everyday nursery puddings that I still eat at every opportunity – rice pudding, jelly, blancmange, custard, junket, semolina and tapioca – all infantile and deeply comforting, but none of which ever graced the dinner table.

After their first outing, the half-eaten puddings would reappear at lunch the next day, with some of their glamour lost, but none of their appeal. Absolutely nothing was thrown away, and a pudding would reappear until it was all eaten up.

Vanilla ice cream

Like all homemade ice creams, this is
infinitely better than anything you can buy.
It is fabulous served with hot chocolate sauce
(page 355) or alcoholic sultanas (see right).

Makes about 800ml
250ml whole milk
1 vanilla pod, split lengthways
4 egg yolks
100g sugar
250ml whipping cream or double cream

Put the milk into a saucepan with the
vanilla pod. Heat just until small bubbles
appear around the edges of the pan; be
careful not to let it boil. Remove from the
heat and allow to infuse for 10 minutes.
Remove the pod and reserve.

In a bowl, whisk the egg yolks with
the sugar, then stir in the hot milk. Strain
the custard mixture into a clean saucepan
and cook over a low heat, stirring
constantly, until the mixture thickens
enough to coat the back of a wooden spoon.

Scrape the seeds from the vanilla pod
with the point of a small, sharp knife and
stir into the custard with the cream. When
the mixture is completely cold, churn it
in an ice-cream machine according to
the manufacturer's instructions before
spooning into a plastic container and
freezing for at least 1 hour.

To make this recipe without an ice-
cream machine, see page 191.

Alcoholic sultanas

These sultanas have enough of a kick to
revive you if you are in need of a lift, and
are a good standby to have in the cupboard
if you need to create an instant pudding.
Spooned over ordinary vanilla ice cream,
they transform it into a richer treat.

500g sultanas or raisins
4 tablespoons light muscovado sugar
375ml brandy

Fill the bottom of a scrupulously clean
1 litre Kilner-type jar with the dried fruit,
layering it with the sugar as you go. Pour
over enough brandy to cover the fruit.

Leave for at least a week, shaking the
jar from time to time to help dissolve the
sugar, until the fruit swells up in the
brandy. The sultanas will keep in the
closed jar for several years.

Rhubarb
ice cream

The first of the forced rhubarb from Yorkshire appears in greengrocers in January, and has startling pink stems with lime green leaves. It is a delicacy that we look forward to each year before our own rhubarb comes up in the garden in early March. The slender stems are best poached in syrup (page 16) to show off their shocking pink colour.

If you don't have time to make the ice cream, make a fruit fool instead, using equal amounts of poached fruit and whipped cream stirred together. Serve the ice cream or fool with shortbread biscuits (page 230).

Serves 6
1 vanilla pod
200g caster sugar
1kg rhubarb, trimmed and cut
*   into 5cm lengths*
About 500g Greek yoghurt

Scrape the seeds from the vanilla pod with the tip of a sharp knife. Pour 400ml water into a saucepan, add the sugar, vanilla seeds and pod. Warm over a medium heat, stirring to dissolve the sugar, then bring to the boil. Simmer the syrup for about 5 minutes to reduce it.

Add the pieces of rhubarb and poach them over a gentle heat until they are cooked but still firm enough to hold their shape. They can turn to mush very quickly, so watch that they don't get to too soft and start to break up. (Mind you, I have often eaten rhubarb in restaurants when it is rock hard and clearly under-cooked, which is probably worse.)

Carefully remove some of the rhubarb pieces and set them aside to serve whole with the ice cream. Remove the vanilla pod.

To make the ice cream, measure the rhubarb and syrup in a measuring jug, making a note of their combined volume. Measure out an equal quantity of Greek yoghurt. Reserve about 6 tablespoons of the syrup, then whizz the rest with the rhubarb and yoghurt in a food processor. Churn in an ice-cream machine according to the manufacturer's instructions before spooning into a plastic container and freezing for at least an hour.

To make this recipe without an ice-cream machine, see page 191.

When you are ready to serve it, put a scoop or two of ice cream in each bowl with a few bright pink pieces of rhubarb and a spoonful of syrup.

Coffee ice cream

It is very hard to buy coffee ice cream, so we make it ourselves as a treat. For a more grown-up version, use very strong espresso rather than instant coffee.

Serves 6
250ml whole milk
4 egg yolks
100g caster sugar
250ml double cream
*2 tablespoons instant coffee dissolved
    in 1 tablespoon boiling water, or
    3 double espressos*

Put the milk into a saucepan and heat just until small bubbles appear around the edges of the pan; be careful not to let it boil.

In a bowl, whisk the egg yolks with the sugar, then pour in the hot milk in a slow stream, stirring as you go. Strain the custard mixture into a clean saucepan and cook over a low heat, stirring constantly, until the mixture thickens enough to coat the back of a wooden spoon. Stir in the cream and coffee, cool completely, then churn in an ice-cream machine, according to the manufacturer's instructions. Spoon the ice cream into a plastic container and freeze for a couple of hours.

To make this recipe without an ice-cream machine, see page 191.

Eat within a couple of days of making it, in cornets or little glasses.

Chocolate sauce

My childhood version of this was a Mars bar, cut up and melted with a couple of tablespoons of double cream, which I then poured over vanilla ice cream from the village shop. My love of chocolate goes back a long way. Apparently, as a tiny toddler I climbed over the garden gate, found my way to the shop and said, using almost my entire vocabulary, 'Choccy please.' It worked because I was given a little chocolate bar. Here is a grown-up version. It's fantastic on ice cream and meringues.

Serves 4–6
2 tablespoons caster sugar
*100g dark chocolate, about 70 per cent
    cocoa solids*
15g unsalted butter
4 tablespoons double cream

Put the sugar and 75ml water in a saucepan over a medium heat and stir, without boiling, until the sugar dissolves. Remove from the heat. Break the chocolate into pieces and put them in the sugar syrup, add the butter and stir until smooth. Finally, stir in the cream. Serve warm.

Chocolate mousse

To paraphrase the socialite Lady Diana Cooper, a successful dinner needs plenty to drink and a chocolate pudding. There is a desire for sweetness at the end of a meal, and a richly intense chocolate mousse provides a perfect finish. This one is made from only three ingredients, which appeals to my minimalist nature and, although simple, needs to be made with care. The more I make it, the easier it gets.

This is not everyday food and we tend to make it for more formal meals or celebrations. It is worth, as ever, using the best ingredients – good dark chocolate and the freshest eggs. Adjust the sugar to taste as how much you need depends on how sweet the chocolate is. Sometimes I serve the mousse in one bowl, dusted with cocoa, though it is more conventional to serve it in pots, ramekins or small cups. It is good served with a jug of double cream to pass around the table.

Serves 4
120g dark chocolate, 70 per cent
  cocoa solids
4 eggs, separated
1 tablespoon caster sugar (optional)

Break the chocolate into small pieces and place them in a medium-sized heatproof bowl. Put the bowl over a pan of barely simmering water, ensuring the bottom of the bowl doesn't touch the water or the chocolate will overheat and become grainy. As soon as the chocolate has melted, take it off the heat.

In a scrupulously clean bowl, whisk the egg whites until they form stiff peaks, just as you would for meringues. Stir in the sugar, if using, and whisk again for a moment.

In a bowl, whisk the yolks together, then beat them into the melted chocolate with a wooden spoon. This can be hard work as the mixture becomes quite stiff.

Spoon a big dollop of the beaten egg whites into the chocolate and stir to loosen the mixture. Gently fold in the rest of the egg whites with a light touch so that the mousse is full of air, yet at the same time ensuring that everything is evenly combined.

Spoon the mixture into individual pots or one large bowl, cover and allow to set in the fridge for at least 4 hours before serving.

Syllabub

Historically, syllabubs were one of the many inventive ways of using milk before it lost its freshness. They were a favourite eighteenth-century dessert made with wine or cider sweetened with sugar and spices, to which cream or milk was added, ideally from a height so that it would froth up. In fact, the perfect syllabub is supposed to be made by squirting the warm milk into the alcohol straight from the cow's udder.

First catch your cow… But failing that, use good double cream and the syllabub will taste as lovely as its name. It's very rich, so serve it in little glasses, perhaps with shortbread biscuits (page 230).

At Christmas, we double the quantities and serve a big bowl of syllabub as an alternative to the heavy pudding usually eaten after the dinner.

You can serve this immediately, or prepare it in advance and chill in the fridge until ready to serve.

Serves 4–6
2 unwaxed lemons
120g caster sugar
2 tablespoons dry sherry
2 tablespoons brandy
500ml double cream
Freshly grated nutmeg

Pare the zest from the lemons using a lemon zester, which will produce delicate strands. You can use a fine grater instead of a zester if you prefer, though be careful not to remove any of the bitter white pith.

Squeeze the juice from the lemons into a bowl. Add the zest, sugar, sherry and brandy and stir until the sugar has dissolved. Traditionally, you are supposed to leave this mixture overnight for the lemon flavour to develop, but I often make it in one go and it still tastes lemony and good. However, if you have the time, it's better to leave it for several hours to infuse. After infusing, strain the liquid into a chilled bowl and reserve the macerated zest to decorate the syllabub.

Lightly whip the cream. Fold in the infused lemon syrup, then spoon the syllabub into small glasses. Decorate with the zest and grate nutmeg over the top.

Lemon posset

Lemon posset is a rich, lemon-infused boiled cream that thickens as it cools. It is a dainty pudding, best served in pretty glasses with shortbread biscuits (page 230) and eaten with teaspoons. It can be prepared up to a day ahead.

Serves 6
2 unwaxed lemons
3 tablespoons caster sugar
600ml double cream

Pare the zest from the lemons, preferably with a lemon zester, being careful not to remove any of the bitter pith. If you don't have a lemon zester, carefully remove the zest with a vegetable peeler and chop it into very thin strands. Cut the lemons in half and squeeze out the juice. Dissolve the sugar in the lemon juice.

Pour the cream into a heavy-based saucepan and bring it to the boil over a medium heat. When it is boiling, add the lemon zest and boil for about 10 minutes until the mixture thickens. Take the pan off the heat and stir in the lemon juice and sugar. Strain out the zest, decant the cream into a jug and pour into small cups or glasses. Chill in the fridge for 2–3 hours before serving.

Apple cake

This is a quick apple pudding, a variation on the simple pound cake (page 237). The almonds make the sponge slightly chewy and the lemon cuts through the sweetness.

Many of our apple trees are specific to this area of Herefordshire, which has one of the greatest concentrations of orchards in Britain. The traditional orchards are surrounded by old hedgerows and grazed by flocks of sheep. In spring they are breathtakingly beautiful, with pink blossom stretching for miles.

The early apples keep least well, so get used up first, but some keep for months, even overlapping the first of the apple blossom. One of the best keepers is Herefordshire Beefing. Norfolk Beefing, which we also grow, keeps for even longer. Both apples have a texture that is quite dry and leathery, with less water content than a Bramley, which means that they keep their shape when cooked. They are good for tarts or baking.

Preheat the oven to 180°C/Gas Mark 4. Butter a 23cm flan dish or cake tin; line the base with greaseproof paper and butter the paper.

Cream the butter and sugar together in a bowl until light and fluffy. Add the eggs one at a time, beating well after each addition. In a separate bowl, sift together the flour and baking powder, and fold into the egg mixture, adding the ground almonds and lemon zest.

Peel and core the apples, then slice into eighths. Arrange the apple slices over the base of the flan dish or cake tin, cover with the cake mixture and bake for about 25 minutes, until a skewer pushed into the middle comes out clean. Cool the cake in the tin placed on a rack before turning out onto a plate and serving warm or cold. It's even better with some crème fraîche or double cream.

Serves 6–8
225g unsalted butter, plus more
*   for greasing*
225g caster sugar
3 eggs
100g plain flour
1½ teaspoons baking powder
125g ground almonds
Grated zest of 1 unwaxed lemon
700g cooking apples

Tarte tatin

The sharp flavour of cooking apples contrasts perfectly with caramel, so this classic upside-down tart is always a pleasure to eat. Tarte tatin is usually made with buttery puff pastry, but I more often use shortcrust pastry. I sometimes substitute the apples with pears or fresh figs, which are sweeter and look beautiful.

The important thing to remember is to use a shallow pan that can be transferred from the top of the stove to the oven. I use a heavy frying pan with a metal handle, which works brilliantly.

Serves 6–8
1kg cooking apples (you can use dessert
*   apples but their extra sweetness can be*
*   slightly cloying)*
120g unsalted butter
120g soft brown sugar

For the shortcrust pastry:
200g plain flour, plus a little more for dusting
A pinch of salt
100g unsalted butter, chilled and
*   cut up into small pieces*
1 egg, lightly beaten

Sift the flour into a bowl with the salt and work in the butter with your fingertips until the mixture resembles coarse breadcrumbs. Add the beaten egg and just enough cold water, about 1 tablespoon, to form a ball of dough. Pat the pastry gently into a circle, wrap it in cling film and chill for at least 30 minutes.

Peel, core and slice the apples into eighths.

Melt the butter and sugar in a suitable ovenproof pan about 20cm diameter, then take it off the heat. Place the apple slices in the pan, cramming them together to ensure there are no gaps because the apples collapse as they cook and you need plenty for a generous filling. Put the pan back on a gentle heat and let it bubble away for 10 minutes, shaking gently from time to time, until the apples have soaked up most of the butter and sugar. Allow to cool completely.

Preheat the oven 220°C/Gas Mark 7.

Lightly flour a work surface and rolling pin, then roll the pastry into a circle slightly larger than the circumference of the pan. Place over the fruit, trim the edges, then tuck the pastry firmly around the inner edge of the pan. Make 3 slashes in the top to let the steam out.

Place the tart in the oven and bake for 20 minutes, or until the pastry is cooked and golden. Carefully remove the pan from the oven. Allow to cool for a few minutes, then turn the tart out onto a large plate. The steaming, caramelised apples will now be on the top.

Serve warm with lightly whipped cream.

Poached pears

Our pears seem to ripen all at once in the autumn, so we often have more than we can possibly eat. As the honey-sweet fruit is incomparably delicious eaten fresh, we give away as many as we can, and poach others to prolong the season. We grow Doyenne du Comice and a couple of other varieties, including a single Conference pear, trained against a south-facing wall.

Unlike apples, pears don't keep for long once they're ripe, and need to be used up in other ways. A simple method is to poach them in syrup. Prepared like this, they freeze well too, ready for effortless puddings in winter.

Perry, the alcoholic drink made from hard little Perry pears, is becoming easier to buy, which is a good thing as it helps preserve the lovely, tall Perry pear trees. Perry orchards are such a feature of the Herefordshire countryside in early April, covered in white blossom. If perry is unobtainable, cider works well as a substitute.

Peel the pears, leaving them whole and retaining their stalks. Place them in a saucepan large enough to hold them upright in one layer. Pour over the perry or cider and add the sugar, cinnamon and ginger.

Bring to the boil, reduce the heat and simmer gently, partially covered, for 20–25 minutes, depending on the size and hardness of the pears – you should be able to pierce them easily with a thin, pointed knife. Remove the pears, cinnamon and ginger from the pan with a slotted spoon and transfer them to a serving dish.

Reduce the poaching liquid by boiling it down to half the original quantity. Pour the syrup over the pears and serve them warm or cold with cream, crème fraîche or ice cream.

Serves 6
6 ripe but firm pears
750ml perry or cider
100g caster sugar
2 cinnamon sticks
25g fresh ginger, peeled and sliced

To serve:
Jersey cream, crème fraîche or ice cream

Fruit crumble

I try to get away with not making a pudding every day, but Montagu inevitably asks 'What's for pudding?' This means I get plumper, as the only way I can resist a pudding is not to make one.

Crumbles are a much-loved pudding in our household, made most often in autumn from apples, quinces, damsons or plums. Spring and summer crumbles are good made from rhubarb, gooseberries and raspberries, and even more exotic ones can be made from apricots or peaches.

We tend to make them from our own fruit, often augmented by blackberries. If it's a good year, we pick enough to freeze lots of little bags of them, no more than a handful, ready to add to an apple crumble in the winter.

The crumble layer should be fairly thin, which will result in a crisp, slightly chewy layer. Too much and it sinks into the fruit and can be stodgy. Any excess uncooked crumble mix can be frozen. Serve with custard or cream – whipped cream is particularly delicious.

Serves 4–6

Apple crumble: *750g peeled, cored apples cut into chunks, 70g caster sugar, pinch of cinnamon (optional)*

Gooseberry crumble: *750g gooseberries, topped and tailed, stewed in 140g caster sugar just until slightly softened and the juices begin to run*

Plum crumble: *750g plums, halved, stoned and stewed with 70g caster sugar until starting to soften*

Rhubarb crumble: *750g rhubarb, cut into 4cm pieces, 120g sugar, zest of a small orange or ½ teaspoon ground ginger, juice of ½ an orange*

For the crumble:

200g plain flour, or 150g plain flour and 50g ground almonds

125g unsalted butter, chilled and cut into cubes

100g caster sugar

A pinch of cinnamon (optional)

To serve:

Pouring custard (page 215), lightly whipped cream or double cream

Preheat the oven to 180°C/Gas Mark 4.

First mix the crumble ingredients together. Rub in the butter with a light touch until the mixture resembles coarse breadcrumbs, or pulse briefly in a food processor.

Make your chosen filling mixture, then place in a shallow, ovenproof dish. Scatter the crumble mixture evenly over the fruit in a thin layer.

Bake for 35–40 minutes, until the top is golden and the fruity juices are bubbling up around the edges. Serve immediately with custard, whipped cream or double cream.

Marmalade pudding

This is a winter pudding to look forward to on a cold day. When you tip it out of the pudding bowl, you get a lovely pool of bitter orange sauce that cuts through the undeniable sturdiness of the sponge. It is best enjoyed after a light main course.

Serves 6

100g unsalted butter, softened,
  plus more for greasing
100g caster sugar
2 eggs
1 teaspoon vanilla extract
100g self-raising flour, sifted
3 generous tablespoons good marmalade

To serve:
Pouring custard (page 215)

Preheat the oven to 180°C/Gas Mark 4. Lightly grease a 1 litre pudding basin with butter.

In a mixing bowl, beat the butter and sugar together until light and fluffy. Add the eggs one at a time, beating well after each addition. Beat in the vanilla extract, then fold in the flour.

Put the marmalade in the bottom of the pudding bowl and spoon over the batter. Cover the basin tightly with foil and place it in a roasting tin. Put it into the oven and carefully fill the tin with about 3–4cm of boiling water. Bake for 1 hour, removing the foil after 30 minutes.

To serve, remove the bowl from the roasting tin, slide a knife around the edge to help release the pudding, then turn it upside down onto a plate. Make sure that all the sticky, marmalade sauce is scraped from the bottom of the bowl. Serve immediately with pouring custard.

Sliced oranges in brandy

Oranges always cheer me up. I love the smell of them, the taste of them, their colour. When I was seven, my grandmother gave me twelve Jaffa oranges for my birthday. It was an odd present to give a child, but I was thrilled. I could hardly manage to eat a whole orange in one go as it seemed so enormous.

When oranges start to arrive in December, I still think of them as a treat, and we buy a crate of them to eat over Christmas. They make an instant pudding after a heavy meal. On Christmas Day, or whenever a refreshing balance is needed, a large bowl of orange slices in syrup, livened up with brandy and orange zest, is perfect.

This can be prepared a day in advance, so although the peeling and slicing takes a bit of time, none of the work needs to be done at the last minute. It is delicious served with a syllabub (page 358). You can use the leftover peel to make candied orange peel (page 245).

Serves 6
8 large, unwaxed oranges
100g caster sugar
1 cinnamon stick
4 tablespoons brandy

Cut the top and bottom off 6 of the oranges. Place them on their bases on a chopping board and work around them with a sharp knife, slicing off all the peel, pith and membrane in strips so that the juicy flesh is exposed. Try to capture any of the precious juice in a bowl.

Zest one of the remaining oranges with a zester. Alternatively, pare off the zest with a sharp knife or vegetable peeler, ensuring you've removed all the white pith, and cut the zest it into the thinnest ribbons possible.

Extract the juice from the two extra oranges and pour it into the other bowl of juice. Cut the oranges into slices no more than 1cm thick and add them to the bowl of juice, again saving all the juices that run out if possible.

Pour 200ml water into a small saucepan, place over a medium heat and add the sugar, stirring to dissolve it. When the sugar has dissolved, add the stick of cinnamon and boil for a few minutes to make a syrup. You should end up with about 200ml liquid. Allow it to cool before pouring it over the oranges. Add the brandy and strew the strands of orange zest over the fruit. Chill for at least an hour, or up to a day, before serving.

Celebratory trifle

Trifle is made for celebrations. My mother and aunties always made a trifle to eat over Christmas and at family gatherings. I remember the cut-glass bowl glinting on the sideboard, full of pretty layers and decorated with cherries and angelica.

I always hope that there is a little left over for the next day for a secret spoonful. If I'm making it for children or don't want to use alcohol, I substitute orange juice.

The trifle should be made the day before the party to allow the flavours to develop, and chilled in the fridge until you're ready to serve it.

Serves 10
500g Victoria sponge made in a single tin (page 239)
4 tablespoons raspberry or apricot jam
A small glass of dry sherry, about 50ml
A small glass of brandy, about 50ml

For the custard:
600ml whole milk, or 300ml whole milk and 300ml double cream
5 egg yolks
100g caster sugar
½ teaspoon vanilla extract

To decorate:
600ml whipping cream
30g flaked almonds, toasted
Glacé cherries
Crystallised angelica

Slice the cake in half horizontally and spread the jam over one of the halves. Sandwich the halves together, then cut into slices approximately 2cm thick. Use them to line the base of a large serving bowl, then pour over the sherry and brandy.

To make the custard, pour the milk, or the milk and cream if you want a richer taste, into a saucepan and heat just until small bubbles appear around the edges of the pan; do not let it boil.

In a bowl, whisk the egg yolks with the sugar, then pour in the hot milk in a slow stream, stirring as you go. Strain the custard into a clean saucepan and cook over a low heat, stirring constantly, until the mixture thickens enough to coat the back of a wooden spoon.

Take the custard off the heat, add the vanilla extract and allow it to cool and thicken. This ensures it will form a separate layer rather than running into the sponge below. Spread the cooled custard over the trifle base, cover with cling film and chill overnight.

Just before serving, whip the cream until it holds soft peaks, then spread it over the custard. Sprinkle on the toasted almonds and decorate generously with glacé cherries and angelica. Serve in pretty bowls.

Sloe gin

Sloes are the fruit of the blackthorn bush, which has the earliest blossom of the year, scattered on its bare branches like a fall of snow. The blossom usually seems to coincide with a spell of really cold weather, hence the expression 'blackthorn winter'. It makes a viciously spiny hedge with thorns 5cm long and hard enough to puncture a tractor tyre – certainly when the hedges are cut around us we seem to get at least one puncture as a result of the thorns scattered along the road.

The blackthorn's small, dark blue 'plums' are almost inedible when picked, being hard and mouth-puckeringly sour, but they make a winter-warming drink when converted into sloe gin. Above all, I associate this drink with Christmas. If you make it in the autumn, it will be ready for drinking by the end of the year.

Makes just over a litre
1kg sloes
325g caster sugar
1 litre gin

Pick over the sloes for twigs and leaves, then prick them all over with a fine-tined fork or sharp darning needle. Alternatively, place the sloes in the freezer for a few hours so that the skins split. You need to do this because the alcohol and sugar can't penetrate properly if the berries are macerated as they are.

Find a container large enough to hold the sloes and gin (I use an old cider flagon). Put the sloes in first, then pour the sugar in through a funnel. Finally, top up with the gin and seal the bottle. Shake thoroughly, then shake again daily until the sugar has fully dissolved. This should take only a couple of days.

Store undisturbed in a cool, dark place until Christmas. The gin becomes a dark pink colour in about 6 weeks, ready to be decanted into clean bottles and enjoyed on the long, cold nights of winter.

Hot toddy

This is what helps me sleep on a winter's night in our draughty old house, after a long day outside. I don't usually drink alcohol if I'm alone as I think of it as more of a social pleasure, but this is almost medicinal. Delicious medicine, and so soothing for a cold. I sit by the fire making plans for the next day as I slowly sip my hot toddy.

The recommended ratio of whisky to hot water is one-third whisky to two-thirds water, but this is too strong for me, so I add more water. Montagu prefers cocoa with the occasional splash of whisky as a change from camomile tea when it is really cold.

Makes 1
Generous measure of whisky,
*   to your taste*
2 teaspoons honey
Juice of ½ a lemon
2 cloves stuck into a thick slice of lemon
Small stick of cinnamon

Warm a tall, heatproof glass by filling it with hot water. If you don't have a heatproof glass, stand a spoon in an ordinary glass before adding the hot water to prevent it cracking.

Tip the water away. Pour the whisky into the warm glass, add the honey, lemon juice, lemon slice and cinnamon, top up with hot water and stir. Sip while it is hot.

We would like to thank all the people who helped make this book happen:

Marsha Arnold for her lovely warm and sensitive pictures.

Adam Don for his energy and help over many months.

Caroline Michel for her endless support and ability to keep our spirits up during a hard winter.

Richard Atkinson, Natalie Hunt and Penny Edwards at Bloomsbury for all their tremendous work in bringing the project together against impossible deadlines.

Debora Robertson for her encouragement and humour during long editing sessions.

Will Webb for his bright and clear design.

Rebecca Spring for her calm competence and delicious food.

Emily Hedges for her marvellous eye.

Stuart Forster for coming to the rescue.

Mark and Sally Bailey for their inspiration and practical help.

And to our other children, thank you.

Last but not least, Brender, Barry, Nigel and Peggy.

To our children, with love

First published in Great Britain 2010

Text copyright © 2010 by Monty and Sarah Don
Photography © 2010 by Marsha Arnold

The moral right of the authors has been asserted

Bloomsbury Publishing Plc,
36 Soho Square, London W1D 3QY

Bloomsbury Publishing, London, Berlin, New York and Sydney

A CIP catalogue record for this book is available from the British Library

ISBN 978 1 4088 0439 1

10 9 8 7 6 5 4 3 2 1

Design by willwebb.co.uk
Photography by Marsha Arnold
Index by Hilary Bird

Printed and bound in Italy by Graphicom

All papers used by Bloomsbury Publishing are natural, recyclable products made
from wood grown in well-managed forests. The manufacturing processes conform
to the environmental regulations of the country of origin.

© **Mixed Sources**
Product group from well-managed
forests, controlled sources and
recycled wood or fibre
FSC www.fsc.org Cert no. CQ-COC-000015
© 1996 Forest Stewardship Council

www.bloomsbury.com/montydon
www.bloomsbury.com/sarahdon